BETRAYING OUR TROOPS

The Destructive Results of Privatizing War

Dina Rasor and Robert Bauman

palgrave
macmillan

First published in hardcover in 2007 by
PALGRAVE MACMILLAN™
175 Fifth Avenue, New York, N.Y. 10010 and
Houndmills, Basingstoke, Hampshire, England RG21 6XS.
Companies and representatives throughout the world.

PALGRAVE MACMILLAN is the global academic imprint of the
Palgrave Macmillan division of St. Martin's Press, LLC and
of Palgrave Macmillan Ltd. Macmillan® is a registered trademark
in the United States, United Kingdom and other countries.
Palgrave is a registered trademark in the European Union
and other countries.

ISBN-13: 978-0-230-60408-7 paperback
ISBN-10: 0-230-60408-0 paperback

Library of Congress Cataloging-in-Publication Data
Rasor, Dina, 1956–
     Betraying our troops : the destructive results of privatizing war / Dina Rasor
and Robert Bauman.—1st ed.
          p.   cm.
     Includes bibliographical references.
     ISBN-13: 978-1-4039-8192-9 (cloth)
     ISBN-10: 1-4039-8192-2 (cloth)
     1. United States. Army—Supplies and stores—History—21st century.
2. United States. Army—Transportation—History—21st century.   3. Iraq
War, 2003—Logistics—United States.   4. Privatization—United States.
5. Contracting out—United States.   I. Bauman, Robert.   II. Title.
UC232003-.M66   1990
956.7044'340973—dc22

                                                                                2007000063

A catalogue record of the book is available from the British Library.

Design by Letra Libre

First PALGRAVE MACMILLAN paperback edition: May 2008
10   9   8   7   6   5   4   3   2   1
Printed in the United States of America.

*For the troops and contractor employees
who took a risk to tell the truth
for the greater good of the country.*

CONTENTS

CAST OF CHARACTERS

—Major Rick Lamberth—Was a logistics coordinator for KBR in Kuwait in 2003–04. He was called up on active duty in mid-2004 and deployed to Iraq as a LOGCAP planner assigned to Camp Speicher. He has said he witnessed contract abuses in Kuwait and Iraq and tried to make the Army brass aware of the problems.

—Ray Kimball—West Point graduate, former Army helicopter pilot who served in both Bosnia and Iraq. Was part of the initial invasion of Iraq in March 2003 during which his unit suffered from a lack of critical supplies.

—Perry Jefferies—Twenty-year Army veteran who retired as a staff sergeant after a tour in Iraq. A tough Texan who saw his first duty as protecting his fellow soldiers, he was furious about how his troops were treated in Iraq.

—David List—A command sergeant major and a soldiers' soldier who saw his duty in Iraq as supplying the troops and keeping them safe. His story is told through the eyes of his long-time driver in Iraq, Adam Roe.

—Adam Roe—An Army staff sergeant who drove for David List and then became a truck driver during his second tour in Iraq. Adam is a twenty-year veteran who also served in Somalia and Bosnia and was appalled by the failures of the contractors and his command in Iraq.

—David Wilson—Vietnam era veteran and seasoned truck driver who was employed by KBR to drive trucks in Iraq. Scandalized by what he saw, he questioned KBR's practices and was fired. He owns a long-haul truck and is now back on American highways. He is concerned that the people he meets across America have no idea what is really going on in Iraq.

—James Warren—Another truck driver, he signed up with KBR and worked with Wilson in truck convoys in Iraq. He and his wife, who is also a trucker, drive together around the country. Along with Wilson, he agreed to testify about what he knew on fraud and waste before a congressional hearing.

—Bobby Yen—A graduate of UCLA in computer science from a wealthy San Francisco family. Having always wanted to be a soldier, he enlisted and was sent to Iraq, much to the horror of his family. After one tour as an Army journalist-soldier, he quit in disgust because of what he experienced.

—Michael Battles—West Point graduate who spent seven years in the Army and three in the CIA. He is an ambitious and politically connected Republican who ran unsuccessfully in the Republican primary to challenge Congressman Patrick Kennedy in Rhode Island in 2002. Hoping to become a big player in the new war service industry, he formed a company called Custer Battles.

—Scott Custer—Former Army Ranger who teamed with Michael Battles during the early Iraqi occupation period. Prior to that he had done some non-profit work in the Balkans, Africa, and Afghanistan, but he went to Iraq intending to play with the corporate big boys.

—Robert Isakson—Former FBI agent who built an international company to help during disasters and the aftermath of war. He became an unhappy subcontractor to Custer Battles in the early part of the Iraqi occupation.

—Franklin Willis—Career State Department bureaucrat who helped staff the Coalition Provisional Authority (CPA) during the early part of the occupation. He was upset at the chaos, cronyism, and lack of accountability in the CPA's contracting office.

—Blackwater Four

    —Scott Helvenston—Former Navy SEAL, stuntman, and actor who joined Blackwater Security and went to Iraq to make money as a private security guard after a divorce.

    —Jerko "Jerry" Zovko—Former Army Ranger who spoke Arabic well and had already trained Iraqi soldiers before the disastrous Fallujah mission.

    —Mike Teague—Decorated twelve-year Army veteran who served in a Special Operations unit in Afghanistan, Panama, and Grenada before joining Blackwater in Iraq.

    —Wesley Batalona—Twenty-year Army Ranger who retired as a sergeant. He was a veteran of the Gulf War and Panama. He was also a surfer and a native of Hawaii.

—Will Hough—Former Marine, body builder, and trainer, Hough signed up to do personal security work with Custer Battles and has reported to the press allegations of horrendous violence perpetrated against civilians by private security contractors in Iraq.

—Ben Carter—Former water quality manager who was hired by KBR to monitor water quality at one of the big bases in Iraq. He soon has reported that the contractor's failure to test or properly purify water was putting soldiers and KBR employees at great risk of illness.

—Representative Henry Waxman—A diminutive and bespectacled career member of Congress. Representing Beverly Hills, he shuns the glamour of his district and seems happiest investigating large corporations. He is best known for his long and successful crusade against the big tobacco companies.

—Representative Tom Davis—An attractive and outgoing Virginia Republican, he is the outgoing Chairman of the Government Reform Committee in the House of Representatives. The bane of his existence is Henry Waxman, the ranking Democrat and former chair of his committee. As a former legal counsel to a federal consulting firm, his constituents in his district include many of the companies who now have major contracts in Iraq.

FOREWORD

Jonathan Alter

When the history of the early years of the 21st century is written, the fiasco of the war in Iraq will loom large. How did the United States get in? How did the United States get out? And, most tantalizing for historians: how did the world's only superpower manage to mismanage the war so horrendously?

The key to understanding the staggering level of incompetence is the privatizing of the Iraq War. For the first time in American history, a huge chunk of the personnel involved in a war—nearly half by some accounts— are neither active duty military nor reservists but contractors. These men and women may be patriotic Americans, but winning the war is not their job. Their duty, as explained to them by their superiors before they ship out, is to make as much money for their companies as they possibly can.

Contractor abuses go back to the Revolutionary War. But as recently as the Cold War, the main role for contractors was in building weapons, not shouldering battlefield security and logistics. More important, the hands-off attitude of the executive branch and (until recently) the Congress is new. During World War II, for instance, hearings about war profiteering were held by an obscure senator from Missouri. Did critics tell him that such inquiries were unpatriotic during wartime? Did the White House stiff him? To the contrary, President Franklin D. Roosevelt selected

Harry Truman as his choice for vice president in 1944. The Congress, press, public and even the president wanted to know how the system was broken and how it could be fixed.

Compare that approach to the one that has dominated Washington for the last four years. Only now, with the election of a Democratic Congress, can we expect real oversight of the way thousands of troops have been betrayed by companies that were meant to supply and protect them. Only now might we get to the bottom of a taxpayer rip-off so large—tens of billions of dollars—that it will likely dwarf any scandal in this country's history.

The news media have reported sporadically about privatization. But few reporters have the patience to sift through the details of an obscure yet immensely powerful Army unit called the Logistics Civil Augmentation Program (LOGCAP), which was charged with underwriting the combat support mission during the invasion of Iraq. Until this book, the many accounts of whistleblowers and other truthtellers inside the Halliburton subsidiary Kellogg Brown and Root (KBR), Blackwater, Custer Battles, and other contractors have not been brought together in one place.

As I read the stories of these private sector patriots willing to sacrifice their careers to expose the abuses of their own companies, I was reminded of how much we owe groups like the Project on Government Oversight (POGO) and the authors' new Follow the Money Project. Dina Rasor, the founder and former director of POGO, and her co-author Robert Bauman do heroic work encouraging whistleblowers to come out from the shadows, and then stick by them when the inevitable retaliation begins.

The stories here will make you angry: KBR employees who billed the Army for 84 hours a week (that's twelve hours a day, seven days a week), when they worked only a fraction of that and could frequently be found poolside in their fancy villas in Kuwait; the SUVs leased for $3,000 to $3,500 a month, ten times the stateside price; the Balkan girlfriends of contractors put on the KBR payroll as "logistics coordinators" and "administrative assistants"; the $1.2 billion dollar discrepancy, according to the Government Accountability Office (GAO), between the amount of materials shipped into the region and the materials that were registered as having actually been received.

You will learn about contractors who threatened work stoppages in Iraq and Kuwait if they weren't paid, and Army officers who allowed private companies to be the main convoy link in the supply chain (a critical command role in the past). You will recoil in disgust to read about nonsensical

KBR instructions that new trucks arriving for convoys be stripped of their spare tires; about trucks sent on dangerous routes empty, putting the drivers' lives put at risk while running up the bills; about concentrated wastewater from what is supposed to be the purifier unit being used for showering by U.S. soldiers at Camp Ar Ramadi.

How could this be? The explanation lies in the nature of KBR's $16 billion contract, which is structured so that the more the company spends, the more it keeps. In such a system, supervision of the spending makes no sense for either the contractor or the government, which would pay even more for strict cost controls. Not only has the army failed to fire or penalize these contractors, it has bestowed on them more than $70 million in bonuses. It hardly needs to be added that Halliburton is politically connected at the highest level. In fact, newspaper accounts have revealed that Vice President Cheney's office has personally approved many of the contracts with his old employer. You will read about how all of the big contractors are represented by top lobbyists, many of them veterans of the Bush Administration.

But even as the war grinds on, this book ends on a hopeful note. Rep. Henry Waxman, who revealed that 40,000 troops lacked protective Kevlar plates for their body armor vests, is back in the chairmanship of the Committee on Oversight and Government Reform, replacing Republican Tom Davis, who saw his job as defending contractors, not probing them. With Waxman's help—and the contribution of books like *Betraying Our Troops*—we are finally seeing the return of a precious value at the heart of American democracy—accountability.

INTRODUCTION

Camp Speicher, Iraq, late summer 2004.

The air in the room hung with tension. Even the air conditioning in the heat-baked environment did not stop the sweat from forming on the foreheads of the Army staff. The brigadier general in charge of the meeting shifted uncomfortably in his chair. The Army's logistics' contract manager at the camp could not believe what he was hearing. A KBR manager responsible for supplying the troops in this camp with food, water, and all other services and supplies, had just threatened to stop KBR's work at Camp Speicher—to stop cooking and feeding the troops, to stop supplying the troops outside the base—unless the Army paid KBR's submitted invoices.

Granted, his company, KBR, a subsidiary of Halliburton, was operating "at risk" by overrunning it's budgeted spending and had been late in sending its invoices to the Army. And the Army was slow in paying because of its concerns over the accuracy of the company's invoices. Even so, the KBR manager had just threatened the Army brass that his employees were going to stay in their housing containers and do nothing until the money was paid. Essentially this would amount to a work stoppage, or labor strike, on the battlefield—perhaps the Army's biggest fear regarding the Pentagon's new experiment of having private contractors supply the basic needs of its troops on the battlefield.

The Army manager and his assistant wondered if KBR really could do this. If soldiers or officers tried to pull this same stunt in the old Army, the general would court-martial them, and they could be sent to prison. However, according to federal contracting rules, a company has the right to stop work if that company is risking a large amount of its own money and the government is unable to pay due to funding problems. Clearly, wartime conditions should be an exception when soldiers' lives are on the line, but there is no legal basis for a general to force a company's employees to work beyond the contracting rules. The company or its employees can stop work or go home, and there is nothing that military commanders can do about it, except seek drawn-out legal-contract remedies in the courts back in the United States.

The Army logistics contract manager and the camp's general officer faced the disaster of having to explain to their men, their superior officers, and the public that there might not be any food, water, or other vital supplies the next day because the Army didn't have a backup plan. Since the Army had outsourced these traditionally Army-provided services to one company, they did not have any choice. The Army was short of troops, so there were no back-up soldiers to take on these tasks.

KBR ended up working the next day because the Army ultimately relented and agreed to come up with new money to pay its invoices. But this was not the first or last time the company would threaten the Army with work stoppages. It was like negotiating with the only plumber within a thousand miles when your basement is filling with water. KBR was in the driver's seat, and the company knew it.

No subject is harder to write about than government procurement, especially defense procurement. The mind-boggling complexity of its rules, requirements, and procedures, not to mention company (contractor) performance, presents anyone writing on the subject with a daunting task. How do you adequately describe a system in which specifications for making sugar cookies run 15 pages and building the C–5A cargo aircraft resulted in a 240,000-page proposal? How do you dramatize contractor accounting fraud that often takes up to five years for the government to investigate and resolve?

We have spent our careers working to understand, expose, reform, and correct this complicated system so that our defense dollars work for the soldiers and the taxpayers. One of us, Robert Bauman, was a career investigator for the Pentagon with the Defense Criminal Investigative Service and is a certified fraud examiner. The other, Dina Rasor, founded and ran a non-profit group called Project on Military Procurement (now called the Project on Government Oversight) that worked with whistleblowers inside the Pentagon to expose many of the weapon scandals during the 1980s and early 1990s, including the high-priced spare parts scandals. We have been working together, in a small company called The Bauman and Rasor Group, as investigators and consultants for over a decade with whistleblowers who file lawsuits designed to return to the federal government money obtained by fraudulent contractor practices. Dina Rasor also has been monitoring military spending via the Follow the Money Project to try to expose problems with defense contracting in general, but with a particular emphasis on private contracting in the Iraq war theater.

In the course of our work, we began to receive emails from soldiers stationed in Iraq that raised questions about the effectiveness of private contractors providing basic services. In the past, problems with logistics typically were not discovered until years after a war, which meant it was not possible to remedy the situation or go after the companies that caused the problems. However, with access to email and the creation of Internet blogs, soldiers in Iraq could describe what they were seeing, in real time, to their families. Soldier emails began to arrive in our in-box along with emails from outraged and frustrated war contractor employees. Many of those employees were concerned with the wasted money and emphasis on profit associated with private contractors in the war theater, which came at the expense of serving the soldiers.

At first these emails focused on reports of troops in the field not getting enough food, water, or vital spare parts. Then came reports of private security companies causing unrest and turmoil among the Iraqi civilians by their overaggressive behavior and apparent lack of rules, in effect undermining the military's efforts to win the "hearts and minds" of Iraqis. More recently, the emails have focused on spoiled food and contaminated water at the forward bases, which could result in serious illnesses to our troops.

Since their accounts are much more illustrative and interesting than anything we could write explaining the failures of the Byzantine military procurement system, we have reproduced their stories, but have kept the acronyms, jargon, and technical explanation to a minimum. That has required us to greatly simplify our descriptions so that the reader can understand these compelling stories.

Anyone who wants a deeper explanation of this war procurement system can go to the Appendix section of the book and read detailed descriptions of cost reimbursement contracts, allowable billing, task orders, and other areas of contracting. We also have provided chapter notes and an extensive reading list of books and reports to back up much of the individual experiences that are recounted in this book.

In addition, we have confirmed the occurrence of the problems exposed in each major story we tell by interviewing others who were familiar with the events. There are many people in the military, and even private contractor ex-employees, who were afraid to come forward publicly but were willing to validate the problems raised in these accounts. The people who told us their story on the record did so at some risk, especially those still in active military service. These accounts are told in chronological order, starting with the run-up to the war and ending well into the occupation, in the fall of 2006. Some of our sources served only a short time in Iraq; others found themselves being sent back to Iraq again and again. All were profoundly changed by their experience, and many of the soldiers were disillusioned and heartbroken to see how dysfunctional and dangerous their beloved Army had become.

We decided to write this book using the eyes and experiences of the troops and contractor employees in order to illustrate that the Army cannot adequately supply the troops on the battlefield using contractor support. We are concerned that a new industry of war service contractors is emerging, one that has little consideration for whether this dramatic change in how war is waged will work for the troops who are actually fighting the battles.

President George W. Bush placed the planning, execution, and postwar responsibilities for Iraq on the Pentagon, under the leadership of Defense Secretary Donald Rumsfeld. Secretary Rumsfeld decided to invade Iraq with as few troops as possible, so that the troops would quickly enter Baghdad and topple Saddam Hussein, and then, just as quickly, win the peace and leave. The mindset within the Pentagon was that it would be a short war.[1] The Pentagon civilian hierarchy imagined that the troops would be welcomed with flowers and cheers and that stability would quickly be achieved. This plan would make it easy for contractors, such as KBR, to be able to move in easily with supplies and set up bases, with all the perks, for the troops.

Not all the military brass thought that it would be that easy, and some tried to put together plans for a postwar occupation of Iraq, but Rumsfeld once reportedly threatened to fire any general who suggested the need to plan for troops in postwar Iraq. It is not known whether any senior military officials had reservations about depending on private contractors, since no one was about to risk his or her career to warn Rumsfeld about it under that environment.

Rumsfeld was in full control, and the military had little say in the matter.[2] Rumsfeld's mandate of going into Iraq "light" on troops meant going in "heavy" on contractors. Despite the best-laid plans of the Pentagon and its contractors, the occupation of Iraq deteriorated into insurgency warfare, extending military involvement far beyond what was anticipated. Both the Government Accountability Office (GAO)[3] and the Pentagon's Inspector General[4] had warned the Army that it could not count on private companies to be there for them when it counted on the battlefield. This is the Achilles' heel of privatizing war—private companies can "just say no" and not provide services during active military operations.

Without a steady flow of supplies, an invading army will be compromised and have to retreat. In fact, we know from history that one of the most important goals in the conduct of war by any military force is to disrupt the enemy's supply lines. Napoleon's famous dictum that "an Army travels on its stomach" points this out all too well. Both Napoleon and Hitler found out how important preserving a constant flow of supplies was to their armies when they were forced to retreat from their respective invasions of Eastern Europe and Russia.

In the past, military support personnel were required by military law to fight and deliver supplies and equipment to the troops. If they refused, they could be jailed under the Uniform Code of Military Justice (UCMJ). Contractors, on the other hand, cannot be legally ordered to deliver vital supplies to the troops under combat conditions; they can only be found in breach of contract, a long and bureaucratic remedy. Despite the attempt by Congress to place contractors under the UCMJ by a change in the applicability of the UCMJ, in 2006, to include "contingency operations" such as Iraq, constitutional issues will be raised if there are any attempts to prosecute civilian contractors under the UCMJ. Another legal tool is the Military Extraterritorial Jurisdiction Act of 2000 (MEJA). Signed by President Clinton in 2000, it gives the federal government jurisdiction over contractor crimes committed outside the U.S. However, MEJA only applies to felonies committed that would constitute a punishment of imprisonment for more than one year if committed within the U.S. Still, the "just say no" factor is the most pressing problem with using contractors on the battlefield.

Counting on private contractors on the battlefield was a big roll of the dice. The failure of contractors to deliver supplies and services would put our troops at risk and ultimately affect the military's mission.

In fairness to both the Army and KBR, the preparation for and execution of the invasion of Iraq were done under considerable pressure, due to inadequate planning, confusion over requirements, and the short time span between the decision to go to war and the actual invasion. The Army Material Command, the agency responsible for Army logistics and for overseeing the LOGCAP contract, was extremely pressed in this rush to war. Likewise, KBR was under pressure to perform quickly with many new employees and equipment to meet its new requirements.[5]

The use of private contractors in war is not new; their involvement in American warfare can be traced back to the Revolutionary War. But they have never been used to the extent seen in Iraq. And more importantly, contractors in Iraq have been used to transport supplies and feed the troops, a job that had been performed by soldiers in previous wars. Also, private security contractors in Iraq have been assigned duties traditionally performed by military police and military intelligence, such as escorting convoys and interrogating prisoners. Since the mid-1990s, this new industry, which we call the war service industry, has been the fastest growing industry in the world. During the Cold War, big-dollar defense contracts were traditionally awarded to contractors who built tanks, planes, and missiles. Now, the new big-dollar contracts are going to private contractors who provide services, such as logistics, security, and intelligence support, rather than hardware.

With the rush to war and the use of an unprecedented number of contractors, the military found that their policy of managing contractors on the battlefield was inadequate or even nonexistent. The military was forced to make up the rules as it went along in the midst of a war. The Army's planning process had not anticipated the numbers of contractor employees and had not educated its commanders on how to handle them. How do you protect the contractors in the middle of a war zone? What if the contractors refuse to do the work or quit and go home? There was no handbook or policy guidance for the commanders of this war; they had to improvise on the battlefield because they did not have any alternatives. "Deal with it" became the order of the day.

What are the costs to the taxpayer of replacing military personnel with private contractors? Can the public really expect to see the promised savings? Neither the Congress nor the Pentagon have been able to come up with an answer to these questions. But one only has to look at the cost of producing weapons and supplies, using contractors in the past, in order to have a hint of the answer. Remember the hammers that cost $435 apiece and the outrageous prices for simple screwdrivers, toilet seats, and coffee pots exposed in the 1980s? Those prices were derived using the same "cost controls" now being used for the LOGCAP contract with the same re-sults–skyrocketing prices. And now the Pentagon is relying even more on contractors to control costs in the life-and-death situation of a real war.

With the passage of a supplemental spending bill in mid-2006, the cost of the war in Iraq has reached almost $320 billion. That total is ex-pected to more than double before the war ends.[6] As of late 2006, we had already spent, in constant dollars, about half of what we did during the Vietnam War or even World War I. Both of these conflicts were hot and active wars, not merely "occupations," and had much higher troop levels. By the end of 2006, LOGCAP expenses were rising to $18 billion. With KBR billing the Pentagon an average of $450 million per month, one won-ders how this expense is affecting the Army's ability to buy, repair, and re-place necessary combat equipment for its troops.

On December 5, 2006, the *Washington Post* ran two different stories on the management of money and resources in the Iraq war. The first article stated that there were about 100,000 contractor employees in Iraq, ac-cording to a new Pentagon survey.[7] This number did not include subcon-tractors, so the actual number may be significantly higher. The Pentagon's previous estimate had been 25,000. Since there were, in the fall of 2006, approximately 140,000 troops in Iraq, this means that there is one con-tractor for every 1.4 troops. In contrast, there were only 9200 contractors in the Gulf War, which was much shorter but had significantly higher troop levels.[8]

At the same time, another article tells of "fields upon fields of more than 1,000 battered M1 tanks, howitzers and other armored vehicles sit-ting amid weeds here at the 15,000-acre Anniston Army Depot—the idle, hulking formations of an Army that is wearing out faster than it is being rebuilt." The story goes on to say that these deadlined and battle-damaged weapons are making many U.S. military units "unready" to de-ploy. "Despite the work piling up, the Army's depots have been operating at about half their capacity because of a lack of funding for repairs. In the spring [2006], a funding gap caused Anniston and other depots to lose about a month's worth of work, said Brigadier General Robert Radin, deputy chief of staff for operations at the Army Material Command at

Fort Belvoir." The Congress has begun to appropriate money to fix the equipment, but there is now a backlog in the middle of a war, and the Army chief of staff, General Peter J. Schoomaker, has told the Congress that additional funds are not enough.[9]

The contractor sponge has soaked up much of this money, with too much going to nonessentials and not enough trickling down for the basic needs of the troops who are away from the "safe" zones in Iraq and lack the battlefield equipment that may save their lives.

This new war service industry is not your father's military industrial complex, which President Eisenhower warned us about. Alive and well, the old military industrial complex is still fat and wasteful, filled with cronyism, congressional pork, and fraud. However, the big difference is that this industry prefers to just bend metal—build planes and ships that look tough but are not likely to be used. It was perfect during the Cold War era after Vietnam, when it did not need to provide beans and bullets for troops in a protracted hot war and occupation. The implications and consequences of this new war service industry were not well thought out before the rapid events leading to the Iraq war. Privatizing military roles introduced a profit motive to performance on the battlefield. This is the "corporatization of the military," as termed by author David Morse.[10] Mixing combat troops, whose goals are to succeed in battle and protect their buddies, with private contractors, whose goals are to make a profit for the shareholders of the corporation, creates an inherent conflict of interest. This conflict of interest has led to higher costs, inefficiency, and the refusal or marked reluctance to deliver goods and services under battlefield conditions, thus endangering the lives of our troops—as you will see in the following stories.

PART I

BLITZKRIEG

"Through LOGCAP, KBR serves the basic needs of America's troops in Iraq and Kuwait. KBR's priority is to make certain the troops have the food, shelter and tolerable living conditions they need while fighting in Iraq."

—Alfred V. Neffgen, Chief Operating officer,
KBR Government Operations,
before the House Committee
on Government Reform,
July 22, 2004.

CHAPTER 1

THE PRIVATE
SIDE OF WAR

Camp Arifjan, Kuwait, March 7, 2003.

On a windy, cool day, Rick Lamberth emerged from his plane at the modern international airport that serves the bustling, Persian Gulf port city of Kuwait City. He immediately noticed the excellent highway and road system that serves the region and marveled at how westernized it all looked. KBR officials met him and the 20-30 other new KBR employees he was traveling with. With the three regal tower spheres—the three pillars of Islam that define Kuwait City—prominent in the background, they traveled in a minibus on a southwesterly route for about 25 miles to Camp Arifjan, a $200 million state-of-the-art facility near the coast, built courtesy of the Kuwaiti government to provide permanent support facilities for American troops in Kuwait.[1] Eventually, it would be Lamberth's new home base as an employee of KBR.

Initially, Lamberth and his fellow employees were housed in luxurious villas leased by KBR at the Hilton Hotel south of Kuwait City, and bused to Camp Arifjan each day for work. The villas were elaborate and ornate, with jogging trails and all the trappings of luxury. It wasn't long before he and the others were moved further south to the luxurious villas at the

Khalifa Resort along the Royal Golden Coast overlooking the Persian Gulf, only about 10 miles from Camp Arifjan. The resort, comprising 84 luxurious villas, overlooks a private white-sand beach and offers guest activities such as windsurfing, banana boat rides, and deep-sea fishing. KBR, which took up residence at the resort in late 2002, pays a hotel tab of at least $1.5 million a month for its employees.[2]

As a newly hired employee, Lamberth was there to work for KBR by providing logistics support for the troops. Having just survived a messy divorce and custody battle that drained his finances and caused him to lose his trucking business, he found himself alone in the late fall of 2002. He needed to find a decent job that would allow him to escape his financial predicament and make enough money to provide support for his children. An opportunity presented itself when he heard that KBR was hiring employees with logistics experience to support the Army in Kuwait. The pay was good and it was also a chance for a new start. A 23-year Army veteran and a Major in an Army reserve unit in Memphis, Tennessee, he was torn: If he had to serve in Iraq, it would be on the delivery end of the supply chain, and his loyalty was naturally with the troops. Straight laced, somewhat headstrong, Lamberth lives by the Army value system of integrity, honor, and loyalty. Integrity, especially, is the foundation of his life.

Before Lamberth arrived in Kuwait, the Army had decided to use the Logistics Civil Augmentation Program contract, known as LOGCAP, to underwrite its combat support mission during the invasion of Iraq. The Army developed a task order under LOGCAP in February 2003 giving KBR the responsibility of setting up a transportation system, called the Theater Transportation Mission and based at Camp Arifjan in Kuwait, to move supplies for military operations to a staging point near the Iraqi border. Along with this responsibility, KBR was also given the task of setting up supply-line operations as a prelude to the invasion of Iraq.

Lamberth arrived in Kuwait having learned nothing of the LOGCAP contract or his duties. He was just told to do whatever he was directed to do by his supervisor. Neither LOGCAP, nor his duties, were included during his two-week KBR orientation in Houston, the headquarters of KBR and its parent company, Halliburton,. The orientation, held at a very nice hotel in the northern part of Houston, included classes on such subjects as the history of KBR, how to use chemical and biological suits and masks, and the Geneva Convention. Although supporting the troops was mentioned, making money was the biggest motivational factor pointed out by some of the instructors for the new employees who were going to risk their lives in Kuwait and Iraq,. During a class on KBR's purpose and mission statement, the speaker provided stories of life overseas and then pulled out his KBR pay stub and waved it to everyone, saying, "Whenever it gets bad and I get pissed off and I want to go home or it gets hot or windy, I just pull this out and look at it." The money was a big motivator. He would say, "Just remember the money." The new employees were told it would be easy to earn $100,000 a year, and that it would be the easiest money they would ever make.

From the moment Lamberth arrived at Camp Arifjan, he felt that supporting the Army took a backseat to KBR's profit margin. Managers drilled into his head, mostly at the daily pre-work meetings, that KBR employees get paid to be there and that KBR was a for-profit organization. They were there to make money for the company.

Once settled at Camp Arifjan, Lamberth dove into his work with abundant energy. He was to help with coordinating the transportation of supplies to staging areas in Kuwait with KBR's trucks and tractor-trailers. In doing his work, he knew only one speed—fast and efficient. But Lamberth felt that his work ethic did not sit well with one KBR project manager in Kuwait. He called Lamberth into his office two or three times and told him he had heard rumors that Lamberth was getting results too quickly, that he was doing too much for the military, and that he needed to slow down and drag his work out. Lamberth would be told when to step up his work effort. It was obvious to Lamberth that someone had said he had been working too fast. The project manager also told Lamberth to hold on to status and completion reports for the Army. This would have the effect of limiting the flow of information given to Army officials and make it appear to the Army that tasks were harder to complete, and more time consuming, than they actually were. Lamberth was to hold back giving them verbal or written information about work efforts. He felt that limiting the flow of work-effort information to the Army was a way for KBR to justify excessive hours. Lamberth believed KBR didn't want to provide any information that would show its actual billable hours.

Such tactics by contractors to limit or even deny information to government contracting or auditing officials are not uncommon in the world of defense procurement. Defense auditors sometimes have to fight long and hard to obtain vital information supporting contractor costs. Also, it is often an unwritten rule with contractor employees that they are not to talk to Defense contracting or auditing officials, referring them instead to a designated company spokesman. When a government auditor does get to talk to a contractor employee, it is common for a number of contractor managers and company legal representatives to be present to limit the questions and answers. These tactics make it difficult for the government to get the spontaneous answers it needs to determine whether costs incurred by a contractor are reasonable or appropriate.

LOGCAP is a cost reimbursable type of contract (cost reimbursable contracts are jokingly referred to around Washington as "defraud me contracts")[3] that provides the contractor a 1 percent fee and a potential award fee of 2 percent, in addition to reimbursement of its incurred costs. In the past, cost reimbursable contracts were not widely used by the Pentagon because of the significant risk to the government of having to reimburse out-of-control costs incurred by a contractor. Usually, they are used when uncertainties involved in contract performance preclude accurate cost estimations, such as in research and development efforts. But, when used, they require a higher level of government oversight to monitor contractor performance.[4] In Kuwait, the Army had very little oversight over KBR performance and costs. And, with little experience or knowledge of what costs were reasonable or appropriate, the Army was operating almost blind in its oversight efforts.

Lamberth began to find this out quickly after observing the way that KBR conducted business. He learned from co-workers that 105 hours a week could be charged on his time cards. He also heard from some co-workers they once could charge 120 hours a week, and eventually to 84 hours only after the Army started to complain about such a high level of incurred labor costs. According to Lamberth, while attending orientation in Houston, he was informed that KBR's goal was to charge 84 hours a week, that is, 12 hours per day, 7 days a week. Not long after arriving in Kuwait, he quickly learned that many of the employees could not have put in this number of hours unless shopping, swimming, and other recreational efforts were counted as work. He felt that some managers considered the Army foolish for its limited oversight.

Even though Lamberth felt KBR was churning time on the contract, he still wanted to do his job as efficiently as he could. This was his work ethic, and he feared personally failing the troops if he didn't get his job done.

By the time Lamberth arrived in Kuwait, he found that KBR had been in the process of buying cargo trucks, tractor-trailers, and fuel tankers from a Saudi company. Because the Saudi businessmen would not cross the border into Kuwait, KBR had to send truck drivers to the Saudi border to receive the vehicles and conduct a "technical inspection" for acceptance by KBR, and then drive them back to Camp Arifjan. The trucks and tractor-trailers, along with KBR drivers, were to be used to supplement the Army's supply vehicles and drivers—the Army didn't have enough vehicles and drivers to haul supplies after the start of the war in Iraq. There was supposed to be a clear delineation between Army vehicles and drivers and contractor vehicles and drivers: Contractor drivers were not going to drive Army vehicles. The Army was thus planning to save the mission by having the capability to supply the troops on the battlefield using both Army and contractor personnel and equipment.

But back in Washington, Secretary of Defense Donald Rumsfeld decided to scrub the Army's traditional comprehensive deployment plan for combat and logistics units, the "Time-Phased Force and Deployment List," known within the Army bureaucracy as TPFDL (pronounced "tip-fiddle," or "tip-fid" for short) for a new type of deployment plan called "Request for Forces." Under this new plan, combat units would be the first to move into the theater, while logistics unit commanders would have to justify the flow of their units and equipment into the theater.

Thus, the plan caused an imbalance of combat and logistics units arriving in the theater and a delay in establishing the Army's Theater Support Command, which was supposed to manage the logistics for the combat units moving into Iraq.[5] As a result, the role of the Army's primary logistics command, the Army Materiel Command, was diminished, causing a lack of coordination during important planning meetings for the mission. Furthermore, the Army excluded the most experienced LOGCAP and contractor personnel during the planning process because of "security concerns."[6] The Army Central Command had raised the security classification beyond the clearance level of the planners, a problem that took some time to resolve. Because of this, neither logistics planning nor contractor personnel were able to take part in the critical planning process,[7] diminishing their effectiveness during preparation for the invasion and subsequent Operation Iraqi Freedom. This lack of planning contributed to many conflicts between the Army and KBR over who was responsible for what.[8]

Army logistics officials were often on site at Camp Arifjan to explain KBR's responsibilities, as they understood them. The contractor learned it would be part of the supply chain, providing direct logistics support with trucks, tractor-trailers, and fuel and other liquid tankers to the Army's Third Corps Support Command, which was responsible for combat service support for the military combat units. In past wars, the Army relied on its own logistics units to keep the supplies moving from arrival in the theater to the soldiers on the battlefield. Thus, for this invasion, contractors would be integrated into the logistics mission of the Army—a fact unknown to the soldiers on the ground.

Part of Rick Lamberth's job as a logistics coordinator was to make certain that the truck drivers conducted daily preventative maintenance checks and service inspections of the vehicles prior to taking them out on their daily runs. He would often be at the motor pool early in the morning to accompany the drivers on their inspections.

While on his morning checks of the trucks and tractor-trailers, Lamberth discovered what he believed to be a major impediment to providing transportation support to the Army. He felt that more than 80 percent of the vehicles were overused and defective. The Army wanted the vehicles up to Department of Transportation standards, and they were not. There were trucks that did not have gas caps—they had rags stuck in the hole instead; seats that were not mounted—they were loose or would slide; transmission problems—some trucks would not go into reverse; speedometers and other gauges that did not work; serious engine problems; oil leaks; bald tires; defective brakes; fifth-wheels that would not release; exhausts leaks; and the list went on. Many trucks simply could not be used. Some of those that had broken down on their way back to Arifjan had to be towed, while others had to be worked on by the drivers in the desert where they broke down. It was obvious to Lamberth that these vehicles would not last in the harsh environment of the desert with its heat, rough roads, and blowing sand. The drivers would be sitting ducks in a war zone, and the supplies would not get to the troops. The Army was counting on them to support the supply mission on the battlefield, but how could they do that with trucks that barely worked?

The drivers themselves were upset at the conditions of the trucks. They complained to Lamberth that KBR managers had told them the trucks would be up to DOT standards. Despite their complaints, however, some of these drivers bragged to Lamberth that the Saudi businessmen had given them three hundred Kuwaiti dinars (equivalent to about $1,000) per truck to accept the vehicles as they were, no questions asked. All they had to do was sign off on proof of delivery so the Saudi company could bill KBR. Hundreds of trucks and tractor-trailers were bought in this manner, Lamberth learned. The drivers also bragged to Lamberth about how they were going downtown to the gold markets or the malls to spend their newly obtained dinars.

Bribery allegations surfaced involving former KBR employees during the contractor's operations in Kuwait in 2003–2004. A former contracting official for KBR, Jeff Mazon, was arrested in March 2005 on an Illinois grand jury indictment related to a kickback scheme in which Mazon was alleged to have received a $1 million payment from a Kuwaiti subcontractor who overcharged the government by approximately $3.5 million. Another former KBR employee, Glenn Powell, pled guilty in August 2005 to accepting $110,000 in kickbacks from an Iraqi subcontractor. Also, former KBR employee Stephen Seamans was charged with accepting $124,000 in kickbacks from Tamimi Global Company in exchange for awarding a dining hall contract in Kuwait. In December 2003, Halliburton publicly announced it had returned $6.3 million to the Army and acknowledged that two of its employees may have taken kickbacks in return for awarding lucrative contracts to a Kuwaiti company.[9]

Lamberth reported the defective vehicle problem to a manager, and his deputy. He told the manager that the trucks and tractor-trailers were substandard and that the Army would reject them. The Army wasn't going to tolerate expenditures on substandard vehicles, and would not allow those vehicles to roll out on convoys in the condition they were in. The manager replied that he wanted Lamberth to keep quiet about it and not to submit any type of written report to the Army on vehicle problems. Lamberth was upset that anyone would try to cover up the problem and potentially risk American lives, but he felt pressure to keep his six-figure job. He felt bad about it, but it was out of his control. Internally, he was in turmoil and found himself eating Rolaids and Tums constantly in order to calm the acids churning in his stomach.

Lamberth also felt that, in addition to the problems with defective trucks and tractor-trailers, KBR managers didn't seem concerned about controlling costs. An example was the leasing of SUVs by KBR from a Kuwaiti company. The SUVs were to be used by the contractor as part of their infrastructure in Kuwait and later in Iraq. During testimony before the House Committee on Government Reform, in 2004, a former KBR buyer said that KBR managers told buyers not to worry about price because they were working on a cost-plus contract. They paid as much as $3,000 to $3,500 a month to lease SUVs; one SUV was leased for $7,500 a month.[10] Such costs, Lamberth learned, would take the Army years to sort out, and by then the contractor could have made its money and the chances of having to pay it back were slim. Without Army oversight to catch such alleged fleecing, nobody could stop what was going on. Lamberth couldn't believe it.

About two weeks after Lamberth reported the defective vehicles to his management, the Army sent a team of transportation specialists to Camp Arifjan to conduct technical inspections of the tractor-trailers and fuel tankers as part of a final acceptance check before the invasion of Iraq. The team started inspecting each vehicle and writing up a technical inspection sheet of results on each one. During the inspection, pages and pages of problems for each vehicle were written. Out of frustration, they stopped the inspections and reported their findings to their officers. The Army was irate. They called a meeting with KBR to air their frustrations about the condition of the vehicles.

The meeting, held in the conference room at KBR headquarters at Arifjan, was presided over by a transportation brigade commander, an Army colonel. KBR officials attending the meeting included a manager and his deputy. The colonel opened the meeting by saying KBR's vehicles were substandard and in violation of the contract. He demanded to know what KBR's plan and timeline for corrective actions would be. He needed to know soon—the invasion was about to kick off and the Army was counting on those vehicles. The colonel was not interested in why the vehicles were substandard; he just wanted them fixed and running. He wanted results.

The KBR manager's reply was that they were going to get the vehicles fixed or replaced with higher quality equipment. The colonel was not happy with the response; he wanted action now and a timeline for future actions. But, Lamberth wondered whether KBR would commit to a timeline and whether it had the both the skilled personnel needed to fix the vehicles and the desire to get the job done quickly. He thought the contractor did not have the same sense of urgency, but rather had an incentive to extend the work as long as possible to increase its profits. It was a classic conflict between corporate and military mentalities. Their objectives simply didn't mesh. The Army was concerned with time and space—the success of the mission, while the corporation was concerned with the bottom line—profits. Contractors on the battlefield represented a wildcard that the military could not control with any sense of reliability.

The colonel also complained that KBR was violating DOT standards for time periods provided to drivers to rest and sleep. KBR allegedly had been working its own drivers beyond the ten-hour limit and in excessive heat conditions. Also, Lamberth noticed that while some KBR managers were staying in plush villas at Kuwaiti resorts, the truck drivers slept in tents, many without operable air conditioners, under extreme heat conditions exceeding one hundred degrees at night. While the KBR deputy was telling the colonel they were following DOT standards for drivers, Lamberth spoke up saying they were actually not. He admitted KBR had not adhered to some of the DOT standards. The KBR manager reacted by squeezing Lamberth's arm under the table as a message he was apparently displeased with his speaking up and wanted him to keep quiet. Despite what Lamberth revealed, the KBR deputy continued to claim DOT rules were being followed, but one of the Army officers who had accompanied the colonel to the meeting spoke up to contradict the deputy. They had been watching the drivers and were well aware that the rules were not being followed for rest and sleep. After the meeting, the KBR deputy was angry at Lamberth. He told him never to talk at a meeting or counter what he says in public. Lamberth believed he was only telling the truth about the matter.

KBR had been running supplies up near the Iraq border at Camp Udairi in preparation for the invasion. Trucks were also breaking down on those runs. Lamberth soon found the poor condition of the trucks and poor living conditions for the drivers were causing many of the newly hired American truck drivers to quit before the war even started. Driving those trucks would be dangerous—that is not what they signed up for; it wasn't worth the money. Lamberth believed that as many as two hundred drivers might have quit, causing a crisis in finding replacements. He saw the pending disaster as the invasion drew closer and agonized that they would fail the troops in a time of war.

Stunned, Lamberth could not believe what he was experiencing. It went against the grain of everything he believed in. But he needed the job. Nearly broke from his divorce, Lamberth had to support his children. He felt he had to bury his concern at what he was seeing and how it would affect the troops. He rationalized his feelings in the only way he could: He had to stay for his kids.

From the beginning, one of the fundamental problems of privatizing combat support functions had been the mismatch of goals. The primary goal of the Army is the success of the mission, while the goal of the contractor is profit. This mismatch manifested itself in the run-up to the war when the Army, although short on logistics support personnel, still worked with a sense of urgency. The contractor, on the other hand, did not have the same sense of urgency, Lamberth thought; it had an economic incentive to extend the work as long as possible with as many employees it could to increase its profits.

CHAPTER 2

SMELLING SMOKE

Washington, D.C., January 2003.

Rick Lamberth wasn't the only person who was beginning to feel dread about the logistics of the war effort. Representative Henry Waxman (D-CA), a career antifraud warrior in Congress, was concerned about an open-ended contract with KBR, a subsidiary to Halliburton, to extinguish the expected oil fires in Iraq after the U.S. military gained control of the country. He knew from the past that this kind of contract could be a big problem for the government and had few safeguards for the taxpayer. He was told by the Army that KBR had the most experience for the job, but it didn't take him long to figure out that a different company had put out the oil fires in the first Gulf War. That company was Bechtel, and the Army did not have it bid on the contract. He also knew that Halliburton's former CEO was Dick Cheney, now the vice president. During the time Cheney was CEO, which was shortly after he served as secretary of defense under George H. W. Bush, the Army gave the troop-logistics contracts exclusively to KBR. Now that more money was about to be poured into these contracts because of the second Iraq war, Waxman's antenna went up. He was certainly experienced enough to suspect that the taxpayer was about to be had.

Waxman, a Democrat from Beverly Hills, California, has one of the wealthiest, but liberal constituencies in the United States. Ironically, this plain and unflashy man represents some of the most glamorous people in the world. He has never been to the Oscars, but his supporters love him anyway. In 2006, *Time Magazine* said that "he stands 5 ft. 5, speaks softly and has all the panache of your parents' dentist. But when it comes to putting powerful people in the hot seat, there is no one tougher and more tenacious . . ." The *Los Angeles Times* also reported, in 2006, that Waxman's "idea of an ideal evening is taking a walk with his wife, Janet, their iPods synchronized." Waxman has built a powerful political base in Los Angeles and has been sent back to Congress by his constituents every two years since 1974. As a result, he has the political freedom to pursue the Pentagon and their contractors during a time of war. According to the *Los Angeles Times,* Waxman has never gotten less than 61 percent of the vote, even though "he doesn't campaign, makes no TV ads, doesn't so much as put up a yard sign."

This makes him unique in the House of Representatives. Since he doesn't need to fundraise in order to win his safe seat, and he doesn't have any higher political ambitions, he can take on many of the big-money industries in Congress without fear of losing an election.

A powerful chairman the last time the Democrats were the majority in Congress, Waxman was, at the beginning of this war, the ranking minority member for the Government Reform Committee. Without the chairmanship and the threat of the subpoena that he had used so successfully in the past to expose giant industries such as Big Tobacco, Waxman was reduced to writing letters to the executive branch and the Pentagon to try to get a handle on what was going on, and to issuing reports when he got any information, usually from frustrated insiders.

Waxman had heard that KBR was getting a big contract to rebuild Iraqi oil fields after the war. He wrote a letter to the Pentagon asking for all the major contracts involving the soon-to-be Iraq war. He received a list that included KBR's main logistics contract, the LOGCAP III contract that Rick Lamberth was working under. He found, to his consternation, that this contract was cost reimbursable, providing KBR reimbursement for its incurred costs, which meant that KBR's profit would go up the more it increased its costs. Because this multibillion dollar contract had no cap on its funding, Waxman realized that it could turn out to be much more than any oil field rebuilding contract. His instincts were right, and he began the patient but dogged gathering of information on KBR and the LOGCAP contract from letters and whistleblowers. Based on his experience, he feared a lack of accountability and a possible failure to provide for our troops when they were at their most vulnerable during a protracted war and occupation.

Even though Waxman was the minority member of the House Government Reform Committee, he decided to start his own investigation to see if there was oversight on these contracts, hoping to make sure that the troops got what they needed at a fair price. He didn't like the answers he was getting. It appeared that there wasn't anyone carefully watching the store in this rush to war. He decided to take on this responsibility himself and had his staff begin a major investigation. He did not know at the time that he would be the key watchdog over the money in this war, or that if he just pulled the thread on these contracts they would completely unravel. While the press and much of the Congress were cheerleading the buildup to the war, Waxman refused to get swept up in the excitement, realizing that someone had to mind the store. He was determined to take on this role because, at the time, he feared that the troops were about to get the shaft and that the taxpayers were going to end up paying through the nose. The troops were about to find out that his hunch was right.

CHAPTER 3

WHERE ARE MY MISSILES?

Kuwait-Iraq border, March 20, 2003.

As the Kiowa helicopters flew overhead, Army Cavalry Captain Raymond Kimball's F "Fury" Troop of the Third Squadron of the Seventh Cavalry (known by the Army as 3–7 Cavalry) rolled across the border in Humvees into the southern desert of Iraq. He now found himself in the crucible of battle in the desert sands where civilization began. Being there in the invasion was what he was born to do. He felt an enormous responsibility to his troops.Captain Kimball was part of the first wave of troops invading Iraq. Born in Reading, Pennsylvania to career Army parents, Kimball grew up on military bases throughout Europe. For Kimball, there was no question he would follow in his parents' footsteps as a career Army officer. He began his career on the grassy fields and asphalt squares high above the Hudson at West Point, where he learned that to lead one must first learn how to follow. Only after mastering the skills of a follower would he be entrusted with the well being of others. Kimball graduated from West Point in 1995, was commissioned as an aviator, and married a 1996 West Point graduate. He trained as a scout helicopter pilot and refined the necessary skills in the harsh, remote deserts of Arizona and the blasted fields and scattered rubble of Bosnia. Kimball learned in his training that the threat of force could be just as effective as the use of force. He would see firsthand in Iraq that there was no glory in war, only suffering, and no victors, only survivors.

Kimball is a natural leader and thinker, who, although fiercely loyal to the Army and the troops, would not hesitate to question authority when necessary. He felt that the troops were the reason for his being. "Fury" Troop was an aviation maintenance and support troop for the squadron's 16 OH–58D Kiowa Warrior scout helicopters, assigned to the Army's Third Infantry Division. Seventh Cavalry, known as a regiment at the time, was famous for its exploits during the nineteenth century in taming the western frontier. It was General George Custer's regiment during his last stand at Little Bighorn.

Getting in position to move into Iraq was not an easy process. In September 2002, while based at Ft. Stewart, Georgia, Kimball was told to get ready to deploy. MILVAN shipping containers showed up to ship their equipment, which was a clear sign they were going somewhere. It was game time. But then, in October, they were unexpectedly told to put their stuff away, to stand down. Kimball heard at the time that Rumsfeld had personally taken over and changed the "tip-fiddle" method of coordinating troop deployment because of the size of the Reserve component planned for use in Iraq. Rumsfeld decided to take control himself of all deployments of military units for the war in Iraq.

Since Desert Storm, The U.S. Army has been going through a "revolution" to modernize its logistical capabilities for improved support on the battlefield. Experiencing a sizeable reduction of military personnel as part of a transformation to a smaller fighting force, Army logistics officials began designing a system to augment the smaller, faster fighting units on the battlefield. Consequently, they adopted what was called "best business practices," focusing on efficiency to streamline operations modeled after the "just in time" and Total Access Visibility systems of such supply-chain giants as Wal-Mart and the auto industry.

"Just in time" logistics meant that supplies arrived at a fighting unit at the time of need.[1] In previous conflicts, the Army has used a "just in case" practice of stockpiling tons of supplies at a fixed location, usually more than what was needed, for use by fighting units when or if needed. Combined with Total Access Visibility, an automated system that assigns a radio frequency tag to each piece of equipment for scanning into computers, this system was designed to provide commanders on the battlefield with real-time knowledge of the location and movement of supplies through the pipeline.[2] Although an efficient and less costly model in a predictable, peaceful environment, its practicality in the unpredictable, hostile environment of the battlefield remains in question.[3] Adding to the unknown element of this new plan was the integration of contractor support into the supply chain that included maintaining radio frequency tags on parts to maintain its visibility for combat commanders in the field.

In contrast to the corporate world with its comparatively stable environment and perfect communications, the battlefield is highly unpredictable, stressful, and confusing.[4] How reliable can "just in time" logistics and parts visibility be in the fog and friction of war, in which communications are highly unreliable? Despite the considerable training, simulations, discussions, seminars, symposiums, and general hand wringing, the Army had devoted to "just in time" and maintaining visibility on critical parts being moved to combat units in need. These concepts had not been tested in the heat of battle before Iraq.

For Rumsfeld, the Iraq war would be a test of his belief in a leaner, meaner fighting force. Going against the recommendations of his senior combat generals, Rumsfeld insisted on using less than 200,000 military personnel for the initial invasion.[5] That meant having to augment military support duties with contractor personnel in order to keep up with the rapidly moving combat units. Further complicating logistics planning in the rush to war was Rumsfeld's decision to throw out the Army's traditional method of deploying units and logistics—the "tip-fiddle."[6] Control was important to Rumsfeld, and the "tip-fiddle" approach took decision making out of his hands.[7] This traditional deployment system operated under the assumption that modern high-intensity warfare is too complex for just one person to keep visibility over everything needed. The military relied on this deployment system to coordinate an orderly and comprehensive deployment of troops and supplies.[8] Now, Rumsfeld alone would determine deployment of units and logistics under the new deployment concept of Request for Forces. The actual effect of this change was to cause confusion in logistics planning over what supplies and equipment would be deployed with units and when. It also put to the test the new concepts of logistics distribution management on the battlefield—Total Access Visibility and "just in time."

For Captain Raymond Kimball, it was back to normal operations at Ft. Stewart until mid-December 2002, when new orders arrived to be ready to deploy to Kuwait again after the first of the year. Kimball found himself in the dark about his troop's level of logistic and equipment support for deployment. No one could tell him who his higher support authority would be. Simple questions up his chain of command, such as "who am I getting my gas from when I get over there," would be answered with, "I don't know, ask when you get over there." "Who am I getting my parts from when I get over there?" "I don't know, they will be able to tell you when you get there." This confusion was in part caused by Rumsfeld's decision to scrub the Army's traditional deployment system and the resultant delays in the establishment of logistics support limits for the war effort.[9]

Fortunately, Kimball had a fair number of Gulf War vets in his troop who told him to expect supply problems. He started worrying about whether his supplies and parts would be there when it counted. Under old Army regulations he was only allotted a certain amount of stockage to deploy with. Kimball feared it would not be enough.

Anticipating logistics problems on the battlefield, he decided to manage the risk by stockpiling supplies and parts over his allotment—four times over, in fact. This meant breaking regulations, but Kimball felt it was necessary so that he could count on the supplies being there for him when he needed them. As it turned out, this decision to overstock was the only way he was able to fulfill his mission of supporting and maintaining the aircraft he was responsible for during the invasion. Kimball did not know who was involved in the supply chain. He was never briefed about the use of logistics contractors for supply functions.

January 8, 2003, Kuwait.

The Seventh Cavalry arrived at Camp Doha in Kuwait, one of the first units from the Third Infantry Division to arrive at the base. At the time, Doha was a sleepy little outpost great for what it had been designed for— the occasional battalion or brigade rotating through for training exercises. But when brigades, aviation units, and other military units, started showing up, it was almost too much for the Kuwaitis assigned to the base. Kimball never got a satisfactory answer as to who was in charge of the warehouses or where the spare parts were located. The military supply troops would say civilians were running the warehouse, and the civilians would say the military would have to approve the release of parts. Kimball was concerned about the availability of parts for his helicopters once the invasion started. To add to his concerns, not all the support units had arrived in theater by the time the invasion started.[10]

As Kimball led his Fury Troop into the desert along some of the worst trails he had ever seen, he felt that he was actually in perpetual service to the soldiers under his command. His troops had loaded every can of oil and every spare part they could find onto their vehicles. They looked like the Beverly Hillbillies going down the road with stuff hanging off all the vehicles—Kimball couldn't believe a military vehicle could look like that. He was told by his command that all he had to do when he needed critical parts was to call them in and they would be airlifted to him, but he instinctively knew that supplies would not be able to keep up with his troops.

Once they rolled into the vast desert of southern Iraq on their way to their first objective, Samawah, Kimball was consumed with getting soldiers from point A to point B, getting to Army refueling points, moving spare parts, and keeping track of his people. It was out of the question for him to pilot a Kiowa or do anything else. Kimball had 136 soldiers under his command, including medics, administrative personnel, and even a cook.

Built for fast-paced armored thrusts, the squadron's mission was to conduct reconnaissance and protect the right flank of the Third Infantry Division.[11] Once they crossed the border into Iraq, they raced up to Samawah, where, according to intelligence reports, they were to expect little to no resistance, just friendly natives waving American flags and maybe even a parade through the town. While the combat units raced ahead, Fury Troop lagged far behind as it attempted to traverse the goat trails and moon dust that were supposed to be roads.

Besides his military personnel, Kimball brought along a contractor field service representative, a manufacturing representative, to assist in aircraft maintenance. Two manufacturing representatives had deployed with the unit to Kuwait, and one was embedded with Fury Troop because he had the expertise to quickly provide maintenance to aircraft so they could return to combat. Because the rep was unarmed, he was told by Kimball to remain in the back of a Humvee.

On their march to Samawah over difficult trails, they encountered additional challenges from dust clouds and confusion. Movement control broke down completely, and it took a day to catch up with the lead elements. Because of constant operations, Kimball started to run low on spare parts for the helicopters. Requests for parts sent through satellite communications network, which worked only intermittently, went unfulfilled. It was later determined that units operating in the theater could not fully use asset visibility systems to track or order parts. This system was not fully operable and so was not capable of exchanging information or transmitting data over the required distances.[12] Kimball only had five radios for 75 soldiers, and two of the radios were in his Humvee—this was all they were authorized to take with them into battle. "Where are the aircraft who are supposed to be pushing me parts?" Kimball asked. "We're working on it," was the reply from the higher-level corps support group in Kuwait. But nothing happened.

Kimball's first re-supply came when his men found an abandoned American ammo truck broken down outside of Samawah. The 8 x 8, 10-ton truck, was loaded with rockets and had been abandoned by another combat unit. The squadron's combat aircraft had used up ammo on their way to Samawah and were in desperate need of rockets. His men asked Kimball, "Sir, are we allowed to take this ammo?" "Your damn right you are," Kimball replied, not thinking twice about it. They were "in the damn desert in the middle of a war." When you are getting nothing from the supply chain, you scrounge where you can. It turned out to be a good move. Instead of waving flags and a parade, the squadron found themselves in a fierce firefight with Iraqi paramilitary forces in and around Samawah. The lead combat elements of the squadron, including the Kiowa helicopters, arrived at Samawah 24 hours before Kimball's troop and had been conducting operations in and around the city ever since. They were still badly in need of parts and ammo and low on rockets at that point. The Kiowas were struggling to fly missions on the minimal support Kimball could get forward. The scrounged rockets were an important asset, but they still needed more supplies.

About two or three days into the fighting, Kimball was told that a Chinook helicopter was flying in with more ammo. "Great, I can use it," he said. The Chinook landed, and Kimball walked to the back of the aircraft where he saw racks of Hellfire missiles he thought his aircraft could use. But after a closer look, he was dismayed. They were Longbow and Apache helicopter Hellfire missiles that did not work with Kiowas. The missiles would have been more useful to Kimball if they had been spilled on the road to block entrances to their assembly areas. Since they were worthless to Kimball, he didn't want to be saddled with them.

He got into a prolonged argument with the Chinook pilot over dropping them off. Kimball told him there was no way in hell he was going to accept those Hellfires. The pilot told Kimball that he had to take them. "No I don't," Kimball barked. "Well, my guys are going to offload them anyway," the pilot yelled. "Well, my guys are going to shoot you if you do," Kimball countered. The pilot looked at Kimball and said, "You wouldn't dare." Kimball retorted, "Try me." He may not have handled it well, but he was on minimal sleep, exhausted, and on a short fuse. He knew that if those Hellfire missiles were dumped on him, he would have to move them out of the way, and he was not going to put his exhausted troops through that. Most likely, he would have had to put guards 24–7 on the stack of sixty missiles so the Iraqis couldn't grab them. Apparently the pilot got the message since he took off with the missiles without saying another word. Kimball was incensed that the correct parts and supplies were not being pushed to his unit. His worst fear was becoming reality—the supply chain was broken.

The squadron was supposed to take control of a series of bridges in Samawah and clear room for brigades to come across. They took the bridges but were not able to get the unarmored support vehicles across without getting chewed up by the Iraqi paramilitary forces operating around the area. The Third Infantry Division scrubbed the plan of crossing the Euphrates River at that location. Instead, they would continue up a route called Appaloosa, west of the Euphrates, and look at the bridges near Hillah and Najaf to find a way across.

They encountered nighttime ambushes along the route. A massive sandstorm descended on them, causing the Kiowas to be grounded and hindering combat operations. The ground troops fought some amazing battles in the midst of the sandstorm to secure their bridge objective, at one point becoming critically short on all supplies, including 9mm ammo. Iraqi paramilitary personnel fiercely defended the bridge. But the squadron prevailed and secured the bridge, enabling them to cross and move north along the east bank of the river. During the battle for the bridge, Fury Troop huddled in their field trains on an elevated dike road in the middle of farmland where they watched the fight, monitored the net, and listened to what was happening. Kimball was convinced some portion of the squadron was going to get overrun and they would have to get into the fight. "Thank God it never happened," Kimball thought.

The squadron soon was fighting simultaneously on three separate fronts on both sides of the Euphrates River while ammunition supply was running low. After gathering at Objective Rams with the Division, about 15 kilometers west of Najaf, to refit for the push north to Baghdad, Kimball and his first sergeant decided that the intense fighting was too much for the manufacturing representative. He was told he was going back to Kuwait. He didn't argue, but also didn't ask to be taken out. Kimball felt he was very scared and shaky. They were about to run the Karbala Gap, a 10-kilometer-wide gap near the city of Karbala, where there was a possibility of encountering Republican Guard units and perhaps being hit by chemical weapons. Intelligence analysis indicated that the Karbala Gap could become an artillery- and missile- killing zone. Everyone was scared, but at least the troops had weapons.

Kimball didn't want to drag the manufacturing representative along if they were going to be hit hard going through the Gap, possibly with chemical weapons. He sent him back on an Army flatbed truck transporting a damaged Kiowa to Kuwait for repairs. It was stunning to Kimball that he could get a flatbed out there to drag the aircraft all the way back to Kuwait, but couldn't get a damn part pushed forward. As it turned out, the expected resistance from the Republican Guard did not materialize, and the Gap was secured against surprisingly light opposition.

Sometime after the manufacturing representative returned to Kuwait, he wrote an email to colleagues detailing his exploits while with the squadron. The representative claimed that he manned a 50-Caliber machine gun after watching a soldier manning the weapon fall asleep several times, and generally criticized tactical decisions made by some of the squadron's officers, Kimball says.

The email was passed around, eventually making its way to the Corps Support Group attached to the Division. As it turned out, the commander of the Corps Support Group was the squadron commander's wife. Not surprisingly, she immediately forwarded the email to her husband with a note that he might be interested in what his contractors were up to. This occurred sometime in April, after the fall of Baghdad. The squadron commander, after reading the email, "launched." "Did the son-of-a-bitch man that .50 cal," he yelled at Kimball? "No, sir, no one put him behind a .50 cal; he didn't touch a weapon," Kimball quickly replied. Two days later, an Army team showed up to gather lessons learned, and the manufacturing representative happened to be with them. The commander wanted to see him "yesterday," and Kimball delighted in taking him there in his Humvee. As they drove in silence, Kimball handed him the email. When they arrived, Kimball walked him into the squadron commander's office and remained outside. It was not pretty. The commander proceeded to tear in to the rep for about 20 minutes. Kimball then was summoned to debunk all the rep's stories. The chewing out ended when the commander told the rep he had 48 hours to clear out of the Middle East.

After clearing the Karbala Gap untouched, the squadron made its way toward Baghdad, stopping in the desert west of the city. After a few days, they entered Baghdad and set up shop in a palace just outside the Baghdad

International Airport. Kimball's troop set up in the old Iraqi Airways engine hanger at the airport. Despite the lack of spare parts, they made it to Baghdad. It was testimony to their hard work, ingenuity, and improvisation; they were able to keep the Kiowas flying. They could not have lasted much longer without parts. Within the Third Infantry Division, battalion commanders agreed they would not have been able to continue offensive operations for another two weeks without repair parts.[13]

Water soon became a contentious subject, as bottled water started running out and replenishments were not forthcoming. The squadron had been using a combination of bottled and purified water from a portable reverse osmosis water purification unit during their march to Baghdad. It was part of the support package. In desperation, Kimball decided to continue to use water from the purifier they had brought with them. Some of the soldiers started getting sick and blamed the purifier-produced water.

They found themselves in a strange country living in a nasty hangar with blowing sand and no port-a-potties, having to use "burn shitters" (make-shift outhouse where waste matter was burned daily using diesel fuel) to dispose of waste. Kimball dropped 25 pounds; almost all the soldiers lost weight, and suffered from dehydration. But in late May 2003, their unit was detached from the squadron and integrated with an aviation brigade that did not have a purifier. Now, they were completely reliant on a limited bottled water supply that was being rationed. It was well into the summer months and very hot, and it started to get ugly. Kimball was concerned about where the food and water was going to come from. He was told not to worry about it—"higher logistics" would send in supplies. But supplies started getting tight because it was very difficult to transport bottled water given the huge amount of space the bottles required.

Kimball had to find parts to keep his Kiowas flying. He raided the Iraqi Airways hangar of about $4.5 million worth of parts. They took everything that could be used. He didn't want to have a soldier die needlessly because he couldn't get an aircraft airborne due to a lack of parts. The aircraft were out there on the front lines supporting troops in battle and keeping them safe.

The supply chain was so bad that Kimball did not see a single part pushed to him for more than two months, starting with the invasion and continuing even after beginning operations at the International Airport. He was angry and felt acquisition and procurement bureaucrats should be put in "GP Mediums" (large green canvas tents) and fed MREs until they figured out the nation was at war. Kimball and many others had nothing but bad things to say about Army logistics after the Iraq war started. In battle, maintenance is a voracious beast that consumes parts and oil and will not be denied. If the beast is not fed, then the systems that rely on it to perform their missions falter and fail in their hour of need, and then soldiers die.

It was the end of May 2003 before Kimball saw a part pushed forward to him. He was given all kinds of explanations. From the end of March to mid-April, it was, "Everyone is strung all over the Iraqi desert. We are trying to catch up with you." From mid-April to early May, it was, "There are all kinds of aviation units flying around the theater, they are all hurting for parts, we are dealing with them as well, be happy with what you got." In early May, it became, "We're pulling you guys back anyway so we are not sending you any parts because they will just get junked up in the pipeline and end up in the desert somewhere."

A lack of spare parts could have resulted in problems that would have affected the mission. Some aircraft would not have flown at all, and some would have flown in such a significantly degraded state that crews' lives would have been at greatly increased risk. Luckily, because Kimball's troops found Iraqi parts and had the ingenuity and skill to modify and use them, those problems did not arise.

Even though the squadron's deployment was eventually extended, Kimball was rotated out of Iraq in June 2003. His unit was staying, and he was going home. It was tough for him to deal with, and it haunted him for six months. Even though his unit got home in August 2003, and everyone returned safe and sound, he still wrestled with coming home before the rest of his troop.

Although no longer in the logistics field, Kimball remains very concerned about both Army logistics and the trend toward outsourcing logistics support. Many of his colleagues have also expressed dismay at the trend. Kimball feels the Army has put itself in an unsustainable position by depending on people who, under the current rules, are unreliable on the battlefield. He firmly believes that while using contractors is a good logistics model in a peacekeeping operation, such as in Bosnia, where you can operate from distributive bases with minimal threat, it is inappropriate for a peace enforcement operation such as Iraq.

As an S–4 Officer (Supply and Logistics) in Bosnia in 1999, Kimball saw the good side of contractor operations supporting troops. Order had been restored in the country, and the Army was providing a peacekeeping mission to keep the various factions from rearming and killing one another. It was, at the time, a stable area with a negligible threat of attack on convoys. The supply convoys drove without escorts. He was so happy with the support that Brown & Root (as KBR was then known) was providing that he emailed his parents in the U.S. to say that the chow was ten times better then any he had ever had in any mess hall, including in the Air Force.

Today, more than three years later, Kimball looks on the logistics problems he encountered on the battlefield with a deep sense of disappointment that the Army did not do a better job of supplying the troops and did not do what it was capable of doing with logistics. He is no longer angry. He is beyond that now. Just disappointed. Historically, there have always been problems with logistics in war, but with the advancements in technology and knowledge, he thought the problems should have been less severe.

Poor decisions at the Pentagon regarding deployment of support personnel, insufficient Army logistics and transportation command personnel, and poor contractor performance contributed to a breakdown in the supply chain, causing the troops to fight their way to Baghdad with depleted supplies. Even if Army logistics had worked perfectly, the contractor's inability to maintain inventory control for parts visibility and its inconsistent performance in hauling supplies to staging areas of Kuwait would have remained a weak link in the supply chain. Under the old system, soldiers were ordered to perform, and they did perform. Under the new system, the Army has to complain, plead, and cajole contractors to perform, and sometimes they still do not perform.

CHAPTER 4

BREAKING DOWN

After much discussion and debate, the Pentagon decided on the strategy of the "running start" for the initial invasion of Iraq in March 2003. This involved starting with a small force to keep the Iraqi soldiers off balance until additional troops arrived in the area.[1] It was Rumsfeld's way to begin the war with the fewest number of troops and a minimum of build up. The difficulty encountered as a consequence of this strategy was in the launching of the invasion before all support units had arrived. The "running start," combined with the elimination of the traditional use of the "tip-fiddle," prevented army logistics personnel and vehicles from arriving in the theater in time to properly set up the supply lines necessary for combat operations.[2]

Camp Arifjan, Kuwait, March 2003.

As the troops began the invasion in March 2003, the Army lacked the logistics personnel and vehicles it needed to keep up with the task of supplying the combat units that had rapidly spread out in the desert and begun moving toward Baghdad.[3] The Army depended on Reserve support personnel to handle supplies pouring into Kuwait. But by early March 2003, there were only 200 Reserves present, even though the authorized staffing level was 965.[4] In addition to the problem of personnel shortages, the

Army lacked sufficient ground transportation, especially cargo trucks, for distribution purposes.[5] Of the 930 light-medium and medium trucks needed, the Army only had 515 on hand, causing a serious strain on the movement of supplies.[6] Thus, the Army relied on KBR to supplement their vehicles and drivers in order to haul supplies to Udairi. But the contractor did not always have enough vehicles to move supplies as needed. Even when trucks were available, they were not always functional.[7] They didn't even have enough container handlers or hammerhead cranes to unload the seagoing containers being trucked into Udairi.

Rick Lamberth's fears were being realized. KBR's vehicles were supposed to transport supplies from the Theater Distribution Center, at Camp Doha, or from the ports at Shuaiba or Doha, for staging at Camp Udairi, near the Iraq border, in preparation for the invasion. Supplies often did not arrive in a timely manner because of mechanical difficulties with the used trucks and tractor-trailers KBR initially purchased. As Lamberth had predicted, the contractor's defective vehicles were breaking down, and many drivers were quitting; some new hires were even quitting immediately after getting off the bus at Arifjan and seeing the austere conditions they were going to operate and live in.

A U.S. Government Accountability Office (GAO) report issued in April 2005 reported that the LOGCAP contractor at one point had only 50 of the 80 trucks needed to move MREs (the soldiers' meals ready to eat) from the ports to the distribution center.[8] Because of insufficient logistics resources, "some troops experienced delays in receiving MREs, and other supplies, thereby reducing operational capabilities and increasing risk." While supply delays forced soldiers at some remote military sites in Iraq to use duct tape to hold their boots together, a KBR employee at Arifjan tried to sell Lamberth new tan Army boots that he had removed from the distribution center after breaking open a box of them with a forklift. Even though Lamberth refused the offer, the KBR employee wanted him to find others who might want to buy the boots. Lamberth complained to his manager about the employee and suggested he should be fired. But his manager had other ideas. He told Lamberth he wanted the billable body so gave the employee the option of resigning or transferring to Iraq. He was transferred to Iraq.

Army officials in Kuwait complained to Thomas that they were upset with KBR's poor performance in transporting supplies. They were upset that the task order for the Theater Transportation Mission was costing a lot of money and yet the Army was not getting the results it expected. At meetings attended by Lamberth, the Army continued to voice complaints to the contractor about its inability to keep up with the volume of supplies needed. They demanded answers, but KBR managers, according to Lamberth, delayed providing an explanation until the Army forced their hand. Lamberth recalls being told by his bosses that KBR had a monopoly and that the Army was dependent on them. The Army would get its supplies when KBR was ready to deliver them. Torn between his loyalty to KBR and his loyalty to the troops, Lamberth recalled not knowing how to handle his divided feelings. He wondered whether he should surreptitiously inform Army officers about what was going on, or go over his bosses' heads directly to senior KBR managers. It was a dilemma he couldn't resolve at that point.

At the same time some KBR managers were trying to convince the Army of its ability to perform under LOGCAP, its trucks continued to break down while trying to move supplies into Iraq. Trucks were not showing up to be loaded at Camp Udairi because of defects in the vehicles and a shortage of drivers. Also, some convoys were not finishing their routes to Baghdad, and some of the drivers were unwilling to do their jobs because of the danger of driving in a combat zone. Facing these difficulties, the Army ended up signing over some of its vehicles for KBR to use in place of its own defective trucks.

While Captain Raymond Kimball was struggling to keep his Kiowa scout helicopters flying in Iraq, KBR was having trouble supporting the effort to get spare parts to the foxhole. At Doha and a KBR warehouse in the Kuwait city of Ahmadi, Lamberth observed poor inventory management, caused by incompetent contractor employees. He also learned from some KBR employees that inventory was being lost, that parts were being siphoned off, stolen, misplaced, or damaged, all of which contributed to the problem. The GAO also found some of these problems in its investigation of logistics activities in Kuwait in 2003, noting in its report a backlog of hundreds of pallets and containers of supplies due to transportation constraints and inadequate asset visibility. They also discovered a discrepancy of $1.2 billion between the amount of materiel shipped to the theater of operations and the amount of materiel that was acknowledged as having been received. They found that physical security at the ports and other distribution points were inadequate to prevent supplies from being lost or stolen. In some cases, vehicles and expensive communications and computer equipment had been lost from distribution centers. GAO investigators also observed a wide variety of supplies spread over many acres at the distribution center in Kuwait, including "a mix of broken and usable parts that had not been sorted into the appropriate supply class, unidentified items in containers that had not been opened and inventoried, and items that appeared to be deteriorating due to the harsh desert conditions."[9] Lamberth felt that parts and other supplies were falling into a sort of Twilight Zone or black hole.

The problem of parts visibility, Lamberth found, was partly caused by radio frequency identification tags intended to track supplies not being used or maintained in a consistent manner. He observed that some KBR employees were lax in their job of scanning and maintaining the tags as supplies arrived in Kuwait. Lamberth felt that discipline in enforcing the scanning process did not exist. Even when the parts were there, visibility was lost on many critical parts.

Under LOGCAP, KBR was given the mission of managing the Theater Distribution Center, a task that included transporting supplies, repair parts, and equipment to the Army. But neither the Army nor the Pentagon had enough oversight personnel—investigators, contract managers, auditors, or inspectors—to keep up with the rapidly changing requirements of the contract and monitor the movement of supplies.[10] The scope and scale of the expansion was so dramatic as to preclude adequate management of the contractor.

The difficulty of identifying and moving repair parts into the theater was the most significant problem experienced by logistics personnel. It took almost two weeks for parts to start moving into the theater and then delivery became inadequate to support entire divisions engaged in combat operations. One after-action report by the Marine Corps called repair parts distribution a "near complete failure."[11] These parts shortages were having a significant effect on the Army's ability to wage combat. The Fourth Infantry Division disclosed in its after-action report that, due to a shortage of armored vehicle track shoes and suspension items, only 32 percent of their 176 Bradley Fighting Vehicles were mission capable by July 2003. Moreover, the Third Infantry Division reported that by June 2003, 65 percent of their Bradley's were not mission capable because of supply-related shortages.[12]

In addition to the logistics problems, Lamberth also discovered that some KBR managers who had been in Kosovo with the contractor had brought their Balkan girlfriends with them to Kuwait. Lamberth saw the influx of women at the Khalifa resort and managed to talk to some of them. They told him they were on KBR's payroll as "logistics coordinators" and "administrative assistants." Some of the women also bragged to Lamberth they took two-hour lunches and were able to go shopping using contractor-leased vehicles. Occasionally, Lamberth observed, they would track down a part, but mostly they would be at the Khalifa pool or shopping downtown. Lamberth complained to KBR managers about the issue, but was told to keep it to himself.

Months after the invasion of Iraq, Lamberth was promoted to operations manager and was transferred to Camp Udairi, where Army troops continued to amass in preparation for their move into Iraq. The insurgency was on the rise, and Army troops were finding out that their Humvees were not well protected against Improvised Explosive Devices (known as IEDs). An Army sergeant from a newly arrived unit approached Lamberth and asked if KBR could uparmor his unit's Humvees. He wanted protection for his soldiers, and the Army brass seemed unwilling to give it to them. It would be a large job involving hundreds of vehicles, but Lamberth instantly realized the importance of getting it done and knew that if he went through the KBR bureaucracy, it would take at least six months—too late for the troops. With the approval of his supervisor, Lamberth put together a team of workers and completed the task before the unit deployed into Iraq. He felt good that he was able to help the troops directly and quite possibly save some lives. But there was a price to pay. A KBR manager was livid and he chewed out Lamberth and his supervisor for allowing the uparmor job to be done. The manager told him that he wanted to expand the statement of work within the task order to include the uparmor task thereby being able to hire more employees and purchasing more equipment and materials. Lamberth felt that it would have unnecessarily raised the costs to the Army.

In another move, KBR management ordered all spare tires, jacks, and repair tools removed from their trucks before deploying into Iraq on their long journey through the harsh desert to Baghdad. Soon after arriving in Kuwait, Lamberth noticed that this vehicle equipment was being consolidated within the dispatch area at Arifjan. He asked a KBR manager why the equipment was being stored there. He was told the reason was to set up an operation where KBR employees could drive the equipment in a dispatch maintenance truck to the broken-down vehicles from a storage site in a newly leased building. This would result in a larger employee count and put to use a building already leased. Lamberth found this logic was crazy; he couldn't rationalize it. He felt it would increase the costs to the Army at the possible expense of the driver's safety.

Performance issues aside, conflicts between the Army and KBR in Kuwait over payment problems also developed, leading KBR to threaten a cessation of operations. Funding for the LOGCAP contract had been appropriated to the Army on an incremental basis, and as a result, the Army could only pay KBR with whatever funds it had available during a given incremental period.[13] It could not spend money it didn't have. Payments to the contractor were based on billings received for work performed and approved by the Army. KBR was having a problem with timely submission of invoices, and that affected the disbursement of funds for payment.[14] On the other hand, the Army was slow in approving and paying KBR for billings they did submit.[15] Aggravating the delay was a directive by the Defense Contract Audit Agency, the primary contract-auditing agency for the Pentagon, negating KBR's direct billing to the Army. KBR was now required to submit its invoices first to the audit agency for review and provisional approval, because the contractor's billing system was found to be inadequate.[16]

These billing and payment delays, coupled with the funding gaps created by the restrictions on the Army's disbursement of funds, caused KBR to operate "at risk," meaning that it had to use its own money—up to between $500 million and $1 billion at one point—to finance operations, a practice called "cash flowing." When they encounter funding gaps, contractors usually keep their work going with the expectation the government will eventually pay. However, under the Defense supplement to the Federal Acquisition Regulation's Limitation of Government's Obligation clause, known by the acronym LOGO, a contractor "will not be obligated to continue work . . .beyond that point" at which billings have exceeded the Army's funding limits.[17]

The LOGO clause creates another "just say no" problem for the military when contractors operate "at risk" during a contingency operation such as in Kuwait, Iraq, and Afghanistan. This problem reared its ugly head in Kuwait in late 2003 when KBR threatened to cease operations unless the Army paid it s bills. The Army had been in arrears in its payments to KBR for work on the contract in Kuwait, and KBR wanted its money. The threat to stop work was noticed by the GAO, which cited in their July 2004 report that, according to an administrative contracting officer in Kuwait, during November 2003, "the contractor was refusing to perform work because of its contention that no funding remained available."[18]

Lamberth recalled attending a meeting that occurred in the conference room at the Khalifa Resort late in 2003, attended by about twenty to thirty people from KBR and the Army. A senior KBR manager represented the contractor, and the military contracting officer for the LOG-

CAP contract in Kuwait represented the Army. All the military administrative contracting officers assigned to Kuwait were also there. The KBR manager told the contracting officer that, on orders from a senior level manager from KBR in Houston they would cease operations if KBR didn't get more money on their outstanding invoices. The contracting officer replied that he couldn't do that; the Army was good for it, and KBR was going to get their money. The work was documented. There was no need to take such a confrontational stance.

After the military personnel left the meeting, the KBR manager told the KBR employees who attended the meeting, including Lamberth, to be prepared to cease operations until they got more money. But the issue was resolved, and a work stoppage didn't take place. A work stoppage—going on strike on the battlefield, if you will—would have had dire consequences for the troops, who were already short on food and water, along with other supplies and parts. The near disaster is a good example of the conflicting objectives between the Army and corporate interests on the battlefield. It is "just say no" taken to extreme.

Although Lamberth noticed that KBR's overall performance in Kuwait improved a little as time went on, there were still many problems with transporting supplies from the ports and the distribution center to Udairi, and then from Udairi to Baghdad or the major bases springing up around Iraq. The truck problem improved when KBR started buying better trucks, but the driver situation worsened. Drivers continued to quit, while others didn't show up to drive. Some drivers just did not want to be put in harm's way, which presented a constant problem given the perilous journey across the almost 400 miles to Baghdad from the Kuwait-Iraq border.

American truck drivers were also getting hard to recruit and expensive to employ. The Theater Transportation Mission began to decrease in scope because of driver shortages, vehicle problems, and skyrocketing costs. According to Lamberth, the Army, frustrated with the expense and unavailability of American drivers and KBR's poor performance in operating the transportation mission, started awarding contracts for logistics transportation in Kuwait to another company, Public Warehouse Company (PWC), a huge Kuwaiti firm owned by the royal family. Retired Lieutenant General Paul Kern, former commander of the Army Materiel Command, further explained the switch to PWC was prompted by KBR's slowdown of the transportation process when convoys started to come under attack and their requests for better security.[19]

KBR also started bringing in foreign nationals as drivers, which actually led to improved driving, Lamberth felt. Even though foreign nationals were paid a much lower wage than American drivers, coming from very poor countries, they still saw significant economic advantage in working for KBR. They also had the motivation and the willingness to drive in Iraq.

The Achilles' heel of privatizing combat logistics support is the "just say no" factor: the contractor unwilling to perform critical services; drivers quitting on the battlefield; the threat of a contractor ceasing operations altogether putting the Army and its soldiers in a bind. The Army cannot force the contractor to perform in the hostile, dangerous environment of a war. Much to the detriment of its mission and to the soldiers who depend on supplies being available, the Army has failed to seriously address this problem.

By March 2004, Lamberth had tried to do his job as effectively as he could. He complained to managers many times over about the waste and efficiency he observed, but to no avail. In March, his employment with KBR was terminated for allegedly "raising his voice to a travel agent." While at the human resources office to get a ticket for a two week rest and recreation trip, the travel agent, a woman from the Balkans, was rude and disrespectful to him, Lamberth says. He asked to see her supervisor, but was not able to. She complained that Lamberth had raised his voice to her, Lamberth says. He was quickly terminated by the same manager he had been complaining to about KBR's business practices. Lamberth returned to the U.S. and settled in the northern Virginia area. He decided the best thing to do would be to utilize his knowledge of logistics, and LOGCAP, by joining an Army LOGCAP Support Unit at Ft. Belvoir, Virginia, located near Alexandria. A new adventure was about to begin.

CHAPTER 5

RUMSFELD'S ARMY

Fort Hood Texas, January 2003.

First Sergeant Perry Jefferies had drawn the short straw in Iraq, although he did not know it when he kissed his wife and four kids goodbye and left central Texas for the beginning of the Iraqi invasion. He knew it would be hard but he was not an infantryman. His job was in logistics, following the combat troops and making sure they had enough food, water, and vital equipment parts to keep advancing. A fierce and proud Texan in his early forties, he had been in the Army for 22 years and was well trained in logistics. He understood that life in a war zone was chaotic and hard, but he had confidence that after the main invasion was over, the Army would supply the troops with the basics.

A sinking feeling came over him about the invasion while preparing his unit—part of the I-10 Cavalry at Fort Hood, Texas in January 2003. He began to prepare the logistics for the 1700 men he had to equip. In looking around at what was available to his unit at Fort Hood, he instantly knew there were going to be problems. He began to see the problems that Rick Lamberth was already fretting about as a KBR employee. There were not enough trucks to carry the supplies, not enough water buffalos (water trucks), and the supply stocks, including vital replacement parts, were low. This could spell disaster at the beginning of an invasion. The existing logistics systems, he feared, would not keep enough supplies for his men in the pipeline. Little did he know that the invasion was going to be the least of his problems.

When he took his concerns to his superiors, they told him not to worry, assuring him that after he entered Iraq, the Army logistics supply chain would be right behind the troops, who would be welcomed as liberators. Based on what he had learned about logistics from past experience, he wasn't so sure. Had he known that the Army logistics chain was counting on KBR to move their supplies and that Rick Lambert believed KBR was not ready for the task—he might have been even less confident. The responsibility of supplying 1700 men facing battle began to keep Jefferies awake at night, but he still had no idea just how bad it would turn out to be.

.The top people in his command were obsessing over GPS gadgets, maps, and grids, predicting that they would know exactly where every unit was and even be able to locate every man to within a few meters. They also were completely certain they would be going through Turkey (of course, this never happened because Turkey refused access) and even picked a bridge in Turkey to use for their entry into Iraq, though they were bothered by their lack of intelligence on it.

This obsession with GPS gadgets infuriated Jefferies, who feared that the troops were headed for a logistical disaster once they got into Iraq. He knew that once the war started, all this GPS grid crap and other micromanagement would go out the window. He even tried to get the command to stop worrying about the lack of intelligence on the bridge. He downloaded a picture of the bridge from the Internet and showed them that it would not support the number of troops they planned to send over it. Although they were excited he had found this "intelligence," they continued to happy-talk him about the logistics. But he wasn't a kid like many around him and he didn't share their excitement and happy talk.

Within four days of invading Iraq from Kuwait, his unit was losing vehicles due to lack of parts and running low on food, water, and fuel. His superiors had promised that the necessary supplies would be pushed forward with them, but he soon realized that after his unit had used up the food and parts they had brought with them, they were on their own. His superiors bragged that the logistics would be run on an effective business model, but he found early on that he had to find supplies on an ad hoc basis. Jefferies and his officers had to make up a new way to find supplies; there was no backup plan.

Jefferies realized that Iraq was the first war in which the supplies were not firmly in place when the Army launched the main assault. Because the

Army thought they would be able to attack Iraq through Turkey, the supplies for the war were sent from Germany to Turkey. However, once the Turkish government refused to have the war launched through their country, these supplies and contingency equipment had to be moved into Kuwait. The base in Kuwait, Camp Doha, was not really equipped to accept the sudden onslaught of materiel. Since there was a rush to start the war, the Army logistics support was already strained even before the war began.

A GAO report noted that the Army had problems with private contractors who promised, by contract, to deliver "door-to-door" but failed to do so. They also claimed that ineffective logistical planning caused a shortage of tires, body armor, and MREs in the battlefield.

While moving from area to area in Iraq, Jefferies hoped the situation would improve as time went on. He was waking up at night with charley horses in his legs caused by dehydration and poor food and he knew that ground soldiers facing combat had to be even worse off. He thought they had hit bottom and that things would start looking up as the war turned to occupation. He could not believe this was happening in the Army he knew and loved. This was not the Army he had spent his career working for; this was a new dysfunctional army, which he now started to think of as "Rumsfeld's Army."

And it was Rumsfeld's Army. What Jefferies and the other troops did not know was that Rumsfeld insisted on being personally involved with most aspects of the war, including the logistics. Many top officers looked on with dismay when he put a troop cap on the invasion. The generals who were planning the logistics faced the same lack of personnel as the generals making plans for the troops who would fight. As you will see in a later chapter, this forced them to use the KBR support contract in ways they had never imagined.

Jefferies could not know that, while he was scraping by, Rumsfeld was fighting two wars in Washington, one with the generals and one with the State Department. As Bob Woodward mentioned in his book, *State of Denial,* Rumsfeld "personally took charge of the mobilization and deployment system. . . . He believed that he had lifted up a big rock and found a system that was totally screwed up. Soon he was personally deciding which units would deploy and when. It was an extraordinary degree of micromanagement that frustrated and enraged the military." Jefferies was right: Rumsfeld was determined to make it his Army.

PART II

MISSION ACCOMPLISHED

Major combat operations in Iraq have ended. In the Battle of Iraq, the United States and our allies have prevailed and now our coalition is engaged in securing and reconstructing that country.

—President George W. Bush, Mission Accomplished Speech, aboard the USS Abraham Lincoln, May 1, 2003.

CHAPTER 6

DUST AND DESPERATION

The scene is now familiar to the American public. On May 1, 2003, President George Bush helped pilot and land a Navy S–3B Viking aircraft onto the deck of the aircraft carrier *Abraham Lincoln* cruising off the coast of San Diego. After climbing out of the plane in full flight suit and joshing with the pilots, he delivered a speech, under a fluttering "Mission Accomplished" banner, declaring the major combat over. It was a public relations dream that would later become a nightmare as the occupation slipped more and more into civil war and chaos. But at the time, Bush seemed politically invincible as the troops on the carrier cheered him on.

The "Dustbowl," Iraq, May 2003.

Around the same time that Bush declared victory, Perry Jefferies and his units were sent to a place they called the Dustbowl, a hot and dusty area between two hills in the blistering desert near the Iraq-Iran border. They were still only eating two MREs a day and experiencing daily dehydration because of an insufficient water supply. Jefferies would stay there trying to feed and supply his men until the fall of 2003 until they were moved to another camp. He loved these men and felt a tremendous camaraderie with them because they had been through combat together. However, he didn't feel the same way about his top-level Brigade and Division commanding officers. They were not taking care of their troops as required by Army tradition. But his commanding officer at the Dustbowl, Lieutenant Colonel Theodore Martin, was a different breed. Martin greatly impressed Jefferies by refusing to sleep on a bed if any of his soldiers were wanting, eating the same food they did, and doing everything in his power to support his men. As he saw his men do without so many basic necessities, Jefferies realized there were not enough officers like Martin in this conflict.

Jefferies and his men had very little access to mail or information. It even took over two months for them to find out that Bush had landed on the aircraft carrier and declared "Mission Accomplished." He could not believe that he and his men had been abandoned by their country. How in the hell did it come to this? He was furious that his men were down to just two MREs per day.

They had no bathrooms, no showers, and rationed water in the 114-degree heat. They had infrequent mail delivery, very limited fuel, and scarce spare parts for their broken trucks and other equipment, including tanks. Because of these transportation problems, they rarely could travel even short distances to try to scrounge for what they needed. He saw that his men were suffering and thought that it would be considered unjust to treat convicts like this in the U.S.; but apparently it was OK in the Rumsfeld Army.

Jefferies realized they only had each other. The soldiers in his unit became amazing scavengers and improvisers. They worked hard every day to keep a few trucks running for an occasional attempt to get supplies from a far-away base, and they tried to help each other by making sure the food and water went to those who were the thinnest or most dehydrated. He made lifelong bonds with these men, bonds beyond the usual battlefield bonds, because they had to share such hard times.

When an Army Bath and Shower unit showed up after eight weeks, Jefferies astounded them by commandeering the trucks of water intended for showers and hoarding it instead for precious drinking water.

Jefferies and the others in this dire condition would occasionally hear from outside visitors and newcomers that in the Brigade commands, where the top officers stayed, there were three hot meals a day, cybercafés, ice, rec tents, mail, and plenty of water and snacks. They heard about the big contractor-run mess tents with all the food you wanted to eat. He knew from experience that the contractors would deliver what they promised as long as there were top brass around. He also knew that his top commanders were going to sleep each night with a full stomach, while he was rationing food to young kids. However, he would not eat any more than his troops ate. Skinny at the beginning of the war at 5'6" and 135 pounds, he had slipped to 112 pounds during the occupation. As the hot, sand-whipped days went on and on for months and he still could not fix the situation, he finally began to believe that Rumsfeld and the commanders who allowed this were woefully negligent. He knew that contractors were being used to make life easy for anyone who was lucky enough to be near a big city or a command brigade. .

He knew where his senior commanding officers were. They weren't at the closest camp to the Dustbowl, Camp Warhorse, but further away, working and living in Saddam Hussein's hometown palace compound in Tikrit, called Camp Ironhouse. This was the largest of Saddam's palaces. Jefferies had seen it when his troop had moved through the country during the early part of the occupation. It was, of course, palatial, with many buildings in the compound. With many dining areas, television, air conditioning, Internet, and a marble-decked indoor pool, it was set up to be a rest and recreation (R+R) site for the Fourth Infantry, which was his main unit and where his senior commanders stayed,. KBR was making sure that all who where there, especially the officers in charge, were well cared for. This just made Jefferies all the more bitter. No contractor trucks and very few Army trucks were getting through to them. He could not even get enough parts for his trucks to go get the supplies with his men.

Jefferies was known as the guy who would take it upon himself to complain up the line whenever he could. He and his commander would complain as loudly and bitterly as they dared to get the supplies for their men. Unfortunately it wasn't working, and later Jefferies found out that his top commanders, although well supplied themselves in their fancy bases, were having their own problems trying to get the supplies needed by their subordinates in this new, untested, contractor-reliant logistics chain. KBR was emerging as one of the weak links in the supply chain.

CHAPTER 7

AFFLICT THE COMFORTABLE

"The Dustbowl," Iraq, May 2003.

Even though the occupation had begun, Command Sergeant Major David List of the 1-10 Cavalry was still on the warpath in the Iraqi war zone, pursuing not the Iraqi enemy but the Army brass wherever he could find them. He was not going to allow the Army to neglect his troops. He took his command very seriously, and his troops loved him for it. He now had to fight the brass and cope with the failures of the contractors in a war zone. Wiry and intense with a big thick gray mustache, List is a career warrior-soldier who would track down any officer in his sector to make things better for his beleaguered troops.

As the top sergeant in the unit, Perry Jefferies reported to Command Sergeant Major List. The two men had worked together in Fort Hood to prepare for this war, and Jefferies had suggested that Adam Roe, a support platoon truck driver, become List's driver. Roe was a good ole boy from West Texas who was able to work up from his humble beginnings to a Sergeant E-5 rank. He had spent most of his adult life in the Army and loved it. A jack-of-all-trades, he could drive trucks, did excellent carpentry work, and could do just about any other task asked of him. Jefferies relied on him a lot in their unit at Fort Hood but thought that it would be a great opportunity for Roe to be List's driver. None of them could have guessed the adventure that List was about to take him on in Iraq. Roe was delighted with the new task of driving this larger-than-life character.

List was from Colorado and had also joined the Army as a very young man. After his first stint in the Army, he had worked as a bodyguard in Africa but eventually decided to go back into the Army for good. He was an old tank person and loved the excitement of battle. He would always trade a pen for a bullet and did not want any other job, such as recruiter or drill sergeant.

Like Jefferies, List was adamant about being prepared for battle in Iraq. As they prepared for war in the fall of 2002, he would not tolerate any goofing off and would have Roe drive him from section to section to make sure everyone was in full-court press in preparing for battle. He was surprised and impressed to see the troops working hard when he arrived at each new section. Roe finally had to tell List that the sections were tracking his Humvee by its GPS unit and could all tell when he was approaching their area. A chagrined List told Roe that he was going to have to turn the GPS unit off.

List and Roe were responsible for the whole 1–10 Cavalry's convoy into Iraq. In early April 2003, they left Kuwait and started for the Iraqi border. List would have Roe drive up and down the convoys to make sure everything was ready. When they reached the Iraqi border and officially entered the battle zone, List told Roe to stop at the head of the convoy. In the old Cavalry tradition, they both put on their spurs (you earn them when you finally go into a combat zone), and then List put on a large Cavalry hat, drew his saber, and raised it to go into battle. Roe remembers the sight of this warrior leading the charge to battle in his Humvee, spurs and hat on and saber drawn.

It took the convoy 26 hours to get to the staging area, and List had Roe driving up and down the convoy during the whole trip. Once the actual battles were over, List took on a new role. When their initial supplies and parts began to dry up and new parts were not pushed to them as promised, he took it upon himself to track down the brass to see what he could do for his men.

Dressed in full battle gear, List would have Roe speed his overdriven Humvee into the comfortable established camps where officers would stay and track them down in mess tents, church services, and even a latrine. List would find them and would bedevil them with requests and complaints that his troops were not getting the supplies, food, and parts they needed and tell them he expected something to be done about it. His zeal for his men made sure that no officer within his area would be comfortable while the troops were suffering. And he had plenty to be angry about. Soldiers living in dire conditions just a short drive away from the bases would inspire him to jump in his Humvee, and speed to the nearest commander. He once found an Air Force officer and asked him how many boots he had. The officer told him two pairs, and List insisted that he surrender one pair for the soldiers at various checkpoints who were living with one taped-up pair.

The men at the checkpoints had the worst time of it. They would be posted out in obscure areas next to a dusty road for weeks at a time with just a few Humvees, MREs, water, and primitive tent shelters. Because there were miles of roads between these checkpoints and they were very far away from any bases, the conditions were even worse than what Jefferies was experiencing. List and Roe would continually make the rounds at these checkpoints, and List made sure that he had picked up ice and other supplies from locals or from the Forward Operating Bases (FOBs). These men were clearly "away from the flagpole," and without List's dogged determination they would have been in even worse condition. List ended up putting the most mileage in the unit on his Humvee in his endless work to help his troops.

List would not stay in comfortable buildings while men under him slept on the ground. List and Roe kept sleeping bags in the ever-present Humvee, and they would throw themselves on the hard desert ground next to the Humvee to sleep. Roe remembers that they did not sleep in a building until June 2003 and List did not sleep in a bed until November. He said that the men admired List for his dedication to their well being.

Roe claimed that List did not complain to him about the logistics failures affecting his troops. But Roe watched him go into the comfortable, air-conditioned offices in the FOBs where the higher brass and even some of his counterparts were living and let it fly. List began to realize that the failure went much higher up the logistics chain than he originally thought when he discovered that even some of the bigger bases could not get a steady stream of supplies. One big problem was that KBR could not be relieved of its command for nonperformance, as the Army brass was always able to do with its commanders in the past. Whatever the reason for his troops not getting served, List would still afflict the comfortable to get whatever he could for his troops.

As often as possible, they would get supplies out to the troops in the field and in the Dustbowl where Jefferies was stuck, which List called the "asscrack of the world." In June, Roe got appendicitis and had to be airlifted out. After his surgery, he returned to Iraq, but List could not wait and had gotten another driver to tear around the desert with him. Roe was assigned to help Jefferies and his men deal with the dire conditions at their next post in any way he could. Meanwhile, List pressured the brass until early 2004, when he was rotated home to Fort Carson, Colorado. He went back to Iraq for another hitch, and Roe knows that List, on this new tour, still bedeviled the brass on behalf of his soldiers.

CHAPTER 8

FOR THE MONEY

September 2003, Venus, Florida.

At age fifty, David Wilson was bored. Owning his truck, which he leased to major trucking companies and drove himself, made a good living. His sons were grown, and he did not have any other family obligations. He decided that he wanted to go to Iraq as a truck driver or manager of truck convoys, hoping that the experience would lead to trucking jobs around the world. KBR was advertising for truckers, and he took the plunge in late 2003.

A Vietnam-era veteran, he was not naïve about life in a war zone. Though he would not say where he was during the war, he said enough for you to know that he had seen action.

Wilson was impressed that KBR put him up in a five-star hotel in Houston for his five-day orientation. It was gold plated all the way, with tuxedoed waiters serving hors d'oeuvres to groups of truckers. This was quite a change from the Motel 6 that some of the leasing companies put him in. We are really going first class, he thought.

Much of the orientation went as expected, with physicals and information sessions. The State Department issued the truckers Army IDs that just said "other" in the blank for rank. At the end of the orientation, Wilson found himself in a surreal motivational session with hundreds of other truckers. The truckers were delayed in getting their visas and tickets, so

KBR wanted to give the men a pep talk about their mission in Iraq. According to Wilson, the speaker told them they were going to Iraq "for the money." He then went on to say they were not going to be heroes, and had the group chant a response of "FOR THE MONEY" as he repeatedly asked them why they were going. Wilson claimed this continued with the same chanting answer when he told them they were not going to help the troops, not going to help the Iraqi people, not going for America. As the group continued to chant "FOR THE MONEY" over and over, Wilson looked around in amazement at the open greed and ambition. Halliburton was not even trying to sugarcoat their motives in this war—no pseudo-patriotic talk here.

James Warren, who eventually served in the truck convoy Wilson commanded, had gone through the orientation a few weeks before Wilson. Warren was from the mountains of North Carolina and had been driving a truck since 1990. For the past few years, he had been driving his truck across country with his wife, who was also a truck driver.

A friend of his told him about KBR, so he decided to call the 800 number for KBR. He was hired on the spot with just a phone interview, with the caveat that he needed to pass the security check. He was also placed in nice hotels and fed fancy meals. Warren could not understand why KBR would hire people and fly them down to Houston to wait in fancy hotels even before they passed the security check. He saw it as a big waste of taxpayers' money. KBR had trouble getting his group of truckers deployed and gave several excuses, such as lack of body armor and or lack of parts for the trucks, so these truckers sat at their luxury hotels for three weeks while still being paid daily.

Warren also remembers that during all the motivational talks KBR gave them, the emphasis was on how much money they were going to make. The KBR speakers told them that they were going for the money and that they would have very happy wives because they would be making so much money tax-free. There was a hitch, though. The truckers had to spend at least 330 days outside U.S. territory or they would have to pay taxes on their earnings when they got home. Warren and Wilson would come to realize the advantage of keeping their mouths shut to avoid being sent home early.

Warren was sent to Kuwait in October 2003, and Wilson followed in November 2003, six months after the war had ended and the occupation had begun. They were put up in a five-star hotel with hundreds of other truckers to await their assignments. This time they were in overcrowded shared suites, and many truckers had to resort to sleeping on rolls in cots. Because of his experience, Wilson had confidence that he could handle any assignment given to him. But he started to worry when he saw how KBR was deciding who, from this myriad of truckers with varied background, would be picked for convoys. One of the managers came into the gilded ballroom where they were awaiting assignment and told the foreman that he needed 40 fuel truckers, a tricky and dangerous assignment in a war zone. Instead of finding truckers who have driven a tanker, according to Wilson, the foreman just called up the first 40 guys on the list. Wilson started to get a sinking feeling that he had placed his life in the hands of people who might not know what they were doing. Warren met a man who had been hired as a truck driver although he had never even driven a truck, and another young man who had just graduated from trucking school but never had been out on the road. It would only get worse.

Each convoy included about 30 trucks and stretched over a mile-and-a-half long. When Wilson's first convoy took off from Kuwait for the Iraqi border, there was no security. On the way to the border, Wilson drove in the middle of the convoy, where he could watch the truck drivers ahead of him. Some were all right but others were weaving, clear indication that they were not familiar with big trucks. He decided that he was not really afraid of the possible insurgent attacks they would face once they got into Iraq, but he was definitely afraid of some of these weaving drivers. He could imagine the domino-like collision that would ensue if one of 30 trucks jackknifed and they were all left vulnerable on a long stretch of road. They picked up Army escorts when they hit the border.

Warren was assigned during the last 30 days of his employment with KBR to oversee some foreign workers, loading the trucks from the supply warehouse in Kuwait. He was dismayed to find that these men had no idea how to load a truck, that they could not speak English so he could not communicate with them, and that there was no inventory control over the items they were loading. Seeing that the supplies came from the United States, the workers assumed that they must be needed by the troops and loaded them haphazardly onto the trucks.

In the beginning of Wilson's convoy runs, Army trucks driven by Army drivers were sprinkled throughout the KBR convoys. By early December, however, the Army pulled out their trucks and drivers and left KBR in charge of the convoys and all the drivers. From that point on, the Army only supplied troops to guard the convoys.

Wilson was happy to discover that the Army escorts dedicated to his convoy group really knew what they were doing. They picked up Wilson's convoy at the Kuwait-Iraq border and escorted them to Camp Cedar II, next to the Tallil Air Force Base located in southern Iraq near An Nasiriyeh, approximately 310 kilometers south of Baghdad. Wilson was arriving in Iraq at about the same time Perry Jefferies was leaving. Camp Cedar II was also called a convoy pit stop. During his entire stay in Iraq, about four months, Wilson was part of daily convoys that shuttled vital supplies back and forth between Camp Cedar and Camp Anaconda, located about 40 miles north of Baghdad. These camps had supplies and facilities that Jefferies could only dream about: air-conditioned tents and latrines, Internet cafés, major dining facilities, movie theaters, fitness centers, and, shortly before Wilson left, even mobile Burger Kings. This was also where the main brass would stay and where KBR pulled out all the fancy amenities to impress the senior officers. So even though Wilson's grueling convoys often required 20-hour days, he and the troops who rotated in and out of these camps really saw them as oases of American comfort in a primitive, strange land of few comforts.

One of the stickiest problems on the route was going through parts of Baghdad. Wilson was amazed at the Iraqis and their rock-throwing ability. They threw rocks at everyone, strangers, military, truck convoys, even their wives. It was disconcerting to drive through these suburbs of Baghdad and some of the smaller towns while being pelted with rocks. One of the worst places was a small town called Samarrah a holy Islamic town 124 kilometers north of Baghdad, which had a traffic circle. As the trucks slowed to go around the circle, the rock pelting hit peak intensity and truck windows were often shattered. But putting himself in the Iraqis' place, Wilson wondered if he might also throw rocks if convoys were speeding, 30 trucks strong, right through his town with supplies he did not have. Warren had four smashed windshields during his time in Iraq.

Later on, when Wilson became a convoy commander, he and the Army sergeant dedicated to his convoy decided to change the way they drove through the traffic circle and town square. They sent the Army escorts ahead of the entire convoy and blocked off the traffic circle so that their trucks would not threaten any cars in the circle, and then slowed the convoy down to drive through the town square at a respectful speed. As a result, the Iraqis stopped throwing rocks and began watching politely and even waving as the convoys went by. Wilson believed that the Iraqis just wanted their town to be treated with respect. However, in other towns with narrow roads and multi-storied buildings, he knew that they had to watch for snipers or IEDs.

Usually the Army protection consisted of four groups—two Humvees, not necessarily uparmored, and two 915s, low-armored Army trucks not considered combat vehicles. At least one of the Humvees was supposed to have a machine gun mounted on top. Once, Wilson's Army convoy escort arrived with a Humvee with a fiberglass roof and no turret mount. Wilson knew that the Army was required by the contract to have a Humvee equipped with a SAW (Squad Automatic Weapon), but his complaint to his supervisor was to no avail. Going on that mission without the protection necessary for the truckers and the troops, the convoy was attacked twice. Before the next mission, Wilson raised hell with the KBR management and the sergeant attached to Wilson's convoy, finally got his gun-mounted Humvee.

For some unexplained reason, KBR did not always buy the kind of closed trailers for their trucks that you see on American freeways, or even flatbed trucks with shipping containers attached to them. Instead, they often used flatbed trucks with no covers. Supplies had to be strapped down by the truckers, which took many hours, and then driven with no protection from sand or rain. Anyone could see what was on the trucks, and when they were delayed on the road, the truckers had to make sure that local Iraqis did not "go shopping" on the stopped trucks. Iraqi kids learned to use knives on sticks to cut the straps when the convoys crept by and retrieve the goods that fell off the flatbeds. Warren thought that it was a security problem and just a bad idea to have all these consumer goods visible to the Iraqis, especially since they had so little after the many years of embargo and two wars. He estimated that at least 10 percent of the cargo on every truckload was looted. At the end of the run, the Army would check off the categories of the items they had delivered, but did not count the individual items themselves and thus had no way of knowing how many had been pilfered.

Wilson also could not figure out why KBR did not systematically have a bill of lading or any paperwork recording what was on the truck. Not seeing any RDIF (radio frequency tracking tags) on the material, he did not understand how they knew what was being shipped or used or lost and how to bill the government for the supplies. It was total chaos compared to the accountability and management of trucking companies at home. He would often try to sort out the paperwork that he did have on the number of trucks in the convoy, but it was usually wrong and chaotic.

His frustration grew and he felt that some of the problems arose from stupidity and mismanagement due to the lack of experience. The trucks would run the same run every day at the same time. He knew from experience it was crazy to do anything like that with insurgents plotting to disrupt the supply chain. It was very easy for the insurgency to set an IED on the side of the road and just put a timer on it. To the chagrin of his Army escorts, KBR set the rules of the convoy. When the Army decided to have a contractor be the main convoy link in the supply chain, they also gave up quality control on the management, equipment, and personnel. Wilson would try to tell the managers about this problem and others but he was mostly ignored. They did promote him to alternate convoy manager, but he wasn't impressed with the title once he saw the inexperience and ignorance of his convoy commander. That inexperience and ignorance, he says, almost got them killed.

CHAPTER 9

A DIFFERENT
KIND OF SUBURB

March 2004, Camp Anaconda.

David Wilson had survived his convoy driving in Iraq, but he was becoming more and more concerned about the KBR decisions that he believed were potentially putting drivers at risk.

For example, one convoy was going through a Baghdad suburb when it had to come to a complete halt because vehicles in another convoy up ahead had been hit by an IED. The KBR convoy commander grew impatient and wanted to move on, but the road was clearly blocked. He told Wilson they were going to try to get off the main road with 30 trucks and wind through the back roads of the suburb. When Wilson protested about the danger and the impracticality of backing up so many trucks, the convoy commander insisted. The Army escorts, who were nervous and unhappy about this order, were told by the convoy commander to run over some guardrails on the road so the trucks could back up and get on a side road. The Army personnel followed the KBR convoy commander's orders.

Wilson was horrified when he saw where they were going. They were driving at a snail's pace through one of the poorest and worst slums of Baghdad. The soldiers had their rifles ready. There were over a thousand Iraqis on the street watching them in amazement that any American would dare come in their neighborhood. Warren, who was also on that convoy run, expected that one of the Iraqis would fire a bullet or RPG (Rocket Propelled Grenade) through his window at any moment. Wilson believed they made it through because of the bravery of the Army escorts and the dumbfounded re-action of the Iraqis, who might have suspected that the stupid stunt was some sort of trap. Warren was driving near the end of that convoy and saw the Iraqis starting to throw rocks at the trucks at the back. The convoy made it through, but Wilson was determined not to place himself and others at such risk again.

He complained bitterly to his superiors when they returned and the con-voy commander was put back on truck driving duty. Wilson was promoted to convoy commander during his last few months in Iraq. KBR was beginning to hire more and more foreign nationals to drive their trucks and they tried to get Wilson to take over the foreign national's convoys. He turned down the offer because of the obvious danger of taking these poorly trained drivers on the road and stayed with his convoy group of American drivers. He had been con-cerned about the driving of some of his American drivers until he saw the poor driving skills of the foreign nationals. Other convoy managers had told him that the foreign drivers would sometimes break away from the convoy and just drive across the desert, stealing the truck and supplies. With only four units to guard the entire 30-truck convoy, the Army could not afford to send anyone to chase after the thieves, so they just had to watch as the stolen trucks sped over the desert, eventually disappearing into the haze and dust.

Warren did go on some runs set up such that a convoy commander was in the first truck, all foreign drivers in the middle, and his truck at the end as the bobtail. He knew that most of the foreign drivers did not know how to put their trucks in reverse and worried that if they had to stop and back up because of an attack, many of them would be killed.

Wilson considered many things insisted on by upper management as being beyond stupidity, and he could not understand how the company could allow them all to be placed in such jeopardy. For instance, when brand new trucks arrived for the convoys, KBR would have all the spare tires removed. This guaranteed that a truck would have to be abandoned if it got a flat tire. Wilson could not believe that this company was willing to risk an $85,000 truck over a spare tire. What in the world was in their minds? The Army convoy escorts would sometimes torch a disabled truck and all of its cargo so that the Iraqis could not acquire the assets. Wilson thought that some of the trucks could be towed and the supplies saved. He could not imagine why the military would allow such waste when supplies were so short. Moreover, the company had nowhere to do regular mainte-nance for the trucks. Even the convoy pit stops were poorly stocked and poorly managed and could not supply the truckers or the managers with oil filters in the gritty desert climate. This caused many failures along the way, and often the trucks could not be saved.

Sometimes KBR would haul supplies for an Infantry unit rotating through one of the camps but fail to reach the camp before the unit deployed. When that happened, KBR would instruct the convoys to return the cargo even though there were other units coming in from the countryside desperate for supplies. Many of the units in isolated areas, such as where Jefferies was located, had to drive long distances at great peril to raid a convoy for supplies when it stopped for the night. Wilson would feel the trucks rocking as the Army soldiers scavenged for anything of use. He felt very sorry for their plight and did not complain when he and others would have to repeat the strap-down process for whatever was left in the morning.

Warren also believed that some of the pilfering was carried out by unscrupulous Army and KBR people taking advantage of the lack of security and paperwork to make a profit on the black market. Items such as Army boots, uniforms, and even laptops disappeared and made him so angry that he personally called Randy Hurl, the head of Halliburton, to tell him about the theft that was going on at night with the KBR trucks at Camp Anaconda. Hurl thanked him and told him that he would look into it. Warren never heard back from him and the pilfering continued.

Wilson was the most puzzled when KBR ordered the entire convoy to go ahead with the daily run even if the many trucks were mostly empty. Once, only one of the trucks had any supplies on it, but all 30 had to accompany it, despite the additional costs in wear and tear, hourly pay for the drivers, and fuel for the empty trucks. This was very demoralizing for the KBR truckers, who had to put their lives on the line to drive empty trucks that were not helping anyone in uniform.

One time, after the insurgency got a foothold and IEDs became very common, four KBR truckers refused to drive empty trucks. This shut down the convoy for a while, but KBR simply pulled other truckers to from their pool to replace the recalcitrant drivers. They were not interested in addressing their employees' concerns or trying to be more efficient in solving problems. The truckers knew that if they refused to drive, KBR could replace them and send them home, forcing those who had not met the 330-day threshold to pay taxes on their salaries. Even with this threat, however, the rate of American truck drivers quitting and returning to the United States increased.

Wilson attempted to explain to any management person who would listen how the operations could be made more efficient and less dangerous for everyone. He was ignored and avoided.

Eventually Wilson's manager told him to report back to headquarters in Kuwait. Wilson figured that he had been bumped up to a desk job and was not looking forward to it. He was stunned when his manager told him that he was terminated after just four months because there were reports that trucks in his convoy were running Iraqi vehicles off the road. Although he had not witnessed this himself, he knew that it had happened. Right before they went out on their first convoy, he remembered what one of the KBR managers told the truckers: "We can't tell you to do this, but just remember that if you get captured, you will be raped and beaten, then raped and beaten again. So if you need to put vehicles off the road, that's what you have to do."

Warren, who had received the same instructions as Wilson, was also called in about the Iraqi vehicle problem. The managers demanded he tell them who in his convoy had run vehicles off the road. Both Wilson and Warren were very close with all the men in the convoy and refused to co-operate. Both went back to the United States in early April 2004. Warren had to pay an extra $15,000 on his income tax bill because he did not stay the 330 days outside the United States.

Wilson has resumed driving his truck across the country and has time to reflect on what he saw in Iraq. He felt sorry for the Army escorts and the truck drivers who worked so hard to deliver supplies. He feels even worse for the soldiers who did not get what they needed because of the same seemingly nonsensical rules that kept Perry Jefferies from getting even bare necessities like of food and water. Now, as he rolls down U.S. highways with all their restaurants, malls, hotels, and every other imaginable convenience, it seems surreal to see so many "We Support the Troops" bumper stickers and magnetic yellow ribbons. The public is clueless about the portion of their $2 billion dollars a week being wasted on mismanaged supplies and questionable billings. Because of his experience in Iraq, he knows that greed and waste are preventing the money meant for the troops from benefiting them as much as it should.

Although KBR's rules initially seemed ludicrous to Wilson, a trucker with experience in the competitive U.S. market, he came to understand the scam after it was explained to him upon his return to the United States. KBR's $16 billion contract to supply the troops does not pay according to any indicator of achievement or progress. Rather, the contract is structured so that the more the contractor spends, the higher his profit. Unlike in past wars, the KBR truck convoys in Iraq were run in the interest of profit, not mission.

Therefore, there is no incentive to control the costs; you make more profits if you spend more money, even if it is wasted. Your profit is a percentage of what you spend, so the more you spent, the higher your profit. While it appears crazy to take off spare tires and lose an $85,000 truck, your profit actually increases if you show that you need to buy another one because one was lost on the side of the road. If your supplies are looted, it will be hard to know because there is no bill of lading, no tracking. But when the supplies are looted before making it to their destination, the Army will have to order more, and your profit will increase. The more you waste, the more goods you lose, the more profit you make, because it is based on a percentage of what you spend. With that understanding, KBR's crazy management makes perfect, greedy sense.

But, Wilson wondered, would a company actually do this unpatriotic thing in the middle of a war zone to our soldiers and their employees? It seemed unbelievable, but no more so than being made to chant with his fellow new hires that he was going to Iraq "FOR THE MONEY." This, he felt, must be the company creed.

Out of his fear for himself and for the soldiers accompanying the convoys, Wilson ended up complaining to his superiors so much that he was pushed out of KBR and sent back to the United States. He was so angry about the situation that he was willing to testify to Congress, with the help of Henry Waxman, about some of what he saw. As discussed in a later chapter, some of the members of Congress did not want to hear what he had to say.

Wilson's concerns about the dangers of KBR-managed convoys were realized dramatically on April 9, 2004, when insurgents attacked a KBR fuel convoy, killing, injuring, or kidnapping 18 drivers. Many Americans saw the KBR convoy commander, Tommy Hamill, on television after he was captured and held for 24 days before escaping. Warren also saw Hamill on television after he returned to the United States. He was stunned to see that one of the convoy commanders who had been on his flight to Kuwait had been captured by insurgents.

An Army report on the incident revealed a lack of communication and coordination between the Army and KBR. The report claimed that the Army did not trust KBR enough to give its employees classified Army radios, and so the company only had crude radio contact with Hamill. To compound the problem, Hamill had incompatible and conflicting radio contact with his drivers and KBR headquarters. First he would have to use one set of radios to talk to his convoy and other set to talk to the headquarters. This unwieldy system failed during the emergency. The report concluded: "Once engagement began there was a complete lack of ability to communicate under intense enemy fire."

Edward Sanchez and Sean Larvenz, two of the surviving truckers from that ill-fated convoy, are suing KBR over this attack. They claim the company knew that the road was too dangerous to travel and had been warned by the Army not to send any trucks but ordered the convoy sent anyway. KBR denies the charges. In another bizarre twist, Ray Stannard, one of the truck drivers wounded in the same convoy, was considered for the Secretary of Defense Medal for the Defense of Freedom, a medal for government contractors wounded in hostile action. Stannard was told that KBR was going to put his name in for the medal but they needed a release of his medical records for proof. However, when Stannard read the release, he noticed that it required him to promise not to sue the company. The release states:

> I agree that in consideration for the application for a Defense of Freedom Medal on my behalf that . . . I hereby release, acquit and discharge KBR, all KBR employees, the military, and any of their representatives . . . with respect to and from any and all claims and any and all causes of action, of any kind or character, whether now known or unknown, I may have against any of them which exist as of the date of this authorization.

Stannard decided to forgo the medal and sued KBR for his injuries in the convoy.

In early April 2004, due to this attack and other rising violence in Iraq, contractor employees began to leave, actually forcing KBR to stop convoys for just under two weeks. It was the "just say no" policy at work, and it threw logistics into a tailspin. According to T. Christian Miller's book *Blood Money:* "Although the company ceased work for less than two weeks, the coalition faced immediate problems of supplying food and water. U.S. Marines in Al Anbar province west of Baghdad issued rationing orders two days after the April 9 attack on the KBR convoy. . . .By April 17 the situation had grown so bad that Bremer [head of the Coalition Provisional Authority] considered ordering food rationing for the CPA itself."

As a result of the departure of so many of its American truck drivers, KBR had to hire more and more foreign nationals to drive their trucks. As we will see in a later chapter, the Army began to replace more and more KBR trucks with trucks driven by Army drivers—including Adam Roe, David List's former driver—and convoy commanders while still paying KBR for running the convoys.

CHAPTER 10

THE GREEN ZONE

Baghdad International Airport, Iraq, November 2003.

Sergeant Bobby Yen, U.S. Army Reserves, arrived at Baghdad International Airport with his unit, the 222nd Broadcast Operations Detachment from California, having flown in a military cargo plane with the unit's Humvees. As it turned out, it was the perfect time to arrive—after the initial fighting and before the rise of the insurgency. He found the airport relatively modern and open, yet barren. He was trying to get his bearings, but was overwhelmed with the newness of everything. The unit had been rushed to Baghdad as high priority, apparently because the Army needed public relations assets there. But when they arrived, nobody knew who called them or why. It was absurd. The Army rushed them there to sit around? There was confusion, and no one could give them a definitive answer about where they were supposed to go or what they were supposed to do.

Yen joined the Army Reserves at age 19, while a sophomore at UCLA, to serve his country and live out his lifelong dream of being a soldier. The youngest of three, and the son of Taiwanese immigrants, Yen grew up in Atherton, California, a wealthy town of the Silicon Valley elite, south of San Francisco. He was born of well-educated and accomplished parents who placed a premium on education, status, and money. His older sister became a doctor and his older brother was working on his PhD in New York. But his parents were disappointed when Yen only got into UCLA and not a more prestigious school. They became upset when he decided to join the Army Reserves—they felt the move was unnecessary. At the time, Yen did not expect to be deployed anywhere. It was before 9/11, and the Reserves never went anywhere. It was a good balance—being a citizen-soldier while developing a career. Yen was scheduled to end his commitment with the Reserves in January 2004. But in November 2003, after graduating from UCLA with a degree in both computer science and engineering, his TV and Radio Unit was called up to deploy to Iraq. His duty with the Reserves had been involuntarily extended.

Yen was unhappy, but he retained a sense of idealism about the deployment. He believed he would be fighting to defend America and for the good of democracy. He was concerned about weapons of mass destruction in Iraq and felt it was necessary to do something about them.

Before deploying, Yen, and his unit of about 30 reservists were mobilized at Ft. Lewis, Washington, near Tacoma. It was there that Yen discovered they did not have the right armor and other equipment for Iraq. They were given old, Vietnam-era flak jackets that wouldn't protect them from a BB gun. A debate broke out among the soldiers in Yen's unit over the wisdom of purchasing better vests on their own. A few of the soldiers could not afford to buy better body armor. Others felt it wouldn't feel right if they had new vests and other soldiers didn't. Still, some believed that if they needed better vests, the Army would supply them. There was also the belief they wouldn't need vests since they were reporters and not combat soldiers.

Besides the old vests, they were also equipped with old, Vietnam-era Single Channel Ground Airborne Radios, known in the military as SINC-GAR radios, contained in large, bulky backpacks. The problem was that these bulky radios needed a specific type of battery with a short life span. These batteries were hard to get and would be available at only a few main bases in Iraq. As it turned out, Yen could not communicate to his people with the SINCGAR radios and had to borrow better radios from other units. If it was so important for their unit to get to Iraq, he felt, why didn't the Army give them proper equipment to start with?

Along with seven other soldiers, Yen decided to order a new vest before deploying to Iraq. They cost them $1,800 apiece when ordered through a catalog. Concerned about his safety, Yen's parents agreed to finance the vests for Yen and the other soldiers until they were able to pay the money back. He had a difficult time rationalizing the Army's spending priorities. Gourmet food, plasma TVs, and video games seemed to be a priority at main bases; body armor, uparmored Humvees, and night vision goggles, did not. It was muffins over armor. But not to worry, Yen mused. If a soldier was bleeding to death, he could soak up the blood and stop the flow with a muffin. Old, inadequate equipment was seemingly all the Army could afford. They were not well prepared for Iraq.

Once things were sorted out at the airport in Baghdad, Yen's main group was used to establish the American Forces Network in Iraq. This network is the operational arm of the American Forces Radio and Television Service, an agency of the American Forces Information Service that operates under the Assistant Secretary of Defense for Public Affairs. It provides news, information, and entertainment programs through radio and television broadcasts and has been operating since World War II. Robin Williams made the network famous as a broadcaster in the movie *Good Morning Vietnam.*

Army officials determined that not all 30 reservists were needed in Baghdad to establish the network. So, while half of the unit was sent to Baghdad, a quarter of them were sent to the Balad area, where Camp Anaconda was located. The remaining personnel, including Yen, were sent to Mosul in the Kurdish area of northern Iraq. As a reporter for television news broadcasts, Yen was assigned to conduct interviews, mostly about military units and their specific missions, to be broadcast to the troops through the newly formed network.

Assignments were handed down the chain of command, mainly generated from the Coalition Press Information Center, a centralized media information center established in Kuwait during preparations for Operation Iraqi Freedom and later moved to the Green Zone area of Baghdad. Staffed by members of the U.S., British, and Australian military, the information center, Yen later found out, was constantly in a struggle with the Coalition Provisional Authority over editorial control—over what the focus, content, and tone of the stories should be. To Yen, the CPA seemed to be out of touch with what was going on outside the Green Zone. Assignments generated from the Information Center were broad in scope and usually somewhat one-sided, stressing, for example, how secure the troops were, or how the military was working cooperatively with the Iraqis on rebuilding and training projects. On the other hand, the Armed Forces Network wanted more specific stories of soldiers in the field or about armored vehicles. They were not as interested in "the message" as the Information Center was.

Yen, a leader of a three-man team, was assigned to the 101st Airborne Division based at sites in the Mosul area referred to by the Army as "D-Main" and "D-Rear." He found the Kurds to be very friendly toward Americans. It was peaceful, at the time, with no terrorist activity. The Kurdish areas had been part of the "no-fly zone" after Desert Storm, and the area was intact and prosperous, with modern buildings and a decent infrastructure. Once, when shopping at a local music store, an old man came up to Yen and kissed him on the cheeks, thanking Americans for what they had done. The old man encouraged Yen to kill Iraqis. The Kurds considered themselves neither Arab nor Iraqi.

Yen had the opportunity to talk informally with soldiers at the military sites in the Mosul area and began to get a sense of their attitude toward contractors. He learned they weren't angry with them, but bitter about the contractors' higher wages, better benefits, and ability to quit anytime they wanted. There were very few contractors at D-Main at the time, and Yen concluded the soldiers' attitudes were more the product of information floating through the grapevine than of direct interactions with actual contractors.

But at Qayyarah Airfield, known as Q-West, located about 30 miles south of Mosul, soldiers did have good recreation areas, plasma TVs, video game consoles, and basketball courts. They had the best food Yen had tasted in a longtime, prepared by KBR contractor cooks and a pastry chef, the former owner of a restaurant chain in Australia, who would serve four different kinds of deserts at each meal. He told Yen that he left his restaurants in Australia to come to Iraq for the money. He was making more than $120,000 a year. Yen found the dining facility at Q-West to be amazing and eventually wrote a story about it.

However, a smaller military site west of Mosul, near Tal Afar, didn't fare as well. Yen noticed that there were no contractors, and that they had the worst kind of Army food. "Burn shitters" were used because of a lack of proper waste disposal facilities. Yen learned their conditions were much poorer than Q-West because the contractors didn't want to go out there.

While in Mosul, Yen noticed that the 101st made an effort to connect with the Kurds. Determined to win hearts and minds, soldiers often hired Iraqis to service or repair equipment on the base. If a generator broke down, they hired an Iraqi electrician to come in and fix it. Relying on KBR for repair and maintenance was not as necessary as in other areas of Iraq.

The 101st was eventually relieved by the Army's Second Infantry Division, Stryker Brigade. A smaller force than the 101st, the Second took a more defensive posture, probably because of its size. They did what they could, but violence was on the rise.

After about five months in the Mosul area, Yen was reassigned to the Green Zone, where he experienced the sharp contrast between this well fortified oasis within Baghdad and the far more difficult conditions faced by soldiers in the risky, poorly supplied areas outside the Zone. A virtual class system seemed to be developing, dividing soldiers and civilians into "haves" and "have-nots" and creating morale and retention problems among those who lacked even the most basic of supplies. Yen would experience both "classes" as an Army journalist. It was a time of increased insurgent activity. Up to the time Yen left Mosul, there had only been two car bombs, but after he moved to the Green Zone, the car bombings increased in frequency.

Yen was astounded by the contrast between the comfort inside the Green Zone and the misery outside it. The Zone was lush and tropical, with contractors swarming all over to serve the needs of military and civilian officials. It was gold-plated and unrealistic—the Club Med of Iraq. Yen was sickened. Those sequestered in the Green Zone were not experiencing the realities of Iraq, its culture, and its problems. There was a huge disparity between the Green Zone and the remote bases, where soldiers had to put up with eating mostly MREs or other types of basic food, while those in the Green Zone enjoyed gourmet meals and the rich desserts of highly paid pastry chefs. Contractor bus drivers shuttling people around the Green Zone were paid far more than soldiers risking their lives on patrol in the other sectors of the city, sweltering in 120-degree heat.

Yen found that security contractors were a large contingent in the Green Zone. There to guard VIPs and facilities and to escort convoys, most were former Special Forces soldiers. They always stood out, driving SUVs, wearing dark glasses, and traveling well armed. These security operators looked and acted differently then other contractors. Then there was another level of security personnel, mostly foreign nationals, such as Nepalese, who handled the basic security chores, such as guarding gates and doors.

Yen talked to a former soldier who was part of the first wave of the Iraqi invasion. He had gone home, left the military, and hired on with a security firm Yen believed to be Blackwater. He talked of having much shorter tours, longer vacations, good pay, and state-of-the-art equipment. The Pentagon could afford to pay private security contractors for sophisticated armor and weapons, and armored SUVs with tinted windows. This,

Yen thought, was why soldiers were griping and becoming very difficult to retain.

Apart from the month he spent embedded with an Army unit, Yen was not able to venture out of the Green Zone more than six or eight times between March and November 2004 because of the violence that was spreading throughout Iraq. Within the Green Zone, the Armed Forces Network reporters were starved for stories and struggling to meet their quotas of two stories a week. The stories started to get really specific and mundane. Yen recalled one, for example, about a local Iraqi collecting the dates that dropped from the world-class date-producing palms prevalent within the Green Zone and selling them to make a living. Another was about a soldier who played his guitar every Thursday night. Still other stories were on classes offered during the week and the postal backlogs caused by the roads becoming too dangerous to make deliveries from the airport. Yen yearned to be out in the field where the real stories were.

By talking with soldiers and civilians, Yen found out that the palaces within the Green Zone were occupied chiefly by civilians and contractors. The CPA was in charge at the time. Many of the CPA staffers Yen met were young twenty-somethings with little real-life experience and certainly no experience outside the Green Zone where the real Iraq existed. They reminded him of the young political operatives you might see at a Republican convention. Yen would often see them strutting around, very impressed with themselves and boasting about being in charge of water, power, or something else. They all thought they were in charge, Yen felt; it was like a bunch of twenty-year-olds had gotten together and said, "Hey, let's run the country." Their inexperience and limited understanding of what was really going on in Iraq were painfully obvious.

Yen's observations were very similar to those of Rajiv Chandrasekaran, a *Washington Post* writer who was assigned to the Green Zone. In his book *Imperial Life in the Emerald City,* he cites the recruiting efforts of Jim O'Beirne, a Defense Department official who screened applicants for posts with the CPA in Baghdad:

> Many of those chosen by O'Beirne's office to work for the Coalition Provisional Authority, which ran Iraq's government from April 2003 to June 2004, lacked vital skills and experience. A 24-year-old who had never worked in finance—but had applied for a White House job—was sent to reopen Baghdad's stock exchange. The daughter of a prominent neoconservative commentator and a recent graduate from an evangelical univer-

sity for home-schooled children were tapped to manage Iraq's $13 billion budget, even though they didn't have a background in accounting . . ."

"To recruit the people he wanted, O'Beirne sought resumes from the offices of Republican congressmen, conservative think tanks and GOP activists. He discarded applications from those his staff deemed ideologically suspect, even if the applicants possessed Arabic language skills or postwar rebuilding experience. Smith [Frederick Smith, former deputy director of the CPA's Washington office] said O'Beirne once pointed to a young man's resume and pronounced him "an ideal candidate." His chief qualification was that he had worked for the Republican Party in Florida during the presidential election recount in 2000.[1]

Eventually, Yen was given an assignment taking him outside the Green Zone to do real stories. He spent a month embedded with the First Armored Division located at the airport. They were extended beyond their original yearlong tour, but the public affairs personnel had been sent home. Yen was volunteered for public affairs duty with the First because he was the last one slated to go home on leave and therefore could stay with them the longest. The Division had just been booted from their permanent living quarters because another Division had moved in. They had only bare necessities at the airport, but remained stoic after having been there 14 months without leave. And now, the First were living in tents on the grounds of the airport—a bad living arrangement for a group that had been in Iraq so long. Plus, they were not getting the perks soldiers were getting in the Green Zone. Despite the size of the base, there was no KBR entertainment or Morale, Welfare, and Recreation facilities, no gourmet meals or soft-serve ice cream. Despite their long stay in Baghdad, the First Armored Division still conducted patrols around various sectors of the city. Yen accompanied them to do stories from the checkpoints they set up on their patrols. Thankfully, the stories he got this way were a lot better. They were about soldiers doing their jobs, the kinds of stories he expected to do when he was deployed. The first story Yen covered with the Division was a funeral for eight soldiers who had been killed by a car bomb. Yen felt those eight soldiers were such a great representation of America. They were privates and sergeants, young and old, experienced and new. It was very sad. Some were married with children, and one was engaged to be married. A few had joined the Army on September 13th, 2001, motivated by the events that took place two days earlier.

While embedded with the First, Yen continued to hear the standard soldiers' complaint about contractors—the pay differential. Some would tell him that as soon as they got home they were going to get out of the military and come back as a contractor getting paid three times as much and going home every three months. The pay disparity issue between contractors and soldiers was distracting, and Yen felt it affected soldier morale. In the Green Zone, the contractors also were able to drink alcohol and wear civilian clothes, while the soldiers were not. Yen also noticed some animosity directed by soldiers in the field toward soldiers enjoying the safety of being based in the Green Zone.

There was always a level of separation between soldiers who had been in combat and those who had not, and a stigma placed on soldiers who stayed on the main bases and Forward Operating Bases (called "Fobbers") rather than venturing out in the field or on soldiers who did venture in the field but were never in harm's way. For every soldier who left the base there were seven who did not. It was an added gripe among soldiers in the field that contractors were paid big salaries but never had to venture outside a base or face much danger. As one soldier put it to Yen, "The guys in the city hate the guys on the FOBs. It's two different mentalities. You have the war fighter and the people who say, 'I gotta play softball tomorrow.' "

Outside the Green Zone, soldiers were patrolling within the dangerous sectors of Baghdad, often without enough supplies, making do in the squalor that the war created in the city. In his book *The Last True Story I'll Ever Tell*, John Crawford eloquently describes life on patrol without adequate supplies in a sector of Baghdad outside the Green Zone:

> We were put on a water and food ration. No supplies came our way, and soon we began commandeering civilian vehicles, our Humvees all being broken. Without a supply chain, the equipment we needed to perform our mission fell into disarray. Our night-vision devices were useless without the swing arm to mount them. Our retooled Vietnam-era rifles began to show their age, falling apart with the slightest usage. We became shadows of the shock-and-awe troops that Americans saw on television. My uniforms were torn beyond repair and my boots had no soles on them. Still we walked on, day and night, sloshing through the sewage-filled streets.[2]

Soldiers were paid about $250 a month Hostile Fire Pay, or as Yen calls it, "Risk Your Life Pay." "Could I pay you $250 a month to go live in Iraq?" Yen asked. "Forget the vicious weather, the uncomfortable living conditions, and the questionable food. Would you take $250 to let people try to kill you? And yet soldiers are asked to do this day in and day out, and they do so admirably."

While in the field, Yen would also hear complaints about the radio station broadcasts from Baghdad. Soldiers, suffering in 114-plus heat, would hear on the radio, "Why don't you all stop by the pool after work and we'll be there." The soldiers would say to Yen, "Who the hell are those people—drop by the pool? There's no pool anywhere." It was Saddam's pool, at the palace in the Green Zone. Not a realistic option for the soldiers in the field who were going out on missions with 40 pounds of equipment, sweltering in the heat, surviving on MREs, and risking their lives, often without adequate supplies and equipment. Life away from the flagpole was difficult at best.

Back in the Green Zone, after his time with the First Armored Division, Yen was assigned on three-to-four-day missions with other Army units. He noticed that the further away from a civilized base he went, the fewer contractors there were. His specialty did not include covering battles. That was another specialty—combat camera. Yen carried his own camera on his stories and was expected to interview and film at the same time. If he got into a battle, he would throw his camera down and do what he could to preserve his life. Combat reporters were expected to continue rolling their camera during the shooting. That would have been hard to do for him instinctively. Yen was not sent to areas where fighting was possible, but did go to Fallujah a week before the battle of Fallujah, in November 2004, to give the Marines some coverage. It was obvious they were mobilizing for battle. One of his stories was about the Marines building pens to hold prisoners taken during the battle.

Most of Yen's stories were about Army civil affairs teams doing work at orphanages, delivering medical supplies to hospitals, or delivering school supplies to schools. His assignments were meant to show cooperation and goodwill between Iraqis and Americans.

Yen's unit spent a year and a day in Iraq. They returned to the United States together and intact. Reflecting on his time in Iraq, Yen remarked that "as much as you may love your country and as much as you may think a cause is right, a year in a combat zone, risking your life, is not a simple thing to ask. Two years for some troops. With the current pay, current treatment of vets and their families and their problems, how can you ask someone to do that? If things were fair, if things were right, being a soldier wouldn't be a sacrifice, and we wouldn't have to call it a duty. The government either needs to fight limited, decisive wars without peacekeeping duties, or it needs to make being a soldier less of a sacrifice. The security companies have people lining up to go to Iraq because the tours are shorter and they're paid a lot, lot, lot more money. It's a cruel situation when your most patriotic citizens are paid the least and asked the most of."

Certainly no one intended this to be a consequence of privatizing combat logistics, but soldiers have been demoralized by their feelings of resentment toward the contractors. They are seeing contractors performing tasks that soldiers used to do, but for considerable more pay and benefits. Added to that is the contrast between the relative luxury of the Green Zone and other large bases and the much harsher conditions endured by soldiers on smaller or more remote bases. Soldiers are leaving an already strapped Army to hire on with contractors and return to Iraq to make more money. Their rationale is that they would be going back to Iraq with the Army anyway. Why not go back making more money with better benefits?

PART III

DIGGING IN

Private companies can only perform a mission more cheaply when they are allowed to do things their own way. This means cutting corners, something that can't always be tolerated. For privatization to be cheaper, you have to give the contractor flexibility, but if you want control, if you care about how the mission is done, then it's going to be more expensive

—Deborah Avant, Political Scientist,
George Washington University,
Washington, D.C.

CHAPTER 11

FEEDING FRENZY

CPA Headquarters, June 2003.

In late 2002, two men, Scott Custer and Michael Battles were struggling along with their consultant company. They had not even settled on a name. They wanted to establish themselves in the international security and risk management field but they had major competition from more established companies such as Blackwater USA, a consortium of retired military officers who offered security around the world and to the U.S. government.

Custer and Battles did have some experience. Custer worked his way up from enlisted Army to become an officer. Known for charging into situations that might be over his head and having a healthy ego, he could be compared to another Custer: the famous General Custer, who died at Little Big Horn. Scott Custer wanted to be a player in the international private warrior arena. He had done some non-profit contracting in the Balkans, Afghanistan, and various African nations. Now he wanted to make money and play with the big boys.

He teamed up with Michael Battles, a West Point graduate with seven years in the Army and a three-year stint in the CIA. Battles was very proud of his CIA work, even though it was just a few years of experience. He liked the mystique of sitting in bars and letting people know that he worked for the Company (the insider name for the CIA). Battles could be a charmer and was a smoother character than Custer.

He tried to get into the political world by running unsuccessfully in the 2002 Republican primary for the right to challenge Democrat Patrick Kennedy for Congress in Rhode Island. He was given political money for his campaign by surprisingly heavy hitters. According to the Federal Election Commission (FEC) record, Battles had several high-rolling and influential donors to his campaign. Haley Barbour, the former RNC chairman and powerful lobbyist, who is now the Governor of Mississippi, gave $1000. Fred Malek, one of the notorious political partisans in the Nixon White House who was tasked with punishing enemies with government clout, was also an investor in the Texas Rangers baseball team with George W. Bush. Malek is now an investment manager. He gave $2000, the maximum amount allowed. Custer and Battles were obviously very proud of Battles's political connections. After interviewing Scott Custer, the Department of Defense Inspector General investigators wrote in a January 2004 report that "Battles is very active in the Republican Party and speaks to individuals he knows at the White House almost daily, according to Custer." Battles's political contacts opened opportunities as a national security commentator on Fox News and other networks.

But these two men in their thirties wanted more. They wanted to be players in the war service industry. Custer had gotten some indication of the money that could be made in this industry in places like Bosnia, but it was hard to get a start with their fledgling company. They decided to name their company with the improbable but catchy name of Custer Battles—presumably hoping to have more success than General Custer in his last battle.

Michael Battles saw his opening when the United States invaded Iraq. Custer and Battles borrowed money to get the smooth-talking, politically connected Battles to Baghdad to find some action. The center of the action after President Bush declared "mission accomplished" was the Coalition Provisional Authority (CPA), established in order to rule Iraq and oversee the rebuilding of the country. The majority of the money for the country's reconstruction was coming from the United States. The CPA, as a governmental organization, was an odd hybrid of a United Nations resolution and, supposedly, a Presidential Directive. It funding came partly from Iraqi assets seized during the invasion and US Federal monies. Even the methodical, non-partisan Congressional Research Service has not been able to sort out whether the CPA was an international agency or connected to the U.S. Government. Some have gone so far as to claim that it was not a U.S. government agency.

The CPA was staffed with eager young men, mainly from Republican circles such as the conservative Heritage Foundation, who, like Custer and Battles, wanted to get in on the ground floor of this new world. According to the government investigations, many did not have detailed knowledge of government contracting procedures, such as the Federal Acquisition Requirements (FARs), and other legally binding regulations that were designed to protect the taxpayers' dollars.

This environment was all the better for Battles. He went to the headquarters of the CPA and passed his card around in the chaos of the rebuilding of the country. When he heard about a contract to provide security for civilian flights out of Baghdad Airport, he joined the bidding process for the $16 million dollar contract. The contract was hastily thrown together and not well thought out by the CPA. The request for a bid went out on June 19, 2003, and the proposals had to be submitted by June 22, 2003. Custer Battles quickly submitted a proposal and won against larger, well-established corporate military security firms, such as Dyncorp. According to Frank Hatfield, the senior U.S. airport official in Iraq, Custer Battles won the contract because they promised to get 138 guards on the ground in two weeks, which was much sooner than the other bids. Hatfield later told the press that he just wanted assurances that Custer Battles could handle the contract. Since they had no track record and no stable of guards, it is unclear what Battles could have said to reassure him. Later on, Hatfield would have to fend off some unhappy CPA officials who were appalled at the way Custer Battles executed the contract.

Nevertheless, they received the contract. When they admitted to the CPA that they did not have any operating capital, the CPA gave them, at least twice, $2 million *in $100 bills,* which Battles put into a duffle bag and deposited in a Lebanese bank. Frank Willis, the Deputy Senior Advisor for Iraq's Ministry of Transportation and Communications, was one of the people from the CPA initially responsible for overseeing the contract. Willis told the Congress that he had a Marine go down to the basement and fetch $2 million in cash. He said that he understood there was up to $3 billion in cash in the CPA basement to pay contractors. Once the money was stuffed into the duffle bag, the CPA's ability to track how Custer Battles spent it was lost. Willis even provided a picture of himself and another official holding up bricks of the money wrapped in cellophane as they handed it over to Battles.

This was the way the government funds went out. There was no banking system—no way to wire cash. Also, there was no tracking system for the cash transfers. Nearly $12 billion, in cash, was withdrawn from the Federal Reserve; $281 million, loaded on 484 pallets weighing 363 tons, was flown to Baghdad from New York on a 747. It wasn't long before evidence suggesting substantial waste, fraud, and abuse started to accumulate. The federal government later admitted that they had lost track of almost $9 billion of this money.

Willis was concerned about the Custer Battles contract from the moment he came in contact with it. An energetic man in his sixties, he had held numerous government positions before becoming the COO of a major medical group. He was persuaded by one of his former bosses in government to take a leave from his job and come to Iraq for a few months to help kick start the transportation area of the CPA. In general, he was troubled by how chaotic and understaffed the whole effort appeared when he arrived in Iraq, but he was particularly concerned about the Custer Battles contract. He pushed to have the contract "definitized"—that is, to have Custer Battles's tasks be clarified in a more exact manner—but the overwhelmed and under experienced staff below him could not seem to get Custer Battles to give them the information they needed, or even to pay attention to them at all. Willis began to look more carefully at the contractor and alerted other upper-management people to the problems.

Custer Battles immediately went to work not only to fulfill their first contract (though the decision to have civilian planes fly out of the Baghdad Airport was abandoned shortly after the contract was given; Custer Battles was paid anyway) but also to expand their new fiefdom in Iraq beyond the airport contract. Within one year, the company had acquired security contracts reportedly worth $100 million, for jobs as wide-ranging as housing power-line workers to providing security for truck convoys delivering vital war supplies.

By October 2003, just a few months into the first contract, Frank Willis and Charles "Ed" McVaney, the director for Security in the Ministry of Transportation, became alarmed when they discovered that Custer Battles was using parts of the airport as free space for their other contracts. They had housed the Filipino employees of their food operation business in one of the main terminal buildings at the airport and had built a dog kennel for another contract next to a dangerous munitions site. R. C. Shackelford, the Director of the Airport, sent an angry email to Willis outlining some the problems:

Custer Battles has commandeered space on the second floor of the Administration Building between Terminal C and Terminal D. It is my understanding that virtually all of the Iraqi owned furniture has been thrown away, the area carpeted and is being used to quarter foreign labor used in the Custer Battles operation. Needless to say, our Iraqi partners are absolutely livid over this unauthorized, unplanned and, indeed, misuse of need aviation dedicated space. They are also livid over the wanton and total disregard of their property (the furniture) and Custer Battles obvious disregard of any type of civilized process of acquiring space.

Shackelford went on in the email to complain that Custer Battles also built a K–9 dog kennel near a hazardous site at the airport.

By November 2003, the Army Inspector General wanted to review the contract for several reasons, including concerns they had over Custer Battles not being diligent enough with their checkpoints into the airport. Custer's reaction was to say that the Army did not have the jurisdiction to investigate them and that it should consult with attorneys. Wills and McVaney were also trying to get a handle on the situation by sending out cure notices that threatened termination of the contract unless various problems were fixed.

McVaney wrote an action memo on November 21, 2003, suggesting the termination of the Custer Battles contract. His memo pulled no punches:

> Custer Battles in their performance against the BIAP contract . . . has shown themselves to be: (1) unresponsive; (2) uncooperative; (3) incompetent; (4) deceitful/manipulative; and (5) "war profiteers." Other than that, they are "swell fellows."

A week later, the Army Inspector General investigator who was trying to find out how Custer Battles was spending the money was rebuffed by Custer Battles, who thought they were above any auditing. Richard Ballard from the Army IG wrote an email to McVaney complaining about Custer Battles non-cooperation and arrogance. The November 29, 2003 email states in part:

> I personally saw three new employees squatted down on the ground with a stick drawing in the sand, and I asked them what they were doing. They stated that as soon as it got to be dusk, they were going to flush out a young boy in a black t-shirt who had been firing random shots in their di-

rection for the past five days from an AK–47 at about dusk each evening. I asked them if they had ever reported this to the military . . . no. I asked them if their rules of engagement authorized them to offensively conduct such operations, and one of them asked me what the term "rules of engagement" meant. I asked them if they understood that if they engaged in offensive military-like operations they might be considered to be terrorists by the enemy, and summarily tried and executed. They laughed at the thought. I then asked them what their qualifications were with their assigned weapons. All three informed me that they had never received any weapons training whatsoever from [Custer Battles]; they had merely indicated the weapon they felt most qualified to use, and it was provided to them. A former Air Force NCO admitted to me that he had only fired his weapon four times while in the Air Force . . .

. . .I was actually told [by Custer Battles] that the way the contract was written, neither the U.S. military, nor the State Department, nor the U.S. government or any of its agencies had the legal authority to check the contract for specific performances, that they all just had to rely on C-B to do what they were being paid to do.

Both the officials at the CPA and the Army IG felt helpless to stop the Custer Battles questionable billing and lack of effective security since the company had dug in its heels and refused to cooperate. The seeds of the ongoing failures and fraud in the private contracting were planted during the early years at the CPA. This feeding frenzy with poorly qualified and opportunistic contractors set the tone for all the future failures in Iraq, both in the reconstruction and the military supply contracts.

CHAPTER 12

STEPPING INTO THE BREACH

Baghdad International Airport, September 2003.

Custer and Battles had grown an initial $16 million contract into contracts reportedly totaling over $100 million. Since Custer Battles was able to stave off the tough oversight efforts attempted by Willis and McVaney, things would have been fine for the two young entrepreneurs had it not been for a few conscientious employees who were shocked at the way Custer Battles was executing its contracts and failing to deliver on its commitments. William Baldwin, a senior manager with the company, and Robert Isakson, a subcontractor with the company, both began to see practices and billing they thought were highly questionable. Baldwin claimed that Custer Battles owned shell companies that they passed off as subcontractors in order to run up the prices in the contracts. For instance, according to Baldwin, one of the shell subcontractors built a helicopter pad for $95,000, but Custer Battles billed the CPA $157,000 in costs. Baldwin also contended that Custer Battles confiscated Iraqi Army forklifts abandoned at the Baghdad airport, repainted them, and then, through a lease-back scheme using a shell company, leased them back to the CPA at highly inflated prices.

Isakson was hired because he had the experience that Custer and Battles could only dream about. He was a former FBI agent with deep roots in the heartland of Texas. After the FBI, he was able to build up an international company that went around the world to help rebuild after natural disasters or wars. He was right behind the American troops when they retook Kuwait in the first Gulf War and went to work helping to rebuild the infrastructure. He was in the country so early after combat that he was taken hostage by the retreating Iraqis and was barely able to make his escape. He was a man who liked to take risks and saw his new job as a continuing world adventure. He also knew the dangers of this business, and his FBI training instilled in him a strong distaste for fraud. He thought he was the proof that you could do this business honestly. Custer and Battles cultivated him for a subcontractor because of his experience. They told him that they wanted to be like him, with the prestige that comes from running a successful international company. Ironically according to the book, *Blood Money,* one of Isakson's companies was being sued by the USAID (Agency for International Development) for fraud charges but Isakson denied any wrongdoing.

Nevertheless he claimed that his ex-FBI blood was boiling because he was appalled at what he thought were blatant attempts of Custer Battles to defraud the country. He vehemently complained to Custer, Battles, and their in-country manager, Joe Morris. Isakson had helped them build up this company with his war reconstruction experience and understanding of government contracting, and the contracts were now pouring in to the tune of $100 million. He knew that his guidance and efforts helped lead to this success, and he was not going to allow them to cheat. He claimed that the work could be done straight.

He knew they would have some kind of a showdown but he did not think they would go gonzo cowboy on him. Since the Baghdad Airport was secure at that time in the occupation and all of his work was based there, Isakson brought his 14-year-old son to work for a month until he left for a break. He wanted his son to see the world beyond the closed culture of his home in Montgomery, Alabama, and he was afraid that during his long absence his wife and three daughters would make the boy too much of a sissy. Incredibly, he thought that as long as they stayed at the airport and he was armed, the boy would be reasonably safe.

Scott Custer and Joe Morris thought differently. According to testimony, in Isakson's lawsuit against the company, Scott Custer was afraid that his insurance policy would not cover Isakson's son. Isakson told him that since he was a subcontractor, none of his employees nor his son were under Custer's policy. This did not appease Joe Morris and Scott Custer and they said that the son had to leave after a few days. Isakson agreed but also let them know that he was going to go back to the United States in a few days and file a legal suit against them for what Isakson claimed were their questionable activities and their breach of contract with him.

When the day came for his son to leave, Isakson stashed him with a friendly Iraqi family he could trust and went back to the airport to sleep in his office for the night. Joe Morris came in and told him that if he would bring his son back to the airport that they had a plane that they could take the next day.

But when he returned with his son the next morning, Morris, still incensed by Isakson's accusations of fraud and that he had brought his son to Iraq, met him at his office. According to Isakson's testimony, Morris had two armed guards with him and put him and his brother under "arrest" in front of his son. Morris told him that they were going to escort him to his plane and out of the country, Isakson told the court. Isakson claimed that after holding them in the office for about an hour, they went to Morris's office and called Scott Custer. According to Isakson, he called Scott Custer in Washington, who said that he wasn't fired and to come to Washington to work out the problems. Scott Custer since has testified that he did fire Isakson.

Isakson went back to his office and gathered his personal things to leave the country. Isakson claimed in the court proceedings that they were then escorted by Morris and the armed guards to the cargo terminal to get the chartered plane. Joe Morris left them at the terminal with the two armed guards, Isakson asserted. After many hours it was clear that there was no plane and Isakson told the guard that they had to go back to the main terminal. Instead, that Morris ordered the guards to take their identity badges and put them out of the gate of the airport, Isakson alleged in the lawsuit.

Isakson said he then had to travel with his son down the most dangerous road in the world, the seven miles between the Baghdad airport and downtown. Journalists and business people have paid up to $35,000 one-way for an armored car transport on this road. He also knew he might not be able to get a room at the only safe hotel open to him, the Sheraton, because it had no phones to make a reservation.

He and his son made the terrifying journey to Baghdad in a hired car, Isakson said, but there was no room for them at the Sheraton or any other hotel. As night fell, Isakson took the rest of his money and hired two cars and drivers and made an all-night run across the dangerous desert, through the town of Fallujah, to Jordan. He did not know what else to do and was desperate to get his boy out of there, he contended.

He is still amazed about this incident now and just shakes his head when he remembers it. He described Custer Battles as just a bunch of arrogant cowboys. He did make good on his promise to sue Custer Battles and Joe Morris. The court ultimately dismissed the claims against Morris. On November 1, 2005, Isakson won $1.4 million judgment against Custer Battles in civil court, relating to various payment disputes. The company has appealed.

CHAPTER 13

THE BERLIN WALL

Camp Caldwell, Iraq, June 2003.

By the end of May 2003, Jefferies's unit was desperate to get out of the Dustbowl. They wanted to find something, anything, closer to some towns and with a paved road nearby so they could try to improve their living conditions. They needed supplies to repair their broken-down trucks, tanks, and Bradleys and desperately needed to get their helicopters out of the dust. Toward the end of May, they moved to a large area west of the Dustbowl and dubbed it "Disneyland." It was still in the hot and blistering desert, but at least they could take shelter in shells of buildings there.

This camp, later named Camp Caldwell, was an abandoned Iraqi military training camp with unimproved and looted concrete buildings, but it was near two small towns, Baqubah and Balad Ruz, where the unit could make runs for food and even ice. Adam Roe, who had returned to Iraq after getting his appendix removed, served as the camp carpenter, trying to fix up the buildings with scavenged material and anything they could buy locally with what little money they had. It was still very primitive but definitely better than the Dustbowl.

One day, a colonel with the CPA accidentally found Camp Caldwell while searching out another area to use for training the New Iraqi Army (NIA). After disbanding the old Iraqi Army (a decision that military men and other policy makers have since criticized as a big mistake), the CPA decided to start a new army from scratch and needed a base in which to train the new recruits. The United States was planning to hire Vinnell, a division of the Northrop Grumman Corporation, a well-known defense aerospace company, to train the NIA. Vinnell subcontracted the job to MPRI, an Alexandria, Virginia firm that had trained troops in Bosnia and Croatia.

In the past, the Army's Green Berets had trained the armies of allied countries,but in this new era, the pressure was to contract the task out. The CPA gave Vinnell, who had also trained elements of Saudi Arabia's National Guard, a $48 million contract to do the job, and began to scout out an area for the training camp.

Jefferies and his officer, Captain Charles Jack, saw a chance to improve their lot. On the assumption that a rising tide lifts all boats, they reasoned that if they could convince the visiting colonel to base the New Iraqi Army at Caldwell, they would gain access to the supply chain that would naturally come with such an endeavor. Jefferies had made maps and slides of how the base could be improved in case he was ever able to get the ear of some brass, and he now gave his maps, with streets named after his pets and various soldiers' home towns, to the colonel to take with him.

The CPA was impressed enough to send a man named Walter Slockombe, who had been dubbed "the vice president of Iraq," to hear more. Jefferies and Jack fine-tuned their presentation and managed to sell the base as the new training camp. When the Brigade command, who had not paid much attention to Caldwell up to this point, found out that the CPA was serious about using Caldwell for the New Iraqi Army, they showed up to see the briefing.

After the decision was made to make Caldwell the new base for the Iraqi Army, Jefferies and Jack eagerly began planning how they could make life easier for their troops as the plans moved forward to improve the base. Even though a visiting colonel saw that they were, according to Jefferies, "challenged for nearly every class of supply and were deadlining vehicles for the lack of parts, the only comment he could make was that our defenses and front gate area were not up to standard. I thought this weird since we had a 6 km standoff and no one at Baqubah had noticed as somebody placed IEDs within their gates—which were up to standard." Jefferies was disappointed that his senior officer was more worried about a gate standard that hadn't worked in another base than the hazardous conditions that his men had been living in. Now that the CPA was interested, he hoped that the top brass in the Brigade would make sure his men got the vital supplies they needed.

During the walkthroughs by the CPA to fix up the base, Jefferies showed them the "despicable living conditions" they had to endure. This was in mid-June 2003, and the men had not received a hot meal since entering Iraq in late March. The CPA sent in contractors to fix up the base. By design, the camp had been divided in half with a berm and concertina wire to make sure the Iraqi Army recruits were kept separate from the Army for security reasons. However, Jefferies and Jack did not realize that they would also be separated from the supply chain and base reconstruction work. The berm became a Berlin Wall of sorts, with plumbing, electricity, windows, air conditioning, even a media center going up on the Vinnell and NIA side of the base, and Jefferies and his men still scrounging for the basics, using outdoor latrines, and living in buildings with boarded-up windows on their side of the base. A well-supplied chow hall was constructed on the Vinnell side, while Jefferies still had to forage in local areas for enough food to cook the occasional hot meal for his troops.

There was a high turnover of trainers during the training of the first batch of Iraqi soldiers, and some complained bitterly to Jefferies that they should not have to live in such stark surroundings. Angry at the griping, Jefferies wished his men could enjoy even just a few of the Vinnell luxuries, but the soldiers on his side were left in the mud. Promises that KBR would come and make his camp as good as Vinnell's went unfulfilled for months.

One day in early August, Jefferies cornered his commanding officer in their dusty mess hall room and told him he had a bad feeling about the NIA. He was afraid the training effort might fail and the area might turn chaotic, with untrained and undisciplined Iraqi soldiers running around the base. He was especially worried about the NIA getting real weapons and real ammo so close to his base. Just at that moment, the normally haughty Lieutenant Colonel Buster came into the room with an ashen face. As he paced around the room, the officers began to ask if he was all right. He replied, "Well, I don't know—we need to get the word out—the New Iraqi Army just quit."

Jefferies, who had seen these trainees and their trainers get world-class accommodations compared to what his troops had to put up with, laughed hard for several minutes longer than his CO liked. The Lieutenant Colonel, he guessed, did not see the irony of new Iraqi troops being able to quit and refuse to defend their own country, while his stop-lossed soldiers were stuck living in abysmal conditions, defending a foreign land. .

Vinnell started training another group of Iraqi men to become soldiers. Despite a high drop-out rate, they managed to graduate 735 soldiers in early October. Jefferies's side of the camp did not attend the ceremony. There were security considerations behind the decision but Jeffries also believed that "it is embarrassing to have rough-shod Cav soldiers, still living in the dirt present compared to the polish of the Iraqi side and its advisors."

A *Los Angeles Times* reporter, John Daniszewski, wrote an article about attending a "well-orchestrated" media event on the new class of the Iraqi Army. He wrote:

> "The Kirkush base, in a desert area about 25 miles from the Iranian border, had been started by the Iraqis as a military base in the 1980s but was never completed. When the Americans arrived to turn it into the first training camp for the new Iraqi army two months ago, the buildings were just shells, thoroughly looted, without doors on hinges or glass in the windows. They also lacked both heating and air conditioning. Today, the barracks area has been finished, providing air-conditioned mess halls, fan-cooled rooms and indoor showers and toilets with running water. Two weeks ago, the coalition also finished a mosque for the soldiers."

Daniszewski later said in an interview that he did not realize there were American troops living on the other side of the "Berlin Wall" in much different conditions. Jefferies and his fellow soldiers' fates, months after President Bush's "Mission Accomplished" speech, illustrate the hollowness of statements from the Pentagon civilian and military leaders that they always strive for the "best for our boys."

By December of 2003, the Army and the CPA realized that Vinnell was failing disastrously at training and retaining the NIA and that they would never reach the 40,000 trained troops they were shooting for in the first year. Vinnell had already spent $24 million, about half of their total contract, even though they were supposed to train nine battalions of 1000 men each. They decided to allow Vinnell to finish its contract but then to have NIA officers trained by the Jordanian military and to set up a separate academy for the non-commissioned officers. They also had to cut in half their prediction of training 40,000 troops trained by the time United States handed sovereignty over to the Iraqis.

The second battalion of the NIA went on to failure in April 2004 in the first battle of Fallujah, simply quitting or refusing to fight. In the absence of a reliable NIA, sectarian militias began to spring up. General Eaton, who was in charge of building the NIA, admitted on his retirement that the failures of the first "lost" year of trying to train the Iraqi troops made the challenge of controlling the country immensely more difficult. This Vinnell debacle was another lesson in the unintended and unforeseen consequences of abandoning Army traditions, like the practice of having Special Forces train foreign troops, and relying on contractors instead.

The initial failure of the NIA cost the United States much more than just money. Since President Bush has repeatedly said that the United States will "stand down" in Iraq when the Iraqis "stand up," the failure with the contractor put the U.S. policy behind schedule and disillusioned many Iraqis with the lack of security in their country. What happened to Jefferies's unit shows that if the contractors like Vinnell and the CPA wanted to get supplies out to remote areas, it could be done. Ironically, they did it with great fanfare for the NIA while leaving our soldiers in despicable conditions. Also, Vinnell's failure to train an Iraqi Army capable of taking over our troops' mission set the stage for the massive insurgency problem and the drawing out of the American commitment to the war.

Jeffries returned home in December 2003 and retired from the service; his wife now has him fattened him up to 158 pounds. After he left Caldwell, the Army decided to remodel the base, and his unit had to move out. Life was better for them at their new location in Tikrit, closer to supplies and other KBR amenities. Jefferies kept up with his buddies and made sure they knew that KBR was supposed to be serving their needs instead of building nice quarters for themselves.

As a lifelong Army loyalist, he will now tell anyone who asks how bitter he feels about the way the men above him, all the way up to Donald Rumsfeld, abandoned soldiers who were fighting for their country. He is livid about the contractors' profiteering and price gouging while his men were going without enough food and water. He blames his command and the civilian leadership in the DOD for grossly neglecting his men while spending $1 billion a week in Iraq. In 22 years in the Army, he had never seen such dereliction of duty and abandonment of the troops. He did not think that his country was capable of this, and he marvels at a public that puts magnetic yellow "Support the Troops" ribbons on its cars yet remains oblivious to the fact that he and others were rationing their food and water while in horrendous conditions while just trying to serve their country.

CHAPTER 14

CORPORATE COWBOYS IN A WAR ZONE

What follows is a recreation of the tragic events based, in part, on the allegations in a wrongful death lawsuit against Blackwater by the families of the employees killed in Fallujah, Iraq.

Fallujah, Iraq, March 31, 2004.

At about 9:45 a.m. on March 31, 2004, Stephen "Scott" Helvenston shifted into panic mode. He had every reason to do that. The Blackwater USA security operator was designated as the driver for the two-man team in the red Mitsubishi Pajero SUV bringing up the rear of a three-flatbed truck convoy en route to Camp Ridgeway to pick up food equipment. Another two-man team of operators was leading the convoy in a black Pajero. They suddenly found themselves stuck in a traffic jam in the middle of downtown Fallujah. The situation seemed calm and the people friendly, but the alarm in Helvenston's head was going off. His experience, instincts, and training as a former Navy SEAL told him they were in trouble as crowds started gathering near and around their SUV. Being in an SUV told the crowd they were Americans. They were a target, and Helvenston knew it. They were undermanned and under-armed. He felt naked, defenseless. According to the allegations of the lawsuit, they should have had a third team member watching their back with a Squad Automatic Weapon (SAW) Mk 46, which fires up to 850 rounds per minute. The lawsuit charges they were ordered by their managers to go with only two operators per vehicle—a driver and navigator. They were supposed to have an armored vehicle, the lawsuit contends, but their SUV had only reinforced bumpers, affording them little protection. For weapons, all they had were M4 carbines and Glock revolvers. The M4 is a good assault rifle, small and versatile, a favored weapon of law enforcement SWAT teams, but it has nowhere near the firepower of a SAW, which can keep a crowd at bay with its rapid fire, belt-fed, 5.56 x 45 mm cartridges. Helvenston was also feeling ill and hadn't wanted to go on this mission in the first place. He was in poor condition, but (the court papers allege) his boss ordered him out anyway.

Scott Helvenston, known as "The Helv" to his friends, had a warrior mind-set. At age 17, he was the youngest-ever graduate of the Navy SEAL training course.[1] He was strikingly handsome, imposing and muscular with sandy hair and a gleaming smile. A physical fitness buff, Helvenston was a world champion pentathlon athlete. He competed in international adventure races, climbed mountains, and developed a line of SEAL fitness equipment and videotapes. Helvenston also was an actor and stuntman, working with Demi Moore on the 1997 film G.I. Jane as Moore's training instructor, both on and off the set. He also served as a stuntman in the movie Face/Off, worked on the films Hidalgo and Lord of the Rings,[2] acted in the reality show "Combat Missions," produced by Mark Burnett (who also produced "Survivor" and "The Apprentice"), and starred on the television show "Man vs. Beast." He was the only human to beat the beast, winning an obstacle-course race against a chimpanzee.[3]

In 1994, Helvenston left after twelve years in the SEALs because he wanted to work for himself. But his fitness business eventually began to lose money, and by 2002 he had to file for bankruptcy, forcing him to sell the home in Oceanside, California, he shared with his wife and two children and move into a 26-foot trailer. At his new home, he was reduced to being a campground security guard, running around in a golf cart telling visitors to turn down their radios.[4]

Short on money, recently divorced, and with a burning desire to "get back into the game," Helvenston heard of the big money that his former

SEAL buddies were making with private security companies overseas. He first applied to DynCorp, one of the biggest, but turned down a job guarding Afghan President Hamid Karzai because he did not want to be away from his children for a year. He eventually learned that Blackwater USA was offering contracts of just a couple of months in Iraq for $600 a day.[5] Even though money was a big motivation, Helvenston's primary desire was to be back with his buddies again, going out missions where the action was. He told his loved ones that he was going to Iraq to earn some money and maybe make a difference. He believed in what he was doing. He also believed that the United States was right to have gone into Iraq and that Saddam Hussein had been involved with Al Qaeda. "I'll only be away from my kids for a couple of months," he told his mother.[6]

On March 1, 2004, Helvenson arrived in Moyock, North Carolina, a small border town about 30 minutes from downtown Norfolk and the location of Blackwater's 7,000-acre headquarters and training site, near the Great Dismal Swamp at Moyock.[7]

Blackwater was founded by young, baby-faced Erik Prince, also a former Navy SEAL. He was the son of a powerful Michigan Republican family and had served as a White House intern during George H.W. Bush's administration. After leaving the Navy in 1996, Prince took over the family business, Prince Automotive, which was started by his father, Edgar, and produced parts for car interiors. (Prince later sold the business to Johnson Controls for $1.35 billion.[8]) Edgar Prince had also helped to start the Family Research Council with Gary Bauer. Erik Prince's sister, Betsy, is the chairwoman of Michigan's Republican Party. Erik started contributing to the Republican Party at age 19, was one of the first interns at the Family Research Council, and worked as a defense analyst on the staff of U.S. Representative Dana Rohrbacher, a conservative Republican from Orange County, California.

Prince left his internship after only six months with the first Bush administration because of his disagreement with "homosexual groups being invited in, the budget agreement, the Clean Air Act, those kind of bills."[9] He felt that the administration had been indifferent to conservative concerns. Involved in various causes like the Christian Solidarity International and the Institute of World Politics, Prince also contributed to many conservative Republican candidates. At age 27, he founded Blackwater USA. Since then, the company has expanded to include Blackwater Training Center, Blackwater Security Consulting, Blackwater Canine, Blackwater Armor & Targets, Blackwater Logistics, Blackwater Airships, and Raven Development Group.

While in training at the Blackwater site Helvenston excelled—almost too much. He often felt that his instructor, Justin "Shrek" McQuown, according to the complaint, would improperly instruct the class by providing erroneous information, tactics or techniques. Helvenston politely tried to assist McQuown by offering his expertise, the lawsuit says, but this only led McQuown to dislike Helvenston for exposing him as an inadequate instructor. Based on an email she received from her son, Helvenston's mother believed that McQuown feared Helvenston might replace him at the company.[10]

On March 8, 2004, according to the lawsuit, while Helvenston was still training, Blackwater established a partnership with Regency Hotel and Hospital Company, a Kuwaiti firm. They then entered into a contract with Eurest Support Services (ESS) Worldwide, a German company that provided catering support services to the military. This arrangement was made to provide security services for ESS's food convoys to U.S. military bases in Iraq. Regency owner Jameel A. R. Al Sane, who developed a business relationship with a Blackwater employee named John Potter, had proposed that Blackwater and Regency join forces to submit a bid to ESS. ESS itself was a subcontractor to KBR under the LOGCAP contract. Initially, Control Risk Group provided security for ESS operations.[11] Because of the hostile situation in Iraq, the contract mandated that each security detail include at least two armored vehicles with a minimum team size of six operators to support ESS movements at all times, the court papers assert.

But Blackwater managers became concerned about their partnership with Regency over control of security details, according to the complaint. In the hopes of resolving the problems and getting the contract implemented quickly, Blackwater duplicated the primary contract between the two companies into a subcontract that was entered into on March 12.

However, the Blackwater victim's families alleged that when the subcontract was drafted, the armored vehicle provision was surreptitiously deleted. Marc Miles, one of the attorneys representing the families said, by removing the word "armored," that Blackwater would save $1.5 million in costs for each vehicle, thus increasing their profits. Also, if they had to up-armor the SUVs, the start of ESS operations would have been delayed, according to court papers. They were gung-ho to start the mission and impress ESS to win more contracts.

The complaint alleges that John Potter, who became Blackwater's project manager for the ESS project, insisted to Blackwater's management, including Mike Rush, Director of Blackwater, that the contract include armored vehicles in order to protect the security operators who would be working in the dangerous Iraqi environment. The court papers contend that Rush, had previously informed Blackwater president Gary Jackson that the contract problems had been resolved, and therefore refused to re-draft and renegotiate the subcontract.

Potter continued to insist to Blackwater management that the subcontract include armored vehicles to protect the security operators in Iraq, according to the complaint. Blackwater allegedly responded by firing him and replacing him with McQuown. Even though Blackwater was not supposed to become operational on the contract until April 2 at the earliest, they wanted to prove to ESS that they could deliver the security detail ahead of schedule, the families assert. After learning Blackwater would replace them on ESS convoy escort missions, Control Risk Group served notice it would cease operations with ESS by March 29.

Blackwater management is said to have pressured McQuown to hurry-up preparations in order to implement the contract in advance of the April 2 start date, even though, according to the lawsuit, the necessary vehicles, equipment, and support logistics were not yet in place. Blackwater also allegedly rejected Control Risk Group's offer to brief their operators on the routes they would be using to escort ESS convoys and refused to allow their operators to conduct ride-a-longs with Control Risk Group personnel. However, the Blackwater security operators designated to replace the Control Risk Group operators did not arrive in Kuwait until March 18 that would have left them little time for training with Control Risk Group and acclimation to Iraq, court papers say.

The lawsuit alleges that Blackwater management purposely delayed sending security operators for the EES contract in order to cut costs and increase profits. Under their contracts with ESS and Regency, Blackwater was being paid up front regardless of the number of operators they sent to Iraq, the lawsuit asserts. By delaying the deployment of the operators, Blackwater allegedly did not have to pay a higher salary rate, but still received money for the operators pursuant to their contract with ESS.

Helvenston was one of the Blackwater personnel to deploy to Kuwait on March 18. According to attorney, Marc Miles, he was supposed to fly first class so he would be rested when he arrived, but instead he had to fly coach. Also, he was supposed to be in Iraq twenty-one days prior to his first mission in order to acclimate to the country, learn the lay of the land, gather intelligence, and learn safe routes around Iraq, according to the complaint. But Helvenston was not afforded that luxury either. After arriving in Kuwait, he was placed on a six-man security detail team. They were told on March 27 that they would be leaving for Baghdad in two days to start their first mission, the lawsuit says. But that would all change the next evening.

During the evening of March 28, according to the court papers, Helvenston went to dinner with his team at a local restaurant. Miles says that while at the restaurant, the team decided to smoke a hookah pipe, a common custom throughout the Middle East for over 500 years and now often done in restaurants. Helvenston was not a smoker and certainly had never tried a hookah pipe, but he was willing. After all, he was part of a team of operators again. He was back in the game, and the team did everything together in the interests of cohesion. Unfortunately, the hookah's effects made Helvenston physically ill.

At about 10:00 P.M., while still at the restaurant, Helvenston received a call from McQuown, who told him he needed to pack up immediately, the complaint says. He would be leaving at 5:00 a.m. the next morning on a security mission to Baghdad with a different team—a team he had not trained with and didn't even know. A Blackwater security operator named "T-Boy" was supposed to be on the mission, but his plane had been delayed getting to Kuwait.[12] McQuown allegedly decided to have Helvenston take his place. But, Helvenston allegedly told McQuown he was sick and in no condition to leave early in the morning. According to Helvenston's mother, Helvenston told McQuown "You're nuts, you know, I'm not goin' in there to Fallujah. You're out of your mind. That's not what I was hired to do."[13] She further said "McQuown apparently told him that if he didn't do it, he would be fired immediately. He would have to reimburse any monies paid to him and would be on his own to get home.[14]

Helvenston and his teammates wondered why McQuown was taken away from the team and put with another team? Why didn't McQuown just send the whole team? They were ready, and there were six of them. It was virtually unheard of in the world of Special Operations, where team cohesion is all-important, to move an operator from one team to another, the complaint says. Teammates know and trust each other, have trained together, and are familiar with how each would react in a pinch. After some discussion, Chris Wyse, another Blackwater security operator, who had already been operating in the Middle East for some time, offered to take Helvenston's place on the mission, the court papers said.

Since Helvenston was still feeling ill, he returned to his room and didn't even try to pack—all he wanted to do was go to bed and sleep it off. Suddenly, the complaint says, his door burst open. McQuown, along with another Blackwater employee, Jim Graham, barged into the room allegedly screaming at Helvenston, calling him a coward along with many other demeaning and derogatory names. McQuown aggressively approached Helvenston and threatened to fire him if he didn't leave early the next morning for Baghdad, according to the lawsuit. Helvenston allegedly told McQuown, again, that he was sick and not in condition to go on the mission into Iraq, the complaint states. He also told McQuown that Chris Wyse had offered to replace him. McQuown again told Helvenston that HE was going on the mission and no one else, the complaint asserts. At that point, McQuown allegedly became more hostile and came at Helvenston as though he was going to hit him. Helvenston, despite feeling sick, was no one to fool with. He went after McQuown and Graham, chasing them out of the room. McQuown got the last word in, though, screaming, while running down the hall, that Helvenston was fired, the court filings said.

Helvenston wasn't sure what was going to happen next, but he didn't have to wait long to find out. McQuown allegedly returned a few minutes later and confiscated Helvenston's weapons. But then, much to Helvenston's surprise, he turned around and told him he would still be leaving at 5:00 A.M. the next morning for Baghdad, according to the suit. Despite how he felt, he decided to go, but also to inform management at Blackwater headquarters about what had happened. He sat down, opened his laptop, and drafted an email to the "Owner, President and Upper Management" of Blackwater, subject: "extreme unprofessionalism."[15] He described, as he regarded, as McQuown's erratic and unprofessional behavior and his animosity toward him. He explained that the original team leader tried to convince McQuown not to reassign him, but, as reported in *The Nation,* Helvenston wrote, "I think [the team leader] felt that there was a hidden agenda. 'Let's see if we can screw with Scott.'" This was one of Helvenston's very last communications.[16]

The next morning, March 29, Helvenston was still feeling ill. He didn't know where he was going in Baghdad, what the mission was about or who his new teammates were. Helvenston was concerned and confused about the whole situation, but he needed and wanted this job. He was a professional and would do the best he could under the circumstances.

After being dropped in Baghdad, Helvenston was quickly moved to the Blackwater team house, where he met his new teammates for the mission—Mike Teague, Jerko "Jerry" Zovko, and Wesley Batalona. Zovko, a 32-year-old former Army Ranger, was an imposing, heavily muscled figure

at 6-foot 3-inches, 235 lbs. A Croatian-American, he was secretive about
his background but so outgoing that it seemed as though he knew every
westerner in Baghdad. He spoke Arabic well, along with several other lan-
guages. He had left the Army in 2001 and found work with a private security firm as a bodyguard for celebrities, including diet doctor Robert
Atkins. In 2003, Zovko did a brief stint training Iraqi soldiers with another private contractor.[17]

Mike "The Ice Man" Teague, 38 years old and also a former Army
Ranger, was a burly softball player and motorcycle enthusiast. He was a
decorated 12-year Army veteran who had served in Afghanistan, Panama,
and Grenada with a Special Operations helicopter unit nicknamed "Night
Stalkers." Teague had left a low-paying security guard job in Tennessee to
work for Blackwater.[18]

Wesley Batalona, 48 years old, spent 20 years as an Army Ranger and
was known among former Rangers as one of the Army's toughest sergeants. In 1989, Batalona's unit was sent to Panama, where they made a
parachute assault on an airfield to begin the invasion. Nearly two-dozen
soldiers died in Panama, some at the airfield where Batalona fought. He
also fought in the first Gulf War.

A thin, white-haired native of the rural, rainy side of Hawaii's Big Island, Batalona liked to wear colorful Hawaiian floral shirts and flip-flops
while on missions. He was also known for quietly sizing up people, then
using pranks to befriend them. Batalona had been a security guard at a big
hotel resort on the Big Island when he heard about good pay in Iraq for
people with his skills. Like Zovko, he worked with another private security
contractor training Iraqi soldiers before joining Blackwater.[19]

After arriving at the Blackwater team house, the new team was briefed
by the site manager in Baghdad for Blackwater, Tom Powell, who answered
directly to McQuown. They would be escorting an ESS three-flatbed truck
convoy to pick up kitchen and construction equipment at Camp Ridgeway,
a U.S. Military base west of Fallujah, a city of 280,000 about 35 miles west
of Baghdad.[20] Even though Blackwater had enough operators in Baghdad
for a six-man team, the lawsuit says, two of them were directed to stay back
at the team house to take care of paperwork. The complaint also alleges
that McQuown directed Powell to send only four operators on the mission. But, according to the complaint, Powell attempted to credit himself
with saving two lives by proudly claiming that if he had sent a six-man
team, there would have been six deaths. The four-man team would be
using two unarmored SUVs. Helvenston presumably never knew the ar-

mored vehicle requirement had allegedly been eliminated in the subcontract. He may have been upset that they would not have the six-man teams, as (according to the lawsuit) the contracts required. The four would be divided into two two-man teams armed only with M4 Carbines; they would not have a rear gunner to watch their back or the firepower of a SAW. If things got rough, they would be sitting ducks.

Helvenston would drive. In the past, he depended on his teammates to pick up the field of fire, to cover all the angles, but this time, he would not have 360-degree vision. Also, they allegedly were not given maps or any other navigational tools to guide them to their destination. The Blackwater Four were given only a cursory briefing of the route to Camp Ridgeway, which was about 45 minutes from Fallujah along a route directly through the center of the city. No one told the team of an alternate, safer route around the outskirts of Fallujah, which would have taken them only about two and a half hours longer to get to their objective, according to the lawsuit.

Fallujah was a high-risk, war-torn city with a population of about a quarter million, located in the dangerous Sunni Triangle. It was a hotbed of the Sunni insurgency, especially after the dissolution of the Iraqi army and de-Baathification policy of Paul Bremer, the American Envoy who headed the CPA. The insurgents had turned the city into a Wild West environment that was considered a "no go" area by the U.S. Marines, even with their dazzling array of weaponry and vast pool of manpower.[21] A very strong anti-American sentiment existed in the city after U.S. forces killed at least 15 Iraqis there just five days before. This happened after a Marine died and two were wounded when their convoy near Fallujah was attacked. The next day, the Marines sent in 300 troops in a raid into the city. The area had been considered too dangerous for the U.S. military to enter, and the troops feared to venture near Fallujah in groups smaller than two dozen. They had a rule against conducting patrols even in the countryside—let alone Fallujah itself—without at least three vehicles packed with troops. Yet four lightly armed private contractor operators, in two unarmored SUVs that easily identified them as Americans, were about to drive directly into the insurgency cesspool that was Fallujah.

Helvenston felt they were not ready because, according to the lawsuit, they did not have the proper equipment, manpower, or firepower. They also hadn't been given the opportunity to perform a pre-trip risk analysis of their route or intelligence briefings of the anti-American sentiment in the area, the complaint says. Helvenston did not know the route, the terrain, or the risks. It was all going against his training, experience, and instincts regarding carrying out a mission.

Zovko also had many concerns. According to attorney Marc Miles, Zovko sought out and met with Pat Sheehan, a former Marine working as a private security operator, at the Al-Rashid Hotel in Baghdad. He had a serious question about the security in Fallujah. Sheehan handed him two grenades. "Not good," he thought.[22]

Helvenston sought out the Blackwater team supplier at the house, who was in charge of maps and ammunition, to get some maps. Unfortunately, the supplier did not have maps for them. Instead, the complaint says he "callously told him it was too late for maps"—they would just have to do the job with what they had, navigating by the seat of their pants. Despite the promises of Blackwater officials, the lawsuit alleges, they were simply sent on their way without any real preparations according to the complaint.

On March 30, the team picked up the convoy at Taji an Army airfield approximately 27 kilometers northwest of downtown Baghdad, and set off on their mission to Camp Ridgeway. Because they did not have maps, the lawsuit contends they made slow progress and soon got lost. As night began to fall over Iraq and they still hadn't found their way, they decided the safest move was to spend the night at a nearby U.S. Marine base called Camp Fallujah. They approached the main gate by zigzagging through a series of walls, giant sandbags, concrete, and barbed wire, which gave the guards plenty of time to check them out. After arriving at the base, the Marines gave them a place to sleep but distanced themselves from the private contractors. After all, they were not military. They were not troopers. They were civilians who made a lot more money for doing the same kind of work the Marines did. There was little-to-no interaction, and the Marines allegedly shared no information with them about Fallujah or the route they could take to avoid it. Helvenston called his mother late that night, but she had turned the ringer off on her phone and did not get the call. He did leave a message: "Mom, please don't worry, I'm gonna be home soon and I'm gonna see ya. We're gonna go have fun. I'm gonna take care of you."[23]

The next morning, on March 31, the team and truck drivers prepared to set off for Camp Ridgeway. As far as they were concerned, all they had to do was get on Route 10, which would take them through Fallujah, across the Euphrates River, and directly to the base. The truck drivers, who were Iraqi citizens employed by ESS, started up their trucks. Helvenston got into his red Pajero as the driver, and Teague climbed in with him. Batalona slid behind the wheel of his black Pajero, and Zovko rode beside him. The two were buddies, and Batalona had come to Iraq partly because Zovko was there. The convoy left the base with Batalona and Zovko leading and Helvenston and Teague bringing up the rear. Just after 9:30 A.M., the convoy entered the commercial district of Fallujah along Route 10, a narrow four-lane road with a center divider.

Helvenston grew concerned when the convoy came to a sudden stop. Teague's head was moving around, like it was on a swivel, in order to see what the crowd was doing, but he couldn't see much behind them. Helvenston wanted to get the convoy going quickly. Suddenly, a group of men with AK-47 assault rifles sprang into the street just behind and a few feet from Helvenston's SUV. They never saw the assailants coming. The men fired so quickly that Helvenston and Teague had no time to react. They were killed instantly when bullets hit them from behind and from either side of the vehicle. The SUV, with its windows shot out and its passengers slumped in the seat, rolled to a stop at the side of the trailer of the last flatbed truck.

After hearing the shots, the truck drivers jumped out of their trucks and tried to run away. The insurgents caught them and, since they were Iraqi citizens, ordered them back into their trucks and to get out of there. Batalona and Zovko in the lead SUV saw and heard what was happening. They acted quickly to help, making a sudden U-turn into the lanes driving back toward Helvenston and Teague. The assailants immediately shot the tires out on the black SUV, causing the vehicle to crash into the back of a white Toyota sedan. The gunmen then shot into the SUV at point-blank range. Batalona, wearing sunglasses and a shoulder holster, slumped to his right with blood running from his white hair. Zovko was wearing body armor, but it didn't help. The trucks headed back in the direction from which they came. They did not make it to Camp Ridgeway.

A crowd swarmed around the SUVs. Some brought out jugs of fuel, doused the vehicles, and then set them afire. After the fire died down, the bodies were pulled out of the blackened metal that was all that was left of the SUVs. The mob beat and ripped at the bodies. One tied a brick to a charred leg and flung it up where it caught on a power line. Young men danced atop the burned-out vehicles. Two of the bodies, one of which was Helvenston's, were dragged through the streets behind a car to a bridge over the Euphrates, where they were strung up on the metal frames.

Patrick Toohey, a senior executive for Blackwater, raised the question of whether the Blackwater operatives were the victims of a random attack or were lured into a planned ambush. A week after the incident, he told the press that the Blackwater employees were in fact lured into an ambush planned by insurgents disguised as Iraqi Civil Defense Corps personnel. However, Pentagon officials said they could not independently confirm his assertion.[24]

Whatever the nature of the attack, the killings, televised throughout the world, were horrific. Unfortunately, the incident would have a domino effect leading to an explosion of insurgency violence against troops and civilians alike and a grave threat to the stability and future of the country itself. Fallujah turned into "terrorism central," exporting car bombs throughout the country.[25] Senior Marine officials on the ground considered the tragedy the result of a tactical error. They intended to eventually restore stability in the area of Fallujah, but it was a tinderbox at the moment, and the Marines were being careful not to ignite it. But President Bush had other plans. America's resolve was being challenged. "We will not be intimidated, we will finish the job," he said through his spokesperson. This forced U.S. military commanders to plan retaliation. Brigadier General Mark Kimmitt said, "We will be back in Fallujah. . . . We will hunt down the criminals. . . . It's going to be deliberate. It will be precise, and it will be overwhelming. . . . We will pacify that city."[26] General John Abizaid, then head of the U.S. Central Command, called for "a specific and overwhelming attack to restore justice." It was payback time. In April 2004, U.S. and Iraqi forces staged an invasion of Fallujah resulting in the death of hundreds of Iraqi civilians and a number of Marines, before withdrawing and effectively handing the city back to the insurgents.

In November 2004, U.S. forces again laid siege to Fallujah, killing or capturing 1,000 to 2,000 insurgents and leading to over 300,000 residents fleeing the city, which was left in ruins. According to reports, 600 Iraqi civilians died there along with 70 American troops.[27] Al Jazeera was quick to broadcast photos of dead, bleeding, and maimed Iraqis. The invasion triggered hatred of America and led to an increased insurgency. Only an estimated 9,000 residents returned after the battle, many living in tents above the ruins of their homes.

Prompted by the tragic loss of four Americans in this failed mission to pick up kitchen equipment, questions have been raised in the media about the costs of using private contractor security operators to perform functions once performed by the military.

According to the Raleigh, North Carolina *News Observer,* the cost of the Blackwater mission to the taxpayer would have added up as the bill wound its way through a series of corporations who had a stake in the contract. Helvenston and his teammates each earned $600 a day ($180,000 a year) guarding the convoy. Blackwater added a 36 percent markup, plus overhead, and sent the bill to Regency, its contract partner. Regency tacked on its costs for buying vehicles and weapons and added its overhead and profit before sending the bill to ESS. ESS also added its costs, overhead, and profit and sent the bill to the prime contractor, KBR. Finally, KBR, which has an open-ended cost-plus contract under LOGCAP worth about $17 billion to date, would have added its costs, overhead, and profit. Only then would the final bill have been submitted to the government.[28]

It is unknown what the final bill was, but it was certainly far more than what it would have cost if the military had performed the same task. For instance, a soldier of Helvenston's experience and final rank would receive about $38,000 a year in base pay plus housing and subsistence allowances. Also, there would be no overhead or profit added on to the salary.[29]

There is evidence suggesting that the actual costs to the Pentagon may have been even higher than they should have been under the contract with the private companies. For example, the publication *The Nation* discovered a heavily redacted 2005 government audit of Blackwater's contract with the State Department's Worldwide Personal Protective Service program. The audit asserted that Blackwater added profit to its overhead and its total costs, which would have resulted "not only in a duplication of profit but a pyramiding of profit since in effect Blackwater is applying profit to profit." The audit also contended that Blackwater attempted to inflate its profits by representing different divisions as wholly separate companies. Without an audit of Blackwater's submitted costs on the Army contract, it is difficult to know which if any costs should be questioned.[30]

In a hearing before the House Government Reform Committee on September 28, 2006, both the Army and KBR denied in a letter that Blackwater had done any work for them and that they were authorized to guard convoys or carry weapons. But while it may be technically accurate to say Blackwater did not directly work for the Army or KBR, what this statement did not take into account was that Blackwater was a subcontractor to ESS and would have worked directly for them, and ESS, in turn, *did* work for KBR.[31] However, on February 6, 2007, the Army reversed itself by admitting that Blackwater was used as part of the LOGCAP contract run by KBR. Tina Ballard, Deputy Assistant Secretary for Policy and Procurement, U.S. Army, testified before the House Government Oversight and Reform Committee on February 8 that an Army investigation had found that KBR, through its subcontractor,

ESS, used Blackwater for convoy security duties in violation of the LOGCAP contract. As a result, Ballard said the Army would withhold $19.6 million from KBR for using private security for convoy protection when the contract called for the use of Army security only.

Then there were the reconstruction costs of Fallujah. The city was in ruins, with over 9,000 buildings destroyed, and it will eventually be the job of contractors to rebuild it at the U.S. taxpayer's expense.

The Blackwater Four lawsuit contends the mission was a failure, in part, because, the contractors were not given the equipment, vehicles, manpower, maps, or intelligence information on the area. They had no coordination with the military before bungling into Fallujah, according to the lawyer. In addition, they were ill prepared and poorly equipped because Blackwater wanted to prove their worth by accomplishing the mission ahead of schedule, according to the complaint. The trucks ended up heading back where they came from and most likely never reached Camp Ridgeway to finish their mission. The horrific and tragic incident in Fallujah, which became known around the world, prompted the U.S. government to retaliate. With two invasions of Fallujah by U.S. and Iraqi forces. Juan Cole, a professor of Middle Eastern History at the University of Michigan, has said that, "in some ways, the second Fallujah campaign was the end of any hope for success for the United States in Iraq."[32]

According to P. W. Singer, an expert on private contractors and the military at the Brookings Institution in Washington, the shift to private contractors has often been justified as cheaper and more efficient than relying on military personnel. But perhaps the real reason for the use of private contractors is to reduce the political costs of war. Singer explains that, by using private contractors to do work soldiers once did, the administration doesn't have to call up more regular troops or National Guard and Reserves, or persuade allies to send more troops. "We don't need another division there—we've got 20,000 private military contractors," Singer said.[33]

The Fallujah tragedy was not the only loss Blackwater would suffer in Iraq, in 2004, a total of nine of the company's employees were killed in Iraq.[34] Also, in November 2004, in Afghanistan, a twin-engine turboprop airplane operated by a sister company of Blackwater, Presidential Airways, crashed into a mountainside, killing all six aboard, including three U.S. soldiers. The victim's families filed a lawsuit alleging the crew had no flight plan, lacked experience flying in Afghanistan, and were poorly trained.[35] Back in Iraq, seven Blackwater operators were killed on a single day (April

21, 2005), six when their helicopter was shot down on its way from Baghdad to Tikrit for a security detail, and a seventh near Ramadi when an IED exploded next to his armored vehicle. Still, it was not over for Blackwater.[36] The families of the Fallujah victims wanted answers from the company. They wanted to see the After Action Report on the incident. How could Helvenston, Zovko, Teague, and Batalona have ended up in a hotbed of insurgency without the personnel and weapons to defend themselves? Blackwater officials reportedly told the family members that they would have to sue the company if they wanted to see any paperwork.[37] They took them up on it.

Dan Callahan is recognized as one of the top trial lawyers in the state of California and in the nation. His firm, Callahan & Blaine, is located close to the Pacific Ocean near Disneyland. His reputation as one of the top-ten trial lawyers in America caught the attention of two of family members of the Fallujah victims, who soon met with Callahan and hired him to serve as their attorney in a lawsuit against Blackwater.

Callahan and his colleague, senior attorney Marc Miles, quickly encountered a number of legal obstacles, such as the contract, signed by each of the victims, releasing Blackwater from liability for any loss or injury suffered on the job. On January 5, 2005, Callahan and Miles filed a wrongful death lawsuit against Blackwater in Wake County Superior Court, North Carolina, seeking damages for wrongful acts resulting in the deaths of Helvenston, Zovko, Teague, and Batalona.

Blackwater first responded by denying the validity of the allegations. They hired attorney Fred Fielding, former aide to President Nixon and Counsel to President Reagan, to represent them in the lawsuit. In their filed response, Blackwater argued that private contractors on the battlefield have become indistinguishable from uniformed personnel and therefore should enjoy the same immunity as the federal government, which bars soldiers from suing for injuries sustained in battle.

Also, Blackwater claimed that the families of the Fallujah victims were entitled only to government insurance benefits under the Defense Base Act. Passed in 1941, this law was designed to cover all civilian workers on military bases outside the United States. Later amendments extended coverage to all those working for the national security of the United States and its allies. All government contractors today are required by law to obtain insurance for their employees. After the Fallujah tragedy, Blackwater quickly applied for benefits for the families under the Defense Base Act, arguing in motions to the court that the families were only entitled to those payments. Miles has said that Blackwater is using the Defense Base Act as "essentially insurance to kill."[38]

It wasn't long before the legal dance commenced. Soon after filing the lawsuit, Callahan and Miles moved to depose John Potter, hoping to get his testimony on record as soon as possible. Potter, who had been fired by Blackwater and was now living in Alaska, was an important witness in the case. Miles filed a motion with the court in North Carolina to obtain an expedited order to depose Potter. Normally, there is a 30-day hold on discovery after the filing of a complaint. However, the court granted the motion and the deposition was set for January 28, 2005 in Alaska. But Blackwater had other plans for Potter. According to Miles, once Blackwater was notified of the deposition order, they quickly acted to rehire him and immediately flew him to Washington D.C., where he met with the company's attorneys. On January 25, 2005, he was shipped off to Jordan, where he was unavailable for deposition.

This would not be the only frustrating turn of events in the case. Shortly after the lawsuit was filed, Blackwater filed a "Notice of Removal" with the court to transfer the case to Federal Court. The company employed a federal compensation defense, arguing that the Defense Base Act provides an exclusive remedy for the victim's families. Callahan and Miles successfully fought the removal, and after eight months the federal court sent the case back to state court.

Blackwater appealed this ruling to the Fourth Circuit Court of Appeals, replacing Fielding with the Greenberg Traurig law firm, the former employer of disgraced super-lobbyist Jack Abramoff. The previous removal arguments having failed, Blackwater's new lawyers now maintained that the Fallujah victims were actually agents of the federal government since they were en route to a U.S. Army base at the time of their deaths. Thus, because they were legally the same as federal employees, the case belonged in federal court. This argument also failed, however, and on August 24 2006, the Fourth Circuit Court of Appeals ruled that the case should proceed in state court.[39]

But Blackwater was not throwing in the towel. Firing Greenberg Traurig, they brought in former Whitewater investigator Kenneth Starr to file an appeal before the U.S. Supreme Court. Starr and newly hired Chief Operating Officer for The Prince Group, Blackwater's parent company, Joseph Schmitz, former Pentagon Inspector General, were friends based on their work for the archconservative Washington Legal Foundation. On October 18, 2006, Starr submitted a petition to Chief Justice John

Roberts requesting a stay in the state case while Blackwater prepared to submit a petition for a writ of certiorari that would allow the company to argue before the Supreme Court for the case's dismissal. Starr contended that Blackwater is "constitutionally immune" from such lawsuits and would suffer "irreparable harm" if the case were allowed to proceed. Starr stressed to Roberts that the Court was Blackwater's "last resort." However, on October 24, Justice Roberts rejected the request for a stay. Starr followed up by filing a Petition for Writ of Certiorari with the Supreme Court which is asking permission of the Court to hear the case. Starr again argued in his filing that Blackwater can not be sued because it was working for the government and, therefore, is the government.

While Blackwater's request to the Supreme Court is pending, the state court judge lifted the stay on November 27, 2006, and it is proceeding in state court in North Carolina. According to Marc Miles, the first order of business was to obtain an order from the court permitting, again, a deposition of John Potter in Alaska, on January 10, 2007, since he returned to the state from the Middle East. Miles feels that Potter's testimony is important at getting to the truth in the case. But, Blackwater opposed the deposition by bringing in the U.S. Attorney General to argue that Potter may possess classified information and to depose him may raise national security issues. The Government was then given time by the court to determine if Potter's testimony could reveal classified information. Thus, the deposition has been put on hold pending the results of the Government's inquiry.

In the meantime, Miles says, Blackwater filed a $10 million lawsuit against the families, on December 15, 2006, for breech of contract because the Fallujah victims had allegedly signed a contract with the company that contained a covenant not to sue.

Starr fears that this lawsuit could have a severely detrimental effect on the growing private security community. He said, "If companies such as Blackwater must factor the defense costs of state tort lawsuits into the overall costs of doing business in support of U.S. 'public works' contracts overseas . . .American taxpayers will pay more for less operational results."[40] Blackwater must now face the evidence, something it has avoided since the case was filed more than a year and a half ago. Miles believes that the change-of-jurisdiction argument was a stall tactic, and is pleased that the case is on the fast track now. The case is being watched by all the private security firms because an adverse ruling against Blackwater could have a domino effect on the other firms, leading families of their employees to file liability lawsuits of their own.

Since the tragedy in Fallujah, the incident and its aftermath have been closely—and often critically—examined in the media and in a number of books. This prompted Blackwater spokesman Mark Corallo to respond in September 2006 that the media criticisms are just "election-year left-wing politics." The critics "are not objective journalists," Corallo said. "They are agenda-driven . . .This is more about Democratic Party politics than it is about any accurate portrayal of the role of military contractors in our nation's service overseas."[41]

As to the lawsuit, Blackwater denied the allegations in the lawsuit and any liability to the plaintiffs.[42] Justin McQuown, also a defendant in the lawsuit, has also denied liability. According to an article in *The Nation*, McQuown's attorney told them "there are 'numerous serious factual errors' in the lawsuit. 'On behalf of Mr. McQuown, we extend our sincerest sympathies to the families of the deceased. It is regrettable and inaccurate to suggest that Mr. McQuown contributed in any way to this terrible tragedy.'"[43]

The use of private security contractors in a war zone presents many of the same problems seen with logistics contractors—the profit motive simply does not mix well with operations in a war zone. Cutting corners to improve the bottom line can have—and, in the case of the Blackwater Four, did—have tragic consequences for its employees. The domino effect of the events in Fallujah—increased insurgency, counterproductive payback operations by the Marines, and the death of 70 soldiers, is a good example of what can happen when contractors, who operate under a set of rules different from the military's, conduct their own operations in the same environment with the military.

CHAPTER 15

THE HIRED GUNS

Baghdad, Iraq, June 2004.

Retired Marine Will Hough landed at the Baghdad International Airport to start his work as a security operator for Custer Battles. He thought he would be assigned to personal security duty, but was told upon arriving that he would be assigned to convoy security instead. When he complained that he did not sign up to do this very dangerous type of work, Custer Battles responded by promising to add another $1500 a month to his $9000 monthly salary.

He was then taken to a barren side of the airport where Custer Battles had set up crude prefab "hootches" for the men to stay in. He was given very shabby, old body armor and a gun that was so poorly maintained that the bullets often got stuck in the breech. He complained bitterly to his boss, but was told they were short of materiel because, a few nights earlier, some 14 employees of Custer Battles had allegedly taken off in the middle of the night with the best body armor, seventy to eighty guns, and several SUVs, with the intention of starting their own company

KBR had a good deal for their convoy security in Iraq. Their contract required that force protection for their convoys would be the responsibility of the U.S. Army, a guarantee not enjoyed by other contractors, who had to hire private security for their employees and convoys as they moved around

Iraq and on construction sites. It has been estimated that up to 35 percent of construction contracts typically went for security alone. This need caused a huge wave of established security companies and hired-gun wannabes to flood Iraq in search of lucrative contracts. Blackwater remains the gold standard for the international security businesses, but the Fallujah disaster exposed the myriad problems the can result from the mixing of soldiers, hostile war zones, contractor convoys, and hired guns into the complicated dynamics of the Iraqi occupation. In 2005, Blackwater received a Blanket Order Agreement from the U.S. Army to take over security tasks in five major Iraqi cities. They are maneuvering their political connections to become omnipresent in security in the same way that KBR is with logistics.

Hough was a physical machine of a man. A finely toned, muscular black man with an addiction to the adrenaline high that extreme exercise can give you, he spent most of his adult life perfecting his body and teaching others to do the same. In 1979, as a young man just out of high school, Hough joined the Marine Corps Reserve and stayed in for three years before becoming inactive.

After the Marines, he returned to his home in New York City and continued honing his body while making a living as a bodybuilder, bodyguard, ironman racer, actor, and personal trainer. He was constantly training and running 35 races a year with the support of sponsors .

But the training exacted a price. In April 2004, he found out that his heart was so overconditioned that his heart rate had become too low. His cardiologist was alarmed and suggested Hough should have a pacemaker implanted so that his rate would not drop so low as to endanger his life while he was asleep.

Hough did not want to get the pacemaker and realized that he had to cut back on his training and racing. He had heard from friends about the high pay of private security work in Iraq so he decided to see if he could get a job in that area. He sent out his resume and received 11 inquiries of interest from private security companies in just 48 hours. Custer Battles was willing to process him the fastest, and they sounded the most gung ho over the phone.

Custer Battles promised Hough that if he came to work for them, he would have Level 4 body armor especially tailored to him, armored SUVs, and a room at the fancy Al Rasheed hotel in Baghdad. He was told he would be doing bodyguard work, providing personal security detail for VIPs. They also told him he would start at $9000 a month and, with salary increases every three months. It sounded good, and he decided to take the plunge.

He arrived at the Custer Battles' facility in Rhode Island for a three-day orientation during the latter part of May 2004, and the company put him up in a fancy four-star hotel. The next day he joined 22 other new hires for conditioning exercises. The instructor wanted them to run 1.5 miles in twelve minutes. Hough started off with the group but hung back to see how fast the other guys were. He had noticed many of them when they arrived, some swaggering into the hotel with a Special Ops air, smoking and partying hard late into the night. They started to drop out of the run, with one guy leaning over and vomiting on the field. Hough sped up, and only one in the group managed to keep up with him, a red-haired former Army man who was later nicknamed "Garfield" because he looked like the cartoon cat.

As the rest of the group staggered past the finish line, Hough started to become concerned that he would have to count on this out-of-shape group to watch his back in a war zone. Each group member then had to carry a 170-pound dummy for 45 yards and transfer it onto another man's back for his turn. When Hough transferred the dummy to the next man in line, the man collapsed under the weight.

Only 15 of the 22 men in the original group, including Hough, cleared the bar to be hired and shipped to Iraq. They gave each other monikers in true military fashion. Hough became "Cyborg"—half man, half machine— because of his superior physical abilities. These abilities would later save his life in Iraq.

Once in Iraq, Hough found that Custer Battles was not the only company with wild guys and loose rules. In the dining hall, there would often be men looking to convince him and others to quit Custer Battles to come work with their company. One guy approached to tell him that Custer Battles was going to lose its contract, flashing large wads of cash and promising Hough $15,000 per month to come work with him. Although Hough was not happy with Custer Battles, he decided it was better to go with the devil you know. Still, it was an amazing amount of money for Hough, who, in a good year, made about $67,000 with his racing and personal trainer work.

During the first three weeks, Custer Battles had the men complete a sign-in sheet to keep track of their work and hours. After that, however, the sheets disappeared and no one seemed to keep track of how many hours they actually worked. Hough did not know how Custer Battles was keeping track of their costs and wages. He could see that most contractors and their employees were there for the money. "Iraq is a cash-cow place to come and make money," he thought.

He liked many of his fellow employees at Custer Battles but was concerned about the cowboy attitude common in the company. He thought that some of the men he worked with were real "psycho whack jobs" who were not really in touch with reality, while the other half were, like him, guys who wanted to make money but had some sense. The psycho guys made him nervous because he knew that he would have to rely on some of them in a pinch to watch his back. Some of the guys he worked with had been doing some type of war and mercenary work for four years straight.

They ended up living in two-man rooms with air conditioning, at the south side of the airport. The rooms were comfortable compared to what the troops were living in but had cheap generators that needed constant coaxing to run. No one wanted to be without air conditioning in the horrible heat.

Hough ended up doing quite a bit of convoy work in Iraq, approximately 70 to 80 missions. He and his coworkers typically took a convoy of six to eight trucks and four SUVs manned with guards and guns. They would often start out from the Abu Ghraib warehouse to deliver various types of supplies, including new Chevy Trailblazers, Humvees, and other SUVs on flatbed trucks. He wasn't always sure who they were working for, but occasionally he knew they were delivering for the Army.

Along the way on these trips, Hough was surprised at several things. The Army was stretched very thin between bases; sometimes he would drive as long as four hours without ever seeing any military. Clearly, there were far fewer than the million troops he considered to be the minimum number needed to keep order and rebuild the country.

He was also surprised to see large above-ground bunkers full of weapons left over from Saddam's regime. The caches were unguarded, and you could see shells and other weapon parts scattered about for anyone to pick up. He was very concerned that some of this unguarded ammo would eventually be used against them, or against the troops, as IEDs.

He was also appalled at the conditions the Army troops at the checkpoints they went through had to endure . There would be three or four miserable soldiers with just a few Humvees and camouflage netting and no decent food and water. Because he felt so sorry for what they had to put up with, he would carry supplies with him to give out to these guys on his runs

After a few weeks of convoy duty, some of the men started getting killed. One of the men, named Bobby, was killed along with his driver Mohammad after an IED tore through their unarmored SUV. Soon after that a guard whose codename was "Voodoo," and his Gurka assistant "Teka" were killed when their SUV was hit with an IED. The car flipped three times, and "Voodoo" was killed by the shrapnel that ripped through his door and penetrated a gap in his inferior body-armor vest.

Alarmed by the deaths, Hough bolted extra armor on the door of his vehicle, wore several layers of body armor, and got ceramic plates for his body armor from some of the buddies he made at the Abu Ghraib warehouse. He took advantage of the black market in protective gear that was being run out of that warehouse to make sure he made it home. Many of the his fellow employees made fun of his heavily armored car and body, but as more and more of the convoy security guys started dying, they came to him to ask where they could get more protection.

Custer Battles hired Kurdish guards to go along with the American guards on these convoys. Many of the Kurds were barely out of their teens, and Hough worried for them. According to Hough, Custer Battles sometimes would only supply one helmet per SUV, and the American guard usually wore it. Bothered by this, Hough tried to scrounge up enough helmets for the young Kurds. He did not feel right leaving them so unprotected.

When he was traveling with his Kurdish guards through various towns providing protection to convoys, Hough told them not to shoot at any of the civilians unless they were fired upon. They were confused and told him they were taught by the other American guards to shoot randomly at people while going through the town to keep everyone back from the convoys and it was all right to hit civilians with gunfire. It was important to remember these Kurds had a natural animosity toward Iraqis because of Saddam's killing and suppression of the Kurds. However, Hough was stricken when he heard this because he knew that would just cause the civilians to attack them the next time the convoys went through their town. He strongly told them not to shoot the civilians. He taught them hand signals to show to civilians on the street and in cars, they would understand, to "keep back from the convoy."

According to Hough, shortly after that, a leader of one of the convoys told his crew, to not let cars near the convoy on the road and to shoot any car that got near them even if they had families in them. After the mission, one of that crew told Hough he shot up at least four cars with families in them because they came near the convoy and the cars had crashed and burned. Hough was appalled, but the crew member knew they could not be prosecuted by the Iraqi government because they were immune. There weren't any hard rules of engagement for these private security contractors like there were for the U.S. military and they knew it.

Hough thought that the crew member must have felt guilty, though, because he watched him get very drunk that night and he was sent home a few days later. Hough knew that the rest of them would have to live with the animosity created by this type of shooting when they returned to the same towns in the future.

Custer Battles was subcontracting with another American security company and had to rely on those companies, instead of the Army for safety mission information. Hough's team did not have satellite phones, just cell phones that did not always work. One of the Custer Battle operators resorted to contacting his old Army unit to try to find out where it was safe to drive. The Custer Battles employees also had poor maps. Hough realized they were winging it with bad maps, bad information, poor armor on their vehicles, poor body armor, poor and cheap ammunition, and not enough of it. Whenever they complained to the management, they were told, "We're working on it." Hough knew that this unhappy situation was a recipe for trouble.

The trouble started for him on his sixth day in Iraq, when he was part of a team escorting a shipment of SUVs in a convoy that got stuck in a traffic jam. In the rearguard position of the convoy, Hough saw a very nervous and sweating Iraqi man pull up along side his SUV. His instincts told him there was something very wrong, and he jumped out of the back of his SUV to keep traffic away from the vehicle. He stopped traffic back about sixty feet from his SUV when the car that had pulled behind them exploded. He was lucky that he was far enough away from the explosion not to be knocked out. But the driver of his SUV thought Hough had been killed and took off to get away. Hough had to sprint through the blast zone of the car with smoldering parts everywhere to catch up to the SUV. He grabbed on to the back of the luggage rack and pulled himself in. "That was way too close for comfort," he thought.

The next close call occurred when they were escorting a convoy delivering white Chevy Trailblazers to a military post near the Syrian border. Hough wondered at first why they were delivering civilian SUVs to a military post, but then realized they were probably for contractors at the post. They drove through a small town, and the civilians started throwing rocks at the cars. At one point, the rock throwing became so fierce that they had to run their SUV over the sidewalk to get away from it. They did not hit any civilians but smashed some open-air markets. To their chagrin, they then realized they had a bad map, were going the wrong direction, and had to drive back through the unfriendly town.

When they reached the town again, they faced more than just rocks. Now, Iraqis began shooting at the convoy, forcing them to return fire as they raced though as fast as they could. Hough knew they had hit some civilians who were firing at them, but he had tried not to hit any children. They finally made it through the town and to the Army post and dropped off the SUVs. Someone with a working GPS unit showed them how to get back without going through the town.

The very next day, Hough was returning in a SUV for his next assignment with two operators codenamed "Sandman" and "Craftsman." They encountered trouble and one of the guards in the convoy, Phil Otto, wrote about it with great gusto in the December 2004 issue of the mercenary magazine *Soldier of Fortune*:

> I was covering the four to seven o'clock from the rear vehicle, with my AK–47. Cyborg had the seven to twelve o'clock and Craftsman covered the twelve to four o'clock. Eight to ten rounds of AK fire erupted from the nine o'clock area. Usually this kind of fire comes from a drive-by in the opposite lanes, to distract the target and sign the main ambush down the road we are coming . . .

Then they were fired upon but stuck to their assigned positions. The attempt to draw their fire from the main ambush failed. Then they were attacked by four to six men from behind a berm and had to continually return fire while driving by at least going 45 mph. More fire came from other men on the side of the road and one of them had an RPG (Rocket Propelled Grenade.) They knew that they had to keep their wits about them and continue to fire to prevent the RPG from being fired at their vehicle.

Otto was proud that they had made it out alive.

> . . .At the end of the day we accomplished our mission, and returned to the base camp safe, with only minimal damage to equipment, and no loss of life. All in all, not a bad start to a new job.

In August 2004, Hough was assigned to a mission escorting a convoy that began from the Abu Ghraib warehouse and headed to the airport. Along the route, an IED explosion knocked off one of the trucks in front of them. The shrapnel from the explosion hit one of the young Kurds in

Hough's SUV in the head and chest. He did not have body armor or a helmet. At that time they only had seven helmets for thirty-five men. Shortly after the explosion, the air was full of machine gun fire. They defended themselves in the firefight, and after the insurgents fled, the Army showed up and medivac'd the young Kurd out. Hough was angry that this young man might have been saved from severe injury by the proper equipment. He made sure that his vehicle had ceramic plates in the doors.

In his next mission, Hough tested fate again. He was escorting a convoy transporting supplies from Basra to Camp Cooke, a staging area for the battle of Fallujah. They had six trucks in the convoy and four SUVs to guard them. He was riding with "Brooklyn," "Redneck," Bill Craun, Ernie Collings, and their Kurdish guards. He was covering the rear of the convoy with two of the young Kurds.

The Army stopped them, telling them it was too dangerous to continue because the road was littered with IEDs. They instructed the convoy to wait until the Army IED team arrived to clear the road. However, Hough says a supervisor, ordered them to push on because they needed to make the delivery; they had a mission, he said. The team did not want to go but felt pressured to do so . Hough had a very bad feeling about what they were about to do.

They traveled down the road and suddenly saw a 155 mm shell on the side of the road. They made a wide pass around it and sped ahead with the convoy at 60 miles an hour. Hough looked back and realized that the civilian traffic was hanging way back and barely moving. "They know something," he thought. He and the Kurds had their weapons ready.

Instantly, there was a blinding flash of light. His SUV spun around and around with shrapnel flying everywhere, punching holes in metal and flesh. There were even holes in the ceiling of the SUV. Seeing the rest of the convoy speed away, Hough frantically called on the radio to tell them he was hit. They later told him they sped away because they thought, based on the size of the explosion, that he and the Kurds were dead. Once the SUV stopped spinning, he looked around. He could tell he was wounded but he looked in horror at one of the young Kurds who had shrapnel sticking out of his head. The other Kurd wobbled out of the car also holding his head. The Kurd in the SUV started going into shock, and Hough tried to hold the young Kurd's head together with his hands.

Suddenly, a group of insurgents began to fire at them from a nearby building. Hough had had enough. He did not want these Kurds to die. Wounded and bleeding, with his body pumping adrenaline left over from the blast, he leaped out of the SUV with his weapon. Joining another operator, named "Bandito," he raced toward the building, firing as he ran. As the two stormed the building like madmen, the insurgents, Hough claimed, suddenly threw down their weapons and surrendered. Amazingly, there were sixteen of them. He and Bandito had them lie on the ground. Later, his fellow operators did not understand why Hough did not just start shooting them. Hough told them he would not shoot men who surrendered and were on the ground.

The Army soon showed up to take the prisoners and help the wounded Kurds. They were stunned that these two men had been able to take that many insurgents. They then looked at the demolished SUV and could not believe that Hough had even survived the blast. Hough was pushing the medics to attend to the gravely wounded Kurds when they began to realize that he also had injuries. They cut off his jeans and found large pieces of shrapnel in his leg. They thought that most of the tendons in his leg had been cut and that most of the ligaments in his arm had been torn from the bone. His head was also bleeding, and they found that shrapnel had entered his skull,causing one of his eyes to bulge out. They began to look at him like he was a freak because he should have been dead from the blast, and yet he had been able to charge the building with all his serious injuries. He said that they looked at him as if he really was a cyborg.

He was patched up at a local Army hospital, where the doctors decided not to take the shrapnel out of his leg for fear of aggravating the injury. His head was bandaged, and he could barely walk. When they took him back to the Custer Battles camp, the doctor told him he was not to do anything for 48 hours especially because of his serious head wounds. He stumbled into his bed and went to sleep realizing how close the day had come to being his last on earth.

The next day a supervisor told Hough that he needed him to go on another mission. According to Hough, he said, "Cyborg, I need you to be my fullback on this one and take it another 400 yards." Hough told the supervisor that he was crazy and showed him his wounds and his medical papers from the Army. Hough's head was greatly swollen, and he could barely move. The supervisor continued to insist that Hough go on another mission. Hough continued to refuse, and he called him a coward. Hough just turned his back on the man to return to his room, wanting only to go back to bed.

The supervisor lost it. He grabbed Hough's gun from the back of his belt, and Hough thought he was going to shoot him. Hough swung around and grabbed his wrist, putting his arm in a lock. The rest of the team ran toward them while the supervisor began to scream that Hough was crazy and had attacked him. He screamed for them to call the Military Police to have Hough arrested. The team tried to tell him that he couldn't grab a man's gun from him and not provoke a reaction, but he just kept screaming. Hough ignored him and went back to his bed.

One of the Lebanese operators with Custer Battles, called "New York," knew of another Lebanese man who worked for KBR but wanted more action. New York went over to the KBR camp and recruited him that day to replace Hough on the mission. Hough came out of his room, shook the new recruit's hand and wished him luck. The convoy traveled to the Abu Ghraib warehouse with the new recruit to pick up supplies. The Army told them they had shut down all missions that day because it was too dangerous to be on the road. Once again, Hough says a Custer Battles manager told the convoy to push through. The convoy continued on and, predictably, was attacked and hit with an IED. Within five hours from the time Hough shook his hand, the new Lebanese recruit was dead. Hough knew that if he had gone, he might have been the one killed.

Hough then blacked out for about 42 hours because of his head injury. He had a hairline crack in his skull, and the shrapnel had made his one eye bulge out two millimeters from his head. The manager for his unit told him he could take an easier job or go home because of his injuries. Hough had enough and just wanted to go home. He could not fly right away because of his head injuries but finally was able to make the trip two weeks later.

Hough returned to New York to try to put his life back together. It would not be easy. He had double vision and poor hearing in one ear. The blast also shattered the bones in one of his inner ears, throwing his balance off. He has permanent ringing in his ears and still has pain and trouble using his wounded arm and leg. The doctors told him they could try various surgeries to relieve his symptoms, but there was a chance these would make the symptoms worse. Hough decided just to live with the injuries rather than run the risk of becoming more crippled. He is getting by day-to-day and trying to regain his life.

Hough was a finely honed athlete with Herculean abilities when he left for Iraq; now, Hough says he is barely able to ride a bike or run because of his dizziness and the other effects of his injuries. Still, he realizes that he was one of the lucky ones. He believes that his team had killed Iraqi civilians unnecessarily and gotten young Kurds killed with misguided tactics and poor leadership. He also believes that this behavior enraged the civilian population and made it more dangerous for the troops and the other private security contractors that came after him.

Hough says he wrote Scott Custer about the problems he saw, but never heard back from him. He is now working with other veterans to help them merge back into civilian life. His broken body can no longer make a living for him, he can only train others, but he has learned not to take each day for granted.

As Hough's experience and the Blackwater tragedy in Fallujah show, using private security companies on the battlefield can have many unintended consequences. The Army and the civilian authorities have no roadmap to deal with the phenomenon, and the regulations and laws have not caught up to this new type of contracting. It breeds resentment and mistrust from our troops when they see private security guards making much more money than they do. The uncontrolled cowboy tactics of some of these companies threaten the troops who have to live with the anger from the civilians and hurt the military's mission by turning many civilians against the United States.

Hough, along with fellow former Custer Battles employees Bill Craun, Jim Errante, and Ernest Colling, went public with their criticisms of how Custer Battles conducted business in Iraq. Appearing on NBC News in 2005, they accused the company of allowing its poorly trained guards to terrorize civilians and randomly shoot innocent Iraqis.

They told the TV audience how some of the Kurds hired by Custer Battles randomly shot unarmed Iraqi teenagers in the back and rolled over civilian cars loaded with children. Craun, a recipient of the Bronze Star, told NBC: "What we saw, I know the American population wouldn't stand for." Craun also wrote this to a friend in the Pentagon: "I didn't want any part of an organization that deliberately murders children and innocent victims." Colling believes that Custer Battles's negligence was responsible for these actions because the company was "throwing people out there and then forcing us to use these brutal tactics." Errante told NBC that he quit because he did not want to be a witness to activity that "could be classified as a war crime." Craun concluded that if Custer Battles continued this type of freelance cowboying, there would be long-term consequences. "If we continue to let this happen, those people [Iraqis] will hate us even more than they already do."

Calling these men "disgruntled employees," Custer Battles has denied the charges. An Army investigation is underway. According to NBC News,

Custer Battles claimed that Hough was fired and these men still owed the company money. The company also disclaimed any wild shooting and Paul Christopher, a former Iraq country manager told NBC, "there has absolutely never been a case of anyone being hurt for Custer Battles or killed to my knowledge, except for people who were actively engaged in shooting at us first."

PART IV

THE SLOG

It is pretty clear that the coalition can win in Afghanistan and Iraq in one way or another, but it will be a long, hard slog.

—Secretary of Defense, Donald H. Rumsfeld,
from a memorandum to Dick Meyers,
Paul Wolfowitz, General Pete Pace,
and Doug Feith, October 16, 2003.

CHAPTER 16

THE OTHER SIDE
OF THE FORCE

Camp Speicher, Iraq, July 2004.

Major Rick Lamberth, U.S. Army Reserves, arrived at Camp Speicher, near Tikrit, about 170 kilometers north of Baghdad, as the LOGCAP planner for the 1st Infantry Division and later 42nd Infantry Division. Once the Al Sahra Airfield and location of the Iraqi Air Force Academy, Speicher was named after Navy Commander Michael Scott Speicher, who was shot down in his F/A 18 during the first Gulf War on January 17, 1991. Designated as "killed in action, body not recovered," his remains have never been found. Compared to those living outside the base, soldiers stationed at Camp Speicher had good living conditions, according to solders based there. The dining facilities, run by KBR, resembled college dorm cafeterias, with Subway, Burger King, and Pizza Hut restaurants among the options.

In March 2004, after leaving his employment with KBR, Lamberth felt free from the waste, abuse, and incompetence he faced in Kuwait working for the company. He chose to live in the northern Virginia area where he joined an Army reserve LOGCAP Support Unit based at Ft. Belvoir, Virginia. With the occupation in Iraq turning into a long, hard slog and the military needing more personnel, it wasn't long before Lamberth volunteered to deploy to

Iraq to help out in overseeing KBR as part of the Army's LOGCAP team. He already knew how KBR worked on the inside and thought it would be interesting to see how they performed with the troops. He also felt he could contribute his knowledge of KBR operations to Army contracting-officials located where he was assigned.

By the time Lamberth arrived at Camp Speicher, the violent insurgency was on the rise throughout Iraq. In June 2004, the United States had transferred limited sovereignty to an Iraqi caretaker government and ended the Coalition Provisional Authority's reign in Iraq. The Mahdi Militia of Muqtada al-Sadr staged an uprising in Baghdad in an effort to take over the streets of that city. Prior to its termination, the CPA had closed down al-Sadr's popular newspaper, resulting in mass anti-American demonstrations.

KBR had suffered a terrible disaster when, on April 9, 2004 a fuel convoy on its way from Balad to the Baghdad International Airport was attacked by hundreds of insurgents, resulting in the death of six of the contractor's drivers, with two other drivers missing and presumed dead, one known to be kidnapped, and many injured. Insurgency attacks on convoys were increasing, spurred on by the attacks against the Blackwater operators in Fallujah, a few months earlier and the KBR drivers on convoy to the Baghdad airport. As a result, there were no longer any front lines, clear safe routes, or areas in which to operate outside the base. Attacks could come from anywhere at anytime. Contractor drivers were risking their lives driving cargo trucks and tractor-trailers that were not adequately armored. They had no weapons to defend themselves if their Army escorts were unable to protect them.

Lamberth now found himself on the other side of the fence—this time helping the Army oversee KBR. He was at Speicher only about a week when a senior level KBR manager at KBR's headquarters in Houston, sent a letter to the Army's LOGCAP contracting officer at Rock Island, Illinois, wanting him removed due to "run-ins" with KBR employees and that he would not be able to perfom his job in an impartial manner. Lamberth was astounded with the allegations since he had no such "run-ins" with KBR employees. He felt the allegations were made by KBR in an attempt to quickly get rid of him because of his inside knowledge of their operations. Lamberth believed that KBR saw his name on a list of LOGCAP Support Unit personnel deployed to Iraq that was routinely sent to KBR in Houston. In short, Lamberth felt he presented a threat to KBR's methods and tactics and they wanted to get him out of Iraq as soon as possible. The contracting officer at Rock Island sent the letter to Lamberth's boss at Ft. Belvoir, Colonel Eric Smith, Commander of the LOGCAP Support Unit. Col. Smith contacted Lamberth to alert him of the letter and told him the matter was under investigation to determine its merits. It wasn't long before a determination the allegations had no merit and recommendations from the Assistant Division Commander, Brigadier General Stephen Mundt, that Colonel Smith replied to KBR that Lamberth was staying at Speicher.

Lamberth learned that the troops had not been adequately supplied with important combat equipment due to Army budget constraints. He found it odd that soldiers had to make due without night vision goggles or uparmored Humvees, and yet they were able to get plenty of plasma TVs, cybercafés, and soft-serve ice cream cones with seemingly unlimited LOG-CAP money. To Lamberth, it seemed that "we were trying to win the war with soft-serve ice cream."

Under the LOGCAP contract, KBR's transportation duties in Iraq included supplying troops at all remote sites within 100 kilometer radius from the KBR operating base.[1] At the same time, the Army was required to provide force protection to KBR supply convoys.[2] However, Lamberth found that the contractor drivers, and some individual KBR employees, were unwilling to go outside Camp Speicher to transport supplies to the remote sites. According to Lamberth, KBR felt it too dangerous—there was not enough force protection—and their unwillingness to leave the base was having an impact on supplies getting to remote forward operating bases. The pool of available American drivers was starting to dry up, and those still at the camp had become too expensive to use. As a result, KBR started subcontracting for drivers from non-American companies, such as Dubai-based PPI, Turkey-based Kulak, and Kuwait-based First Kuwaiti, all of which employed foreign nationals at a much lower salary than American drivers required.

Camp Caldwell was one of those remote bases suffering from a lack of the kind of supplies trucks from Speicher typically delivered. Caldwell was far from the security of Speicher and trips to the camp were made infrequently. Almost eight months after Sergeant Perry Jefferies left Caldwell at the end of his tour, conditions for the soldiers there remained bad.

It was part of Lamberth's duties to visit the many small remote military sites under the responsibility of Camp Speicher. When Lamberth visited Caldwell, soldiers confided in him that whenever KBR workers were in the camp, they lived better than the soldiers. Their equipment was always of higher quality and better functioning, and the generators at the contractors' part of the base were always running, while the soldiers' generators often failed. "It really pissed them off," Lamberth said.

In addition, soldiers complained to Lamberth that it was common for many of the contractor workers, such as electricians or carpenters, not to know what they were doing. Soldiers, usually Reservists with a background in the trades, such as carpentry, often had to take over the work from the contractors, pushing them aside saying, "Just give me the damn hammer and nails and I'll do the job." The soldiers were frustrated at the contractor personnel because they were getting paid big money and yet they couldn't perform their tasks sufficiently well. Lamberth quipped that it sometimes seemed that the only criterion for being hired by KBR to work generators, for example, was knowing how to spell the word "generator." Lamberth joked that the contractor would then get a worker in Iraq who may have known what a socket wrench was, but didn't know anything about repairing a generator.

Lamberth found the problem of contractor personnel incompetence to be common at Speicher. It was also common, he observed, for arguments to break out between the military's administrative contracting officer and KBR managers over the contractor's inability to perform required tasks. It was a constant battle between the contractor's mind-set and the military's mind-set—a difference that was having an adverse effect on the troops.

Lamberth noticed a lot of pushback from KBR in response to challenges from the administrative contracting officer. In large measure, it was the same dance between contractor and government often seen in the traditional government procurement world. In many ways it was a type of intimidation on the part of the contractor to get what it wanted. It was a marking of territory—the contactor staking a claim of dominance over the government. Pentagon oversight personnel are often overmatched by the contractor's knowledge, expertise, and political connections. It takes a rare breed of government official to stand up to a contractor. When that happens, it isn't unusual for the contractor to complain to higher-level government officials that a difficult military oversight official should be removed or reassigned. When he sent a report to his supervisors criticizing KBR's performance, Lamberth was threatened by a KBR manager with a lawsuit for reporting negative information to his superiors.

The military administrative contracting officer, part of the Defense Contract Management Agency (DCMA), represents the procurement contracting officer in overseeing and managing the contract on site. His or her job is to make certain that a contractor complies with the requirements of its contract, which is spelled out in the "Statement of Work." The contracting officer assigned to Camp Speicher also had contract responsibility for the 28 to 32 smaller military sites located everywhere from the Iranian border in the east, Mosul in the north, Syrian border in the west, to near Balad in the south. This zone of responsibility pretty much encompassed what is known as the "Sunni Triangle."

Camp Speicher had only one administrative contracting officer (ACO), one military quality assurance representative, and one LOGCAP planner, Lamberth, to oversee contract compliance throughout the entire area of what was designated as the "C" camps. They represented the only oversight for the Pentagon and the Army in this large area. The contracting officer's work at Speicher, which involved dealing with compliance issues, changing orders, definitizing requirements, interpreting the Statement of Work, and resolving arguments with KBR, pretty much kept him tied to his office. It was the same for the quality assurance representative. As a result, spot checks of KBR compliance outside of Speicher were not performed very often. The quality representative was supposed to conduct spot checks so that he could confirm that the assigned tasks associated with an invoice had been completed. Continuity in monitoring contractor performance was also a problem in that administrative contracting officers were routinely rotated out of Iraq about every four months. Unlike the ACO, who has a warrant to authorise expenditures of funds for KBR, the LOGCAP planner has no warrant and no authority over KBR's actions.

Among the many problems facing the administrative contracting officer was the threat that KBR would possibly cease important operations because their invoices were not being paid in a timely manner. It was the same threat experienced by the Army in Kuwait rearing its ugly head again—this time at Camp Speicher. Ceasing life-support operations would have a critical impact on the troops. It was déjà vu for Lamberth who witnessed those same threats in Kuwait when he worked for KBR.

In late summer 2004, Lamberth attended a meeting in the General's conference room at Speicher presided over by the Army's Assistant Division Commander for Support, Brigadier General Stephan D. Mundt. KBR was operating again "at risk" and wanted the Army to pay their invoices. It was difficult for Lamberth to assess whether the funding problem was a result of KBR not getting their invoices in, the Army making slow progress in paying those invoices, or a funding gap caused by the Army overrunning its appropriated supplemental money.

Nevertheless, the problem again was coming to a head, with KBR threatening to cease operations and keeping their employees in their housing containers. Such a work stoppage, if done, in the middle of a war would put soldiers at risk. General Mundt responded by telling the senior KBR manager making the threat that if the company ceased operations, he would throw all of KBR's personnel outside the base. He was not going to have the troops suffer from a lack of life support. Lamberth felt that KBR's threat was uncalled for; there was no doubt that they would be paid.

The Army convinced KBR that the invoices would be paid, and KBR's threat was never carried out. But it was still disturbing to the Army that such a close call had caught them unawares. They did not have a back-up plan to resort to if contractors were unable or unwilling to supply the soldiers. Lamberth fumed that the Army buckled under to the threats of work stoppages. It was embarrassing to him how the government reacted to the contractor. "They just gave in," Lamberth said, "by not standing up to them." It appeared to him to be the new reality of contracting for contingency operations.

An example of an actual work stoppage seriously affecting the U.S. military supply chain occurred in August 2004. Kahramanli and Oztur, two Turkish cargo firms that brought supplies for American forces into Iraq from Turkey stopped their convoys after two of its drivers were kidnapped and held hostage by insurgents. This stoppage disrupted two to three hundred daily convoys of supplies into Iraq. Some of the supplies carried by the Turkish convoys included fuel vital to the military.[3] Two days later, after the Turkish firms declared that they would stop transporting supplies to U.S. forces in Iraq, the kidnapped drivers were released.[4] The fact that contractors can quit the battlefield and leave the troops to fend for themselves is a serious problem the Army faces when it privatizes much of the supply chain. Under these circumstances, the Army would have to step in and use troops to provide the supplies. Thus, one of the Pentagon's primary reasons for privatizing the supply chain—freeing up troops to be "trigger pullers"—would not hold water.

Lamberth continued to see supplies failing to get to remote sites because KBR managers were unwilling to allow employees to leave the safety of the base. At another site visited by Lamberth, an Army Tank Company base located between Speicher and Camp Warrior (near Kirkuk), he was appalled at the conditions the soldiers had to endure because they were not being adequately supplied. Their latrine trailer had no water due to plumbing leaks, so they had to use burn barrels to dispose of their waste. Also, there was no cook or mess facilities and the soldiers had to subsist mainly on MREs, unless the First Sergeant there could get an opportunity to go off base himself to find hot food. Electricity was sporadic and the soldiers didn't have enough water to shower regularly. And Morale, Welfare, and Recreation (MWR) facilities didn't exist as it did on the larger bases. Lamberth heard many complaints from the soldiers that KBR had not been out there to supply them or build MWR facilities.

The same problem existed at another remote site being used as a detention facility, about 60 miles south of Speicher and 10 miles north of Camp

Anaconda, a large military base near Balad. According to Lamberth, KBR had been unwilling to transport supplies to the facility because it was too dangerous. The administrative contracting officer at Camp Anaconda, who was also responsible for this detention facility, would not direct the contractor to supply the facility despite the relatively short distance from the base.

After the area serviced by Anaconda was restructured bringing the detention facility within the responsibility of Speicher. The Battalion Commander for the unit assigned to the detention facility, a Lieutenant Colonel was based at Anaconda, disregarded the danger and drove to Speicher herself to see the administrative contracting officer. At a meeting Lamberth attended, the Lieutenant Colonel told the contracting officer that the troops needed to get supplied; they were not getting food, water, or ammunition. She told Lamberth and the contracting officer, "My troops are doing without. You have to make these people (KBR) function." The administrative contracting officer at Speicher directed KBR to convoy down to the facility to service it.

Another incident witnessed by Lamberth during the late spring or early summer of 2005 spoke volumes about the regular conflicts between KBR and the administrative contracting officer. A Special Forces Army Captain and a Lieutenant showed up at the contracting officer's office at Speicher. They had just driven over from the palace at Tikrit, where division headquarters was located. They were operating a safe house across the street from the palace where Iraqis could come in for protection or to safely provide information. The generator the safe house depended on for electricity was constantly going out and had finally quit running altogether. With no air conditioning to combat the sweltering heat, the generator needed to be replaced immediately if the safe house was to continue operating.

The two officers told Lamberth they had gone to the KBR offices at the palace to request assistance in replacing the generator. Lamberth said it was the contractor's responsibility under the contract to repair such equipment, but KBR refused to go to the safe house. According to Lamberth, the KBR thought it was too dangerous, even though it was located only about a block away and the Special Forces soldiers were well armed. They would have shot their own mothers to protect them, Lamberth felt. The Special Forces officers told KBR managers they would personally ensure their physical safety, escorting them the entire way to and from the palace. KBR still refused. Again, it was "just say no" at work.

The Special Forces officers explained their plight to the contracting officer, who immediately contacted a senior KBR manager to direct them to do the job. A KBR manager still refused, again saying it was too dangerous. He also argued that it was outside the scope of the contract in that it was a "safe house," while the contract only mentioned working on Forward Operating Bases. But this was a purely semantic dispute since the safe house was a military facility and the contract covered any and all military facilities in Iraq. When the KBR manager continued to refuse, the contracting officer bucked it up to General Mundt. Mundt, who had not been happy with KBR's performance, emphasized the importance of the task to the manager, who finally agreed to comply. It was typical of the teeth-pulling often necessary to get the contractor to perform tasks outside a base. And when KBR's repairs did not work, it ended up taking several more days of requests, arguments, cajoling, and the muscle of a one-star general to finally persuade them just to replace the generator. Delays like this wreaked havoc on the Army's mission.

Unfortunately the safe house episode wasn't an isolated incident. KBR had the responsibility, under LOGCAP to fix air conditioners and generators theater-wide. The lack of work by KBR became so bad that two soldiers, in 2005, took the risky step of complaining about the company in *Stars & Stripes,* an official military publication:

Major Ralph D. Heady wondered, in his letter to *Stars & Stripes,* why KBR was there at Logistics Support Area Anaconda, Iraq. "Certainly not to repair broken equipment," he wrote. Major Heady revealed that with the third year approaching in Iraq, soldiers were living in housing with a life expectancy of only two years. According to Heady, the generators and air conditioning units were purchased using what the Army calls "field ordering officer (FOO) money." But limits on FOO money, "will not allow replacement of generators." According to Heady, KBR would not work to provide maintenance on the generators without a government purchase order number (known as a GP number by the Army). Unfortunately, most of the generators at LSA Anaconda were purchased from local vendors using FOO money and do not have the GP number, Heady said. The KBR workers are not the problem. The KBR workers are willing to work on the equipment. If KBR is not here to maintain every piece of nonmilitary government-owned equipment in theater, GP numbers be damned, then why is KBR here?"[5]

Sergeant Gary M. Davenport wrote in *Stars &* Stripes that Major Heady was "right on target" about KBR. Davenport, who was located at Camp Speicher at the time he wrote a letter that appeared in *Stars &* Stripes, experienced similar problems with KBR. He observed "hundreds of air-conditioning units sitting idle, yet if you place a work order to have an A/C unit installed, it is denied. 'There's no money for new installations,' you are told by a man wearing a T-shirt and shorts inside a nicely cooled building. So you go back to your oven."

According to Davenport, when A/C units breakdown in a soldier's barracks, it takes a week, and an emergency work order, to get a response from KBR, and then they are unable to fix it because of bureaucratic work rules. Davenport didn't blame the KBR employees. Their hands are tied. If they do work they aren't supposed to, they lose their job," Davenport wrote. He concluded by writing "It seems KBR, at the administrative level, has found a way to get paid for doing a job without ever actually having to do it.[6]

As part of the transportation mission, KBR was tasked to recover all military and commercial transportation assets—five-ton trucks, Humvees, Bradley's, etc., in the event of breakdown or damage sustained under hostile situations. These recovery operations were also done under force protection. If Army vehicles were left unattended for any length of time, Iraqis completely stripped them of anything of value. It was important, then, that recovery operations be done in a timely manner. Because of the limited number of troops in Iraq, the Army did not have the resources to conduct recovery operations on a consistent basis. They needed KBR to supplement the operation.

To be able to do this, KBR was given an expensive, fully loaded wrecker to conduct recovery missions outside Speicher. The problem, as Lamberth learned, was that the KBR driver would not leave the base because he thought that going out was too dangerous. Again, it was "just say no." At times, the driver himself refused to go, and at other times, KBR managers wouldn't allow him to go.

Lamberth often saw him driving the wrecker around the base, listening to CDs, picking up his girlfriend for meals, or giving other females rides back to their work areas. Army officials complained about it to Lamberth and wanted to know how to get the driver to deploy in order to recover broken down or damaged vehicles. He was supposed to go outside the base—it was a requirement under the contract. In an illogical maze of the contract enforcement specifics, the driver could be "directed" to go by the contracting officer, but could not be "forced" to go. He could be terminated, but that did not solve the immediate problem of recovering vehicles. The military faced similar dilemmas throughout Iraq when relying on contractors to perform in a hostile environment.

The Army, on many occasions, addressed the issue of KBR not performing outside the base in meetings among Army officials and between the Army and the contractor. The individual task orders were negotiated and tasks predefined between the Army's LOGCAP officials at Rock Island Arsenal, Illinois, and KBR Headquarters in Houston. The requirements were understood by KBR and documented in the task order. They included performing transportation operations outside a base with force protection. There were no surprises in the wording of the contract. Army force protection officers tried to assuage KBR's concerns about protection. Yes, there would be risks—everywhere outside the base was a potentially hostile area. But protection would be provided at predefined ratios between the number of vehicles and number of troops. Lamberth felt that KBR wanted to be paid for all the tasks set out in the contract while retaining discretion over which of them it would actually perform.

At Camp Speicher, Lamberth discovered the same problems with maintaining the inventory of spare parts that he had experienced when he was in Kuwait working for KBR. Mundt, a former helicopter pilot, was adamant about keeping his operational readiness status up on helicopters, and he knew that he couldn't do this in combat operations without spare parts. Lamberth observed Mundt's frustration at KBR for not maintaining the visibility of helicopter parts. They were losing parts at the Logistics Support Area at Camp Anaconda. Parts would arrive at Speicher and no one would know it. Lamberth attended Battle Update Assessment meetings where Mundt chewed him out along with the administrative contracting officer in front of the staff-represented officers. "Why aren't you guys tracking the stuff?" he would ask. "Because KBR is difficult to control," Lamberth would reply. They were losing traceability of the parts. Parts visibility was a joke. Lamberth knew the importance of those parts to keep the helicopters flying to support combat operations and rescue troops caught in firefights.

In order to address the parts problem, Lamberth approached a senior KBR manager and told him that his KBR counterpart at Anaconda needed to do a better job tracking helicopter repair parts when they arrived. He was also told the parts needed to be tagged, and the crates spray painted to maintain visibility and expedited to Speicher anyway they could, even if it meant having someone fly with them to keep the parts visible. The KBR manager said he would get on it, but he had no control over the KBR workers at Anaconda. Lamberth explained to the manager that it was not a matter of control but rather understanding the chaos they were putting the Army through at Speicher by losing tractability and accountability of the parts.

Lamberth noticed that the parts problem would get a little better for a while, but then eventually become a problem again. This dance kept repeating itself. It would always take someone being chewed out to see an improvement. But even then, the improvements were never consistently maintained. The sense of urgency instilled in KBR always faded with time. Lamberth had a constant slow burn inside because KBR's poor performance was unnecessary and could be detrimental to the Army's mission and to the troops trying to fight.

Lamberth believed that one of the problems with KBR at Speicher was that it hired too many employees, such as trades workers, with the wrong backgrounds—either with no skill sets or the wrong ones. He found that many of the employees were incompetent in the buying, receiving, and delivering of parts and supplies.

Inventory of foodstuffs was also a concern to Lamberth. He found that KBR did not have an accountability officer to oversee inventory, which often caused them to lose track of what food they had on hand that sometimes led to shortages of milk, bread, water, and other food staples. Lamberth even saw some employees taking food intended for the troops for themselves and their friends. Also, when Lamberth requested data from KBR on food staples on hand that is necessary for the Army to determine how many days of supply were available at any given time, KBR managers were reluctant, and sometimes even completely unwilling, to provide the data claiming is was "proprietary."

Lamberth thought this claim ludicrous since the Army paid for the food and was thus entitled to the information; besides, what other company would steal trade secrets on how to order and provide food in the middle of Iraq when KBR had a sole-source contract? A KBR food manager told Lamberth that his superiors made the decision not to provide the information to the Army. Lamberth believed the real reason KBR didn't want to provide the data was that it would show they were over-ordering supplies of food and leaving the excess to sit in trucks and spoil. Later, the contractor tried to tell the Army's administrative contracting officer that KBR did not have the data. Mundt again had to intervene, ordering that the data be turned over.

Lamberth was not the only one frustrated with the difficulty of obtaining important data from KBR. According to the results of a review by the Special Inspector General for Iraq Reconstruction in October 2006, KBR routinely marked almost all of the information it was specifically required to maintain for the government as "proprietary data," including information on its daily dining facility head count. The Special Inspector General charged that the routine use of proprietary markings by KBR was "an abuse of FAR (Federal Acquisition Regulations) procedures, inhibits transparency of government activities and the use of taxpayer funds, and places unnecessary requirements on the government to both protect from public disclosure information received from KBR and to challenge inappropriate proprietary markings."[7]

In addition to Lamberth's discovery that KBR was allowing food to spoil, Rory Mayberry, the KBR food production manager for a dining hall at Camp Anaconda between February and April 2004, found that KBR managers would triple the food order every week to bring in more food than was needed. He told the U.S. Senate Democratic Policy Committee in June 2005 that the contractor did this because it was charging for an extra 5,000 troops they weren't actually feeding. As a result, most of the extra food went to waste.

Mayberry also discovered that some of the food being brought onto the base was past its expiration date, sometimes by as much as a year. The KBR food service managers fed it to the troops anyway. This occurred everyday, sometimes with every meal. KBR, and subsequently the Army, also paid for spoiled food. When Tamimi (a sub-contractor to KBR for food) dropped off food, there was often no room in the base freezers or refrigerators. This food would stay in the refrigeration and freezer trucks until they ran out of fuel. Then, when KBR declined to refuel the trucks, the food would eventually spoil. It happened all the time, and the Army was ultimately responsible for the bill.[8]

Wasted food items were often given away. Lamberth saw pallets of Gatorade powder sitting outside the dining facility in the rain. Soldiers were told by KBR food workers to take as much as they wanted—even a whole case. They even had Near Beer. That upset Lambert: "You got to be kidding me—this is our tax dollars at work? The government is buying stuff like this? It's bad enough they are buying multiple flavored sodas." Lamberth would see the living areas of soldiers stacked with wasted food items. A lot of items on the base were being thrown away, Lamberth said, while many soldiers in the remote sites were having a hard time just getting basic food because KBR was reluctant to transport supplies off base.

Soft-serve ice cream was also a big perk at Speicher. The Army had the contractor order sixteen soft-serve machines for the dining facilities. Lamberth wasn't sure who at KBR was responsible, but they ordered the machines from Iran despite the fact that Iran was on a prohibited list for trade. The machines were to be used to make food for soldiers, and the Army was going to pay $250,000 to $300,000 for each of them. Lamberth was among those who inspected the machines when they arrived. They turned out not to be functional, but the Army couldn't have used them anyway because they came from Iran. KBR had promoted themselves as professionals in procurement. Lamberth wondered how something like that could happen. KBR had to order more machines at the total cost of another $300,000, yet the company was not penalized for the original illicit purchase, and the Army footed the bill for both the original and the replacement machines. KBR was nonchalant about the mistake. They knew they were the only game in town.

As was the case in Kuwait, Lamberth learned that many KBR employees at Camp Speicher were routinely charging 12 hours a day, seven days a week, on their labor time cards. KBR supervisors told Lamberth that some of their employees only worked about two of these 12 hours, and Lamberth himself observed that many KBR workers seemed to have little to do most of the day. That told him there were too many contractor employees. KBR easily could get leaner or, maybe, volunteer to do more work for the Army. Lamberth never saw a guarantee in the LOGCAP contract of 84 hours a week for KBR employees.

Also, Mike West, a labor foreman for KBR at Camp Anaconda in late 2003, provided a statement to the U.S. House Committee on Government Reform in June 2004, asserting that of the 35 or so KBR employees at Anaconda, only a handful had anything to do. At a nightly staff meeting, the question of pay came up because so few people had done any work. The KBR human resources supervisor said, "Don't worry, just write down 12 hours. Walk around, look around, look busy."[9]

Lamberth knew the 84-hour week set a bad precedent—inflated labor costs could cause inflated estimates for future task orders. The work KBR was doing in Iraq could have been done far more economically. KBR was supposed to provide coverage 24 hours a day, seven days a week, but Lamberth did not believe there was a provision in the contract allowing each of the contractor employees to charge 12 hours a day to the contract. Lamberth felt that KBR could get away with charging excessive labor hours only because government oversight of KBR, including audits, in Iraq was minimal at best.

Lamberth did not see a Pentagon auditor at Speicher during the time he was assigned there. At one point, a woman showed up for two or three days from the Government Accountability Office. She was escorted around the camp by a KBR official and ended her stay by saying she found no irregularities. Lamberth did not know what she was supposed to investigate, but it was clear from conversations he had with her that she didn't want to be there; she had come only because her number had come up to go. His impression was she had a "short straw" attitude. She did tell Lamberth that KBR pretty much self-audits. "There's so many of them and too few of us; we count on them to self-audit," she said.

During the rest of Lamberth's tour at Speicher, which lasted until June 2005, he concluded that KBR's performance did not improve. They had too many employees there, many with almost nothing to do. Lamberth would see them hanging out at the PX, wandering around the camp, playing video games, working out at the gym, watching movies, sleeping. He didn't believe the Army was willing to put a stop to it, even though the contractor was burning a lot of money and Army officials at Speicher were unhappy with KBR's performance.

Again, contractor reliability on the battlefield, as Lamberth saw, was a major issue affecting the troops. The ability of a contractor to decide whether it wants to perform its contractual responsibilities when faced with a hostile environment will continue to present a threat to the troops. A contractor's ability to stop work altogether places the Army in a difficult position vis-à-vis life-support supplies for the troops, and this has resulted in the Army's complete surrender to the contractors. Moreover, the lack of government oversight personnel on site to properly monitor contractor performance allows a contractor to pretty much do what it wants. Unfortunately, the Pentagon has been unwilling to raise staffing levels high enough to provide the oversight necessary for contingency contractor operations.

Lamberth returned to Ft. Belvoir in June 2005 to continue his active duty status with the LOGCAP Support Unit. He was deeply shaken by the experience of being on both sides of the fence as a KBR employee and an Army overseer. He believes this new contracting system with the war service industry must be broken if it allows a contractor to grab control over the Army in a wartime situation. He is still very disappointed that his superiors were so intimidated by KBR's monopoly. They may have had no choice, but he believes the whole process is detrimental to the troops, the very people that the Army is supposed to protect as they put their lives on the line. Lamberth felt that upon returning to the U.S., he could provide Army LOGCAP officials with the benefit of his experiences—what he observed on the ground in Iraq with the questionable business practices and poor performance of KBR, and their impact on the troops and taxpayer.

CHAPTER 17

A DIFFERENT KIND
OF BLACK WATER

Camp Ar Ramadi, Iraq, March 2005.

Tyrone Ross was one of the original 12 KBR employees at Camp Ar Ramadi, previously known as Camp Junction City, situated about 70 miles west of Baghdad along the Euphrates River, at the southwest point of the Sunni Triangle." Ross was the labor foreman who managed the foreign national workers doing janitorial work around the camp. On Wednesday morning, March 23, 2005, Ross wandered to the toilet of his housing shipping container hootch and noticed something that looked like a bug swimming in the toilet bowl. Disgusted, he grabbed his radio and summoned Harry Grocholski, an electrical foreman acting as the operations and maintenance manager while the regular manager was on Rest and Recreation. Grocholski showed up at Ross's hootch and also saw something moving around in the toilet bowl.

Ben Carter, the new KBR water specialist at Ramadi, had been working hard to get the new KBR-operated Reverse Osmosis Water Purification Unit, universally known by the acronym ROWPU, up and running to replace the smaller, inadequate military ROWPU that had been purifying the camp's water. He was completely focused on this task.

On that busy Wednesday morning in March, Carter was intent on getting more work done on the water system when his radio came to life with a call from Grocholski, who needed him at Ross's hootch right away. "There was something swimming in his toilet bowl and you need to come and look at it," he said. Irritated about the interruption, Carter nonetheless grabbed his sole test kit and made his way to the hootch. If the water was properly chlorinated, he thought, there shouldn't be any bugs in it.

Carter met with Ross and Grocholski and tried to see the "bug," but because the water was clear, he couldn't make it out. So Ross dumped a bottle of Pine-Sol in the bowl to color the water and make the "bug" more visible, and Carter saw what he thought looked like mosquito larvae wiggling in the bowl. If KBR had chlorinated the water to the required levels, Carter thought, no bugs would be able to survive. He decided to test the water from the sink next to the toilet bowl and quickly discovered that the water contained no chlorine at all. Was this an anomaly? He needed to find out right away by testing the water in other hootches. Little did Carter know that he was about to open Pandora's box.

In October 2004, the 42-year-old Carter found himself building log furniture in the mountains of Southern Utah at Panquitch Lake. A native of Cedar City, Utah, he had been running his own business with his second wife, Sandra, for four years. But there was trouble with his marriage and separation had long seemed inevitable. Then, on October 17, Carter's 20-year old son from his first marriage died unexpectedly in St. George after a bad reaction to a combination of prescription medications. He felt he had to get away from the grief he was feeling over the death of his son.

Until late October, Carter had never heard of contracting in Iraq. At a family get-together, his younger brother, Clayton, mentioned Halliburton and the good money they were paying their employees in Iraq. It sounded like the perfect opportunity to get away. Interested, Carter conducted an Internet search for Halliburton employment opportunities and found an opening for a ROWPU operator with KBR in Iraq. Even though he was familiar with the concept of reverse osmosis, he didn't know a lot about the mechanics of a ROWPU. He had a background in the water industry having worked for Culligan as a water service manager and knew how purification equipment worked, what could go wrong, and how to fix it. Carter started his own water company in Gunnison, Colorado, handling residential, commercial, industrial, and small community water systems for five years. Having worked on all types of filtration systems, from small-cartridge filtering to remove sand to de-ionization and ultra-filtration, he felt he could handle the job in Iraq with KBR

With his knowledge of water systems and purification, Carter applied online for a position with KBR as a ROWPU operator. About a week later, in early November, a KBR recruiter called Carter and offered him a job that he quickly accepted. The recruiter told him he would be assigned to the Green Zone in Baghdad where it was safe, but he learned differently when he arrived in Houston for his orientation during the first week of January 2005. He would not be going to the Green Zone; instead, he would be going to the "frontier," the "Wild West"—Ar Ramadi. While at orientation, Carter learned nothing about what his duties or responsibilities as a ROWPU operator at Ar Ramadi, or about KBR policies regarding water systems and purification. He would have to figure everything out on the job.

Arriving at Ar Ramadi on January 20, 2005, Carter was surprised to learn that he would not immediately be working as a ROWPU Operator. That job was in the hands of a KBR foreman who was about to be reassigned. Also, he discovered that the KBR ROWPU was not in operation. Water was being produced by a military purifier, with a limited output amount of potable and non-potable water per day—not enough for the 7,000 troops and civilian personnel and the additional 1,200 Iraqi National Guard present in the camp. The KBR purifier, when operational, could produce about 360,000 gallons a water a day, enough to sustain the camp's population.

Carter was given a tour of the new KBR ROWPU unit on the first day he arrived at Ar Ramadi. The KBR purifier was located just inside the camp perimeter fence closest to the river, about a quarter- to a half-mile from the main section of the camp, and the military purifier was located outside of the perimeter fence, about another quarter-mile away from the KBR unit.

Carter says that the usual ROWPU operator told him the water was chlorinated and safe. The new ROWPU was not operational because they were awaiting new pumps to be installed. But Carter also found that the staff had only one test kit—a Hach Turbidity Meter, which measured turbidity and cloudiness but not chlorination, meaning that it could not determine the safety of the water. The camp did not have a test kit that measured chlorination. Carter was told those test kits had been on order since the previous August but had not yet arrived, some five months later.

Carter asked for an analysis of the water from the Euphrates River, but was told one did not exist. He got the impression there was a general lack of understanding about water purification or chlorination. Carter was not able to visit the military purifier because it was located outside the base and required a military escort to reach. There was also another KBR purification unit located across the river at Blue Diamond base, but Carter says his request to visit the site was refused.

Carter felt that water treatment information was scarce at Ramadi. Carter never saw water treatment, purification, or testing procedures and policies. Of course, Carter says, they didn't even have test kits to test the water. KBR did have standard operating procedures for the disinfection of the trucks used for transporting water to the storage tanks. Carter would later learn that the contractor's responsibility under the LOGCAP contract was to ensure that both potable and non-potable water were purified, stored, and distributed for use to all bases in Iraq for the troops and contractor personnel. That responsibility included regular testing of water at the consumption points. While the military purifier produced both potable and non-potable water, KBR was responsible for taking possession of the non-potable water at the unit and delivering it to the non-potable water storage tanks for use by base personnel.

Before Carter took over the water responsibilities sometime in late February, a KBR manager wanted Carter to help out "Ms. D," the dining facility director. The dining facility was operated by KBR. Ms. D had received an email from KBR management instructing her to test the potable water for chlorine at the facility's points of use three times a day. Carter was willing to help, but he told the manager that without test kits he couldn't test for chlorine. The manager promised to expedite an order for test kits. Two spectrophotometers, designed for chlorine analysis, arrived two days later. This was surprising, since a foreman said he had ordered test kits back in August 2004 and they had never arrived.

Carter created a water analysis report form and started testing the potable water at the dining facility. He was elated. He actually had something to do. At least three times a day, he had a ten-minute job. The tests did show that there was a sufficient amount of chlorine present in the potable water. The military was responsible for transporting potable water from the military purifier site to the potable water storage tanks.

Even though they were now testing potable water for chlorine at the dining facility, Carter believed they were falling seriously short on other analyses that needed to be done, such as for radiation, biological contaminants, pH, and turbidity. The pH of water is important to measure because its level can affect chlorine's capacity to disinfect water.

With the revelation that testing was required for potable water, water purification equipment starting showing up. A water lab was delivered. The pumps for the KBR purifier arrived and were eventually installed, after a lot of prodding by Carter. He felt progress was finally being made to bring the purifier online.

Carter was facing a new problem, however. The non-potable water, the water that ran through the sinks, showers, and toilets of the base, had not been chlorinated like the potable water had been. That meant that highly polluted water from the Euphrates River was not being disinfected either manually or by the ROWPU, thus potentially exposing the entire population of Camp Ar Ramadi to a risk of serious illness, Carter thought.

By the end of 2005, about 25,800 soldiers had been evacuated to Army hospitals outside Iraq for treatment of both combat and non-combat injuries and illnesses. Of that number, nearly 60 percent had been evacuated due to illness.[1] Illness had taken a major toll on troops already stretched thin in Iraq. Although the causes of illness in Iraq were varied, the Army had concerns over the poor quality of the water supply. The terrible quality of Iraq's water has been blamed for many Iraqi civilian illnesses and has been the leading killer of infants in that country.[2] The Tigris and Euphrates rivers provide an abundance of water for the country, but years of war, destruction, and neglect have left the water badly polluted.

After discovering that the sink water in Ross's hootch had not been chlorinated and was thus unsafe, Carter decided to test the water in the privacy of his own hootch. The result was the same—the water was not chlorinated. With the previous foreman gone, Carter was the only person in camp who could do anything to fix the problem. He rushed over to the communications room and tested the water there. Same results. The non-potable water storage tanks were next. Carter climbed up on top of both tanks and discovered the lids for both were wide open, exposing the water to contamination from the air. About the size of a manhole cover, the openings were used to access the tanks in order to fill them with water. "You could drop a sheep in there," he thought.

Tests showed the water in these tanks also to be without chlorine. Carter was stunned. He was also frightened, not only for himself, but for everyone in the camp—the troops, his coworkers, everyone. No one could claim the water to be fit for human use, Cartrer believed. Carter started formulating in his mind all the things that now had to be fixed. But first he wanted to chlorinate the water and make sure everyone was aware of the problem.

Carter felt really fortunate. A couple of weeks prior to the incident, while at the KBR purification unit, a Marine major stopped by and asked if he wanted some spare granular chlorine he had on hand. "Yes, absolutely," Carter told him. After all, he didn't have any and may need it someday. Now, Carter was thinking that without that chlorine, he would have been in a real predicament. Carter retrieved the chlorine from his office, returned to the storage tanks, and dumped in the required dosage for the quantity of water in the tanks. Now he had to get the chlorine circulated through the water system. He grabbed some pumps from a work area, borrowed several plumbers and electricians, and jerry-rigged a pump system to circulate the chlorinated water. He did the best he could with what he had available. His experience building water systems in Gunnison, Colorado was now being put to good use.

Carter's next task was to determine why the water had not been chlorinated. It should have been done as part of the process at the military unit. He needed to determine if the problem was at that unit level or somewhere else.

At the military purifier, Carter talked to the non-commissioned officer in charge of the unit. He told Carter it was no surprise to him that the non-potable water was not chlorinated; they never had chlorinated the non-potable water. He explained to Carter that they didn't have the production capability to run all the water through the unit. The water flowed through the multi-media filter, but due to the physics of the plumbing, the non-potable water could not be chlorinated. He would have to change the system to allow chlorination, and he was not able to do that.

Carter returned to the camp with his military escort. He had to get on the radio and notify all the KBR employees to go to their hootches and turn on the faucets. He needed to run the water at every single faucet until the chlorine circulated throughout the plumbing. Carter believed that all the employees would then need to be told they had been exposed to contaminated water.

But, Carter says, a KBR supervisor, after he learned of the problem, didn't want the notification to take place. He wanted Carter just to chlorinate the tanks and get it back to normal. They argued about notification, Carter says, until another employee walked up and backed Carter's position. That seemed to settle the argument, as Carter was allowed to get on the radio and notify all the employees to run their faucets.

Once all the employees were told to run their faucets, the cat was out of the bag. Now, it was damage control time. First, Harold "Mo" Orr, the health, safety and environmental manager at Ar Ramadi, demanded to know why he had not been notified when the water hazard was discovered. Orr had been in Iraq since August 2004, and at Ar Ramadi since October. He had been told when he arrived in Iraq that the non-potable water was chlorinated and safe. Now he was stunned to learn it was neither.

Orr considered the incident serious enough to warrant documenting the problem. However, at least one KBR manager claimed that the incident was a "mistaken" identification of the "toilet creature" in Ross's hootch and therefore did not need to be documented. It wasn't Orr's concern—it was none of his business. Anyway, since Carter had now chlorinated the water, all was well. Carter felt that KBR manager's attempt to cast doubt on whether there had been an actual bug in Ross's toilet was nothing more than irrelevant "spin." He was ignoring the bigger issue of the chlorination problem.

Everyone at Camp Ar Ramadi had been exposed to contaminated non-potable water, and that needed to be reported, thought Carter. Once the word got out, many of the employees expressed concern to Carter. Some were panicky because they knew how bad the water from the Euphrates was. Carter was upset that he didn't know before about the lack of chlorination and had just accepted assurances, he had received, that the water was safe. But Carter also wanted to keep his job. He wanted to be loyal to KBR and even had thoughts of spending the next 20 years working for the company.

Orr had Carter write up an incident report, but KBR site management wanted to preview the report before it was submitted to Orr. Carter initially wrote in his report that he discovered mosquito larvae in Ross' toilet bowl. Site management argued that he couldn't be sure it was "mosquito larvae" or any type of living creature. At their insistence, Carter rewrote the report, calling the object in the toilet a "suspected micro-organism," that was eventually authorized as the final version.

Orr called his supervisor, Jay Delahoussaye, the KBR health, safety and environmental manager for Bravo sites, at Al Asad. Bravo sites, also known as "B" sites, included Camp Ar Ramadi and many other sites within the responsibility of the Al Asad base. Delahoussaye wanted to know why Orr had initiated an investigation into the water incident if it was only a "near miss" based on an "employee misinterpretation" of seeing "parasites" in the water.

That same morning, Carter was called in to meet with site management about the incident. He explained to them the risks of exposure to contaminated water. He insisted the military be notified because their water also needed to be chlorinated; they were using the same non-potable water supplied by KBR. Carter says he was told, "the military is none of your fucking concern." Carter was asked if he had done everything he could do for the KBR area of the base. Carter replied that he had, but he knew that this was still not good enough. The water needed to be chlorinated manually every day because the military water purification unit could not chlorinate or filter the water adequately. He decided that his responsibility to the troops was more important than his job at KBR. He had to do the right thing.

Carter then met with Captain Matthew Hing, U.S. Army, Second Infantry Division, Second Brigade, and the command surgeon at Ar Ramadi. He wanted to notify Hing of the lack of chlorination at the military unit so that the military operator could be ordered to start chlorinating. He also wanted to get their determination of the surface water's propensity for biological contamination. Carter understood that if the command surgeon deemed the water hazardous, it would have to be chlorinated for all shower points.Captain Hing told Carter he would look into the matter.

At the same time, Orr was trying to conduct his own investigation into the water problem. It was an immediate health issue, and he felt it was his responsibility to investigate not only the lack of chlorination, but also the lack of caps on the storage tanks that had exposed the water to contamination. He did get a copy of the incident report from Carter, but he also needed statements from witnesses, such as Grocholski and Ross, and everyone else involved in the water distribution system at the site. But, Grocholski told Orr he was forbidden to give him a written statement. Therefore, no statements were taken from anyone except Carter to document the incident. A KBR manager had written a statement insisting that there had been no incident, but they were taking efforts to keep the water supply chlorinated. Grocholski said he could turn in a statement but could not to put anything in it that would imply KBR had done something wrong. "What are you telling me, Harry?" Orr asked. "Well, I can give you a statement, but . . .I can't tell you what happened," Grocholski replied. "I'd give you a statement, but it would be worthless."

Orr was also concerned that the water at the Ar Ramadi camp was not being tested. He knew they had this responsibility, but had only recently realized that they hadn't fulfilled it. Water reports with testing results should have been submitted, but the only reports he saw were for water count—the volume of non-potable water delivered and the volume of wastewater removed.

Orr was appalled. He felt the directive to prevent witness statements and telling supervisors to defy Health, Safety, and Environmental procedures for investigation, was beyond the pale. He decided at that point to resign; in his resignation statement, he said he no longer wanted to work "in an environment where deception and fraud are commonplace."

The same day, emails started flying between Ar Ramadi and Al Asad over the water incident. Delahoussaye agreed with Orr that the only way to guarantee the potability of the water was to test it three or four times a day, and this had not been done. Delahoussaye acknowledged that KBR was not set up to do this kind of testing. Even more disconcerting, this lack of testing, Orr believed, might be happening at bases all over Iraq.

Carter was concerned about the exposure of KBR workers and the troops to possible pathogens and parasites. He did a search on the Internet and found on the Pentagon's website a report from the U.S. Joint Staff, Washington D.C. on health threats in northern Iraq. According to the report, "all fresh water sources in Iraq are subject to biological contamination from man and animal waste and chemical contamination from pesticides and fertilizers. All surface water should, therefore, be treated prior to consumption."

The document proceeded to reveal likely outbreaks such as acute diarrhea brought on by E. coli, shigella, and salmonella, or by protozoa such as Giardia. It also cited the possibility of typhoid and cholera outbreaks. The quality of untreated water was generally poor, and Iraq's rivers "contain biological materials, pollutants, and are laden with bacteria. Unless the water is purified with chlorine, epidemics of such diseases as cholera, hepatitis, and typhoid could occur."

In the spring of 2003, a Naval Environmental and Preventive Medicine Unit conducted a study of Marines involved in the invasion of Iraq. They wanted to see what illnesses the military was facing in Iraq and to determine the risks to the troops' health. They found that gastrointestinal illness was by far the most common reason for "infectious disease sick call." They stressed the importance of water sources being controlled and limited to bottled water or reverse osmosis and chlorine-treated river water. There was concern over the high risk of gastrointestinal illness among the troops.[3]

Carter felt the urgency to get the new KBR purification unit online quickly, and he worked hard all the next week to achieve that goal. He laid out all the water bladders and got it close to starting up. But soon, Carter came to the realization he had to quit. He believed he didn't have a choice unless he was to keep quiet about it. He wanted to be loyal to KBR, but he also wanted to be loyal to the truth. Who was upper-level management going to blame when the incident was exposed, as it surely would be? They were going to blame the water treatment guy. They would blame Carter.

He wanted to quit before that happened. Before he left, he trained the medics to use the chlorine test kit.After telling Grocholski he was quitting, Carter started receiving the silent treatment from the rest of management. It took three days, but finally, on April 28, he choppered out of Ar Ramadi and made his way back to the United States. Ironically, before boarding the helicopter, an assistant site manager walked over and shook Carter's hand, telling him that he had done a good job.

Before he left Ar Ramadi, Carter started experiencing bouts of nausea and fatigue. When he returned to the United States, the same symptoms continued, along with insomnia, irritability, and trouble concentrating. He could only sleep a couple of hours a night. He tried to restart his log-furniture business, but because of his lack of concentration and focus, he was not able to complete the work, and the business failed after only three weeks.

Concerned that he may have been exposed to pathogens or parasites, Carter wanted to be tested. It would be costly—specialized medical tests usually are. But if he was exposed to diseases from the contaminated water, he reasoned, the tests should be covered under worker's compensation. The Defense Base Act covered injuries on the job for contractors in Iraq. Carter filed a claim on April 29, 2005, alleging dermatological, gastrointestinal, and psychiatric injuries from exposure to "unprocessed water."

Halliburton did not automatically approve the claim. Carter had told Halliburton's worker compensation department that he had discussed his claim with an attorney. In response, Halliburton stopped talking to him directly since he was now represented by an attorney.

On May 6, 2005, about the same time Carter was trying to get approval to see a doctor, Wil Granger, KBR's Iraq Water Quality Manager, arrived at Camp Ar Ramadi to investigate the water contamination incident. It had been more than a month since the incident occurred, and Granger found that significant data had been lost and key personnel had left. The loss of hard drives and a "general disregard for data creation" limited his ability to recreate the event and obtain the facts.

Granger found that chlorination of non-potable water, begun by Carter, had been discontinued about April 7, again exposing military and civilian population to non-disinfected non-potable water. In addition, Granger discovered that concentrate wastewater created by the military water purification unit was being used as the source for the non-potable water. It was an important and possibly dangerous revelation. The raw water source from the Euphrates River was highly polluted—a virtual sewer of human and animal waste. The ROWPU wastewater, which concentrates the waste and contaminants removed by the treatment process, is normally about twice as contaminated as the raw water. A Tufts University Medical School professor would later tell congress "They would have been better off being provided with water straight from the Euphrates River." Carter felt the wastewater should have been dumped back into the river or used only for dust abatement or washing vehicle engines. Because this normal procedure wasn't followed, Granger believed, the military and civilian population of Ar Ramadi were potentially at greatly increased risk for Giardia cysts, Cryptosporidium occysts, E. coli, and other diseases. The staff had assumed that all the water passing through the purifier had been disinfected.

Granger validated Carter's findings by concluding that the non-potable water designated for showering use had not been disinfected. An unknown number of military troops and civilians were exposed to potentially harmful water for an undetermined amount of time. Granger felt that the event was a "NEAR MISS as the consequences of these actions could have been VERY SEVERE resulting in mass sickness or death." He also considered it likely that all military camps were facing the same water problems to some extent. Granger summarized his findings in a report, dated May 13, 2005, and submitted them KBR and Halliburton management.[4]

Carter first became aware of Granger's investigation and findings on September 6, when Granger called to ask if he had seen the report. Halliburton attorneys were worried sick that Carter might have a copy. Learning of Granger's findings, Carter was astounded that KBR had allowed concentrate wastewater from the purifier unit to be used for showering.

Carter felt vindicated—Granger had validated his findings. The situation was even worse than he thought, and he believed he was paying the price physically. He had broken out in rashes on his arms and head while still battling nausea, fatigue, and insomnia. Halliburton had still not approved his insurance claim, and he was getting increasingly desperate to see a doctor and resolve his medical problems. Carter did go to an emergency room for treatment, and the doctors there sent him to a dermatologist who diagnosed the cause as flesh-eating bacteria. Carter then decided to seek a settlement with KBR and to make sure that they notified the troops of the problem. His medical expenses continued to rise. Desperate, he, and a former KBR colleague, sent a message to Halliburton management that since Halliburton failed to act, they were ready to expose the issue publicly.

When Halliburton responded that they found no basis to accept his "terms and conditions for resolution of this issue," Carter became convinced that the company was not going to approve his claim. It was time to go public. Carter contacted Jim Donahue, a reporter for the non-profit organization HalliburtonWatch.org.

Donahue was very interested in Carter's story and suggested he also tell it to the House Government Reform Committee, specifically to Henry Waxman. Carter, along with Ken May, a former co-worker at Ramadi, wrote a report on the contamination issue and sent it to Donahue. In early September, Donahue sent a summary of the information to Halliburton's public relations personnel for comment without exposing its source.

On September 8, Halliburton spokesperson Melissa Norcross emailed Donahue to say that KBR had conducted its own inspection of the water at Ar Ramadi and had "found no evidence to substantiate the allegations made by these former employees." She said the "military's own records show that the water produced during this time period contained no bacteriological contamination and was suitable for these non-potable purposes." Further, she said "The unfounded allegations refer to non-potable (non-drinkable) water that was produced at a military base in AR Ramadi, Iraq, prior to May 2005. During that time, bottled water was used for drinking and food preparation, and KBR and military personnel at the base used non-potable water supplied by the military's own water treatment facility for laundry, showers, sinks and toilets. KBR now operates its own water treatment plant at Ar Ramadi to supply potable water for hygienic uses. For drinking and food preparation, KBR continues to supply bottled water throughout Iraq." Norcross contended that there "have been no documented cases of unusual illnesses or health conditions reported at the site during or since that time."[5]

Shortly after receiving Halliburton's response, Donahue published an article on Carter's findings on the HalliburtonWatch.org website. Carter had taken a big step against a very powerful company. The contaminated water issue had gone public.

CHAPTER 18

THE REPLACEMENTS

Camp Arifjan, Kuwait, January 2005.

Just as David Wilson was leaving Iraq in April 2004, he saw that KBR was hiring more and more international truck drivers to drive the risky convoys for much lower pay than the Americans. Many of these foreign nationals did not speak English, and more than a few seemed to have little if any experience. When Wilson saw one trainer desperately trying to show supposedly trained drivers how to back up a truck, he felt glad to be getting out.

The Army soldiers responsible for escorting these convoys didn't have Wilson's options; they had to stay. But some are now being rotated home and are willing to speak. Here is one soldier's anonymous post to the Iraq and Afghanistan Veterans of America (IAVA) website complaining about the problem:

> —KBR is now requesting, and the army is allowing, US soldiers to ride "shot gun" in KBR convoys hauling KBR goods all over Iraq. KBR is afraid to be out on the roads alone and want our US soldiers to risk their lives riding shot gun for their missions.

This soldier was concerned that foreign nationals and Iraqis were being hired as truck drivers and they were not well trained in avoiding ambushes, fire support, IEDs or what to do when they are attacked. He was also angry that these inexperienced drivers that put their lives at risk were paid 5-8 times more than the soldiers who were protecting the convoys.

Even though he acknowledged that Army needed to protect KBR on their missions, he complained that the soldiers' concerns and safety suggestions were being ignored:

> *KBR is requesting that US soldiers risk their lives at the hands of inexperienced and improperly trained individuals to provide them with security . . . We have suggested that we run in the convoys with every third vehicle being a US Army gun truck with proper drivers and fire support. . . . This is the only way that most of us want the missions to be run, the others are just afraid to be opposed to the decisions our leadership is making.*

This soldier did not even know the Army was "under contract" to provide the convoy security for KBR. In October 2006, other soldiers told the *New Hampshire Concord Monitor* that they were fed up with risking their lives to protect luxury items destined for the larger bases, such as Anaconda, or the Baghdad PX. From the *Concord Monitor*:

> *"Soldiers, including National Guard soldiers from Charlie Company, 3rd of the 172nd Mountain Infantry Division, protected KBR trucks and drivers in Iraq. Some soldiers in the Manchester-based unit were irritated that they had to protect trucks filled with things like big-screen televisions, plastic plants and pet goods, which were trucked onto military bases and sold to soldiers at the post exchange or PX.*
>
> *'I'm risking my life for kitty litter,' said Staff Sgt. Patrick Clarke, who deployed to Iraq with Charlie Company and is the Chichester police chief.*

The article went on to say that the PX in Baghdad had so many items that some of the troops compared it to a Wal-Mart.

Adam Roe also came home from his second Iraq deployment troubled by the deep problems he saw with the KBR convoys. He had returned from his first tour of Iraq to Fort Hood in March 2004, about the same time Dave Wilson was leaving Iraq. He decided to volunteer to go back to Iraq as an Army truck driver with the 96th Transportation Company, knowing that he could retire after this additional tour. He was afraid that if he stayed with his old unit, he would be deployed to Iraq and then stop-lossed. By this time, Roe, who had spent most of his adult life in the Army, was very disillusioned by what he had seen in Iraq and, like Perry Jefferies, he wanted out. He knew it was dangerous to go back but saw it as the quickest way to retire and get out once and for all.

He was redeployed to Iraq in January of 2005 and stayed until May 2005, based in Kuwait at Camp Arifjan. Soldiers there were responsible for taking convoys of trucks into Iraq to various forward operating bases, such as Camp Anaconda. But the KBR convoys had drastically changed since Dave Wilson's days as a driver. Before, the Army merely provided the security protection for the convoys, while KBR provided the trucks, the drivers, the convoy commanders, and the fuel.

When Roe returned in 2005, this arrangement had changed. Perhaps out of frustration, or the sheer necessity of getting their supplies through, the Army had taken over the duties of the convoy commanders. Roe said that the convoy commanders were now either Army lieutenants or sergeants. Moreover, the KBR truck drivers were now all foreign nationals; there were no American KBR truck drivers or managers in sight. There were 10 Army trucks and Army drivers, including Roe, interspersed in the convoy of 30 to 80 KBR trucks. The Army felt that the only way to make the convoys reliable was to supplement the KBR staff and equipment with Army drivers and Army trucks; and, adding insult to injury, they had to buy the fuel for the additional trucks from KBR. Now the Army was still paying KBR to run the truck convoys but had to put in their own personnel and trucks to make sure that the supplies got through.

Roe was especially frustrated that there were no KBR managers involved in the entire convoy. The Army would go to the KBR compound in Kuwait and pick up the foreign drivers and their loaded KBR trucks, and the Army convoy commander, truck drivers, and security detail would then direct and watch the KBR truck drivers along the route.

Roe and the other Army truck drivers never had any normal downtime once they reached the base. He was disheartened to hear from his commanders that the KBR foreign nationals were not trustworthy enough to be set loose on the base, which meant that the Army truck drivers had to monitor and "babysit" them until the return convoy the next day.

Roe actually felt sorry for these drivers. Many of them were scared by the dangerous work but came to Iraq to improve their finances for their families. They were paid a fraction of what the KBR American drivers were paid and were not well trained for the dangerous type of truck driving they were hired to do.

The bases did have KBR management people, but they were in the food area and did not oversee the KBR truck drivers. The Army had gone from just supplying security for the KBR convoys, to managing those convoys, adding Army trucks and drivers, buying fuel from KBR, and babysitting KBR's foreign drivers. "So, what exactly is KBR contributing to the effort?" Roe wondered

Roe was also amazed that he, as an Army truck driver, had to haul KBR supplies and equipment around the country. He even hauled broken KBR trucks and trailers back to KBR, as well as some of the supplies for their living quarters.

Leaving Iraq in May 2005, Roe came home to Fort Hood and retired from the Army he loved. It was not the same institution that he once knew, and he was very disillusioned by what is happening in Iraq. He has kept contact with his buddies in the 96th Transportation Company, who tell him that the truck convoy situation remains the same. The Army is now rotating this unit in and out of Iraq every six months because they need the drivers, and some of Roe's buddies are on their fifth deployment. Some say they want to get out and go work for private contractors in Iraq so they can make more money for their families and have shorter rotations with better living conditions.

Roe drove Army trucks in Bosnia with KBR employees. Back then, he says, there was one Army truck driver for every KBR employee in a convoy, an arrangement that worked fine because no one was shooting at them. For many reasons, he thought that the Army's reliance on KBR as the main contractor for supplies and truck convoys in Iraq wasn't working. He had been on the receiving end of the company's incompetence while stuck at the Dustbowl with Perry Jefferies and the rest of the troops, unable to get parts for their vehicles and forced to drink their shower water. He had watched Command Sergeant Major List stalk officers at all levels to get decent boots for the troops. He had seen the abysmal conditions at the checkpoints and met soldiers wanting for food, water, and shelter months after President Bush declared "Mission Accomplished." And finally, he had seen the Army, out of frustration or sheer necessity, take over many of KBR's duties.

He believes these problems could have been avoided in Iraq if the Army had done the logistics in the traditional way, relying on Army truck drivers and Army commanders. From his days in Somalia and Bosnia, he remembers Army drivers going 24/7 to get their supplies through no matter what the conditions. The Army drivers had that kind of dedication, he says, because it wasn't just a job to them; they were doing it for "their brothers and sisters" in the Army. They knew that if they did not do what they were supposed to do, soldiers would have to go without vital supplies and even food and water. Roe is convinced that you cannot get that level of commitment from a contractor, no matter what you pay them.

Roe believes this to be especially true in Iraq because of the IEDs and the overall lawlessness and hostile conditions there. He clenches his teeth when he recalls all the things the soldiers he served with had to do without because some company was not up to the job. Even List, he remembers, had to come to the realization that the Army brass that were powerless to solve the problems plaguing his troops, because the brass, too, had to rely on KBR rather than their own troops.

Like Perry Jefferies, Roe did not want any part of this new Army. He retired and now works for a defense contractor while still living near Fort Hood, Texas. He keeps tabs on many of his buddies who are still serving rotations in Iraq and hears the same stories of frustration from troops just now returning from Iraq.

PART V

EXPOSURE

We are having this hearing today because there are those who believe we have a company, Kellogg, Brown and Root, that is wasting tax dollars or abusing its contracting role, or even defrauding the U.S. taxpayer.
I happen to disagree. I have yet to see any evidence of this. What I see are occasional failures to communicate, inattentiveness in adhering to strict business procedures, and a less than perfect accounting process.

—Chairman Tom Davis (R-VA),
House Committee on Government Reform,
July 22, 2004

CHAPTER 19

THE HAND THAT
FEEDS YOU

After four of its employees were brutally murdered, burned, and dragged through the streets of Fallujah on March 31, 2004, Blackwater USA found itself on the public's radar screen. A day after the attack, co-founder Erik Prince hired the powerful Alexander Strategy Group, founded in 1998 by Edwin Buckham, a former chief of staff and personal evangelical pastor of former House Majority Leader Tom DeLay. Buckham once headed the U.S. Family Network, which was heavily funded by Jack Abramoff's clients perhaps, in part, because of its connections to DeLay. Alexander was staffed primarily by former top DeLay aides, such as Tony Rudy (who pled guilty to conspiring with Abramoff in a lobbying scandal), James Ellis and Karl Gallant, who once ran DeLay's leadership Political Action Committee, and DeLay's wife, Christine.

Alexander was considered the gatekeeper to DeLay for moneyed clients. The firm was closely tied to Abramoff, who eventually became the poster boy for lobbying excesses and pled guilty to corruption charges. As a tradeoff for large donations to Republican House and Senate candidates, Alexander offered its clients direct access to powerful Republicans and an inside track to lucrative defense contracts. The firm also became the go-to lobbying firm for private security contracts in Iraq and other areas of need. A partner at Alexander, Paul Behrends, was a friend of Erik Prince, and the former National Security Advisor to Representative Dana Rohrbacher, for whom Prince also worked in the 1990s.[1]

The move to hire Alexander produced immediate results for Prince. Within a week, he had private meetings with some of the most influential Republicans in the House of Representatives at the time: Tom DeLay, the House Majority Leader; Duncan Hunter, the Chairman of the House Armed Services Committee; Porter Goss, Chairman of the House Intelligence Committee; and Bill Young, Chairman of the House Appropriations Committee. Not long after that, Prince was able to meet with Republican powerhouses from the Senate as well: Ted Stevens, Chairman of the Senate Appropriations Committee; John Warner, Chairman of the Senate Armed Services Committee; George Allen; and Rick Santorum.[2]

Blackwater's investment in Alexander paid off quickly. By mid-November 2004, Blackwater reported a 600 percent growth in additional contract dollars. Soon after, Prince and company president Gary Jackson started making contributions to DeLay and other Alexander-favored lawmakers.[3] After Hurricane Katrina, Blackwater was able to obtain lucrative contracts for work in New Orleans.

While allegedly cutting costs for the protection of their security operators in Iraq, Blackwater had poured money into lobbying efforts in Washington, D.C., in the hopes of gaining political influence and a larger slice of the contract pie. Prince, a staunch right-wing Christian, had been a big-time contributor to Republican candidates and causes since he was 19 years old. His father, billionaire Edgar Prince, started the influential conservative Christian group Family Research Council with Gary Bauer.[4]

In order to repair the negative image of private security firms as "mercenaries," a number of security companies, including Blackwater, joined together under the banner of the International Peace Operations Association (IPOA). IPOA hired Alexander to help achieve their public-relations objectives, using used Rudy, Buckham, and Gallant to lobby for them.[5]

Once Alexander was damaged by the publicity about the investigation into the Abramoff scandal, the firm quickly ceased operations and shut its doors in January 2006. Former Alexander lobbyists fled to other lobbying firms, including Behrends, who was hired by C&M Capitolink, an affiliate of international law firm Crowell & Moring. Behrends signed up Blackwater, as a client, in 2006 and now is a registered lobbyist for the company.

With total costs for the war in Iraq exceeding $320 billion, competition for space at the Pentagon's feeding trough has expanded faster than the rising costs in Iraq. As a result, influence peddling has become about the best way for contractors to obtain lucrative contracts for work in Iraq. Influence peddling has taken two forms—lobbying and the "revolving door," that is, hiring former congressional or other high-ranking government officials to take advantage of their powerful connections.

The more than 2,200 former federal employees (including over 200 former members of Congress) who registered as federal lobbyists between 1998 and 2004[6] have become indispensable to contractors seeking to profit from the emerging war service industry. Lobbyists have been dubbed "the Fourth Branch" due to their ability to influence Congress, the White House, and federal agencies.[7]

Influencing the awarding of war service industry contracts is one goal of lobbyists; influencing policy to keep the war service industry in business in Iraq and future conflicts is another. The latter goal has become increasingly important as contractors make ever-higher profits from contingency contracts. This new industry depends on hot wars, occupations, and natural disasters (which can't always be counted on) to keep it going.

Titan Corp., the largest supplier of translators and linguists to the U.S. military, and also a source of interrogators sent to Iraq, hired the law firm of Copeland, Lowery, Jacquez, Denton and Shockey, which is connected to Representative Jerry Lewis (R-CA) through Letitia White, a longtime staffer to Lewis now employed by Copeland.[8] Prior to the 2006 midterm elections, Lewis was the chairman of the Defense Subcommittee of the House Appropriations Committee. American Defense International, also hired by Titan, includes Van Hipp, a former deputy assistant secretary of the Army under then Defense Secretary Dick Cheney.[9] In addition, NorthPoint Strategies, composed mainly of former staffers to former Representative Randy "Duke" Cunningham (now a convicted felon),[10] including Patrick McSwain and Trey Hardin,[11] was engaged by Titan to represent its interests. Since 2000, Titan has spent $1.29 million on Washington lobbying and garnered revenues of $1.8 billion from government contracts.[12] Titan and its parent company, L3, have lost 216 employees and subcontractors killed in Iraq as of November 2006—almost a third of the total number of contractor deaths in the war and the most for any contractor.[13]

Another major player is security giant CACI, which sent interrogators to Iraq—some of whom were initially mentioned in connection with the

prisoner abuse scandal at Abu Ghraib prison (CACI executives emphasized to the press that later official reports show "that CACI people were
not anywhere close to having conducted or participated in the most egre-
gious things we saw in the photographs and were alleged to have happened"). CACI hired The Livingston Group to lobby in Washington for
more contracts. Livingston founder Bob Livingston, a Louisiana Republican and former House Appropriations Committee chairman, registered as
a lobbyist for CACI along with his former chief of staff J. Allen Martin
and a former staff member, Rick Legendre. The Livingston Group is one
of the ten largest non-law-firm lobbying shops. Having been a chairman of
the House Appropriations Committee, Livingston specializes in appropriations lobbying and prides itself on being able to deliver appropriated dollars to clients.[14] His company's work had helped CACI obtain close to
$800 million in contracts by September 2005.[15]

In addition to The Livingston Group, CACI also hired the PMA
Group, which specializes in defense contracting. According to the Center
for Public Integrity, PMA has received more than $21.7 million since 1998
in lobbying fees from top defense contractors, the most of any defense-
lobbying firm. The fees have paid off handsomely for the company's
clients, who have won $266 billion in contracts from the Pentagon in the
last six years. More strikingly, $167 billion of this was obtained from no-bid
contracts. These results are not surprising given that 30 of the 31 upper-
level employees of PMA were previously employed either with some
branch of the armed forces or with the House and Senate.[16]

Halliburton was not going to be left behind in the influence game.
During the first half of 2004, their spending on lobbying efforts increased
400 percent. Since 2000, they have spent $4.6 million buying influence
via donations and lobbying. The board of directors and their spouses personally gave $828,701 to congressional and presidential candidates. Hal-
liburton's political action committees donated $1.2 million, mostly to
Republicans and political organizations with strong Republican ties.[17] Halliburton's in-house lobbyists, retired Army Lieutenant General Charles E.
Dominy, formerly of the Army Corps of Engineers, Donald A. Deline, a
former counsel to the Senate Armed Services Committee, Barbara Jones,
and George P. Sigalos, a former counsel to the president and press aide to
Representative Philip Crane (R-IL), were very active during 2004.[18]
Dominy was first hired in 1995 by Dick Cheney, the CEO of Halliburton
at the time. He was also an Army general in 1992 when KBR was awarded
the first LOGCAP contract. Dominy succeeded Dave Gribbin as chief

lobbyist when Gribbin joined Cheney in the Bush administration. The Cheney-Dominy-Gribbin trio played a major role in gaining lucrative war service industry contracts for Halliburton.[19] Sigalos serves as the Director of Government Relations for Halliburton-KBR. His federal experience includes serving as press secretary for three members of the presidential cabinet during the Reagan and Bush 41 administrations.

In 2004, Halliburton hired registered outside lobbyists from Covington & Burling to lobby on behalf of its subsidiary, KBR Government Operations. The firm was paid $520,000 to lobby for KBR's construction and service contracts in Iraq. Hoping to garner more influence with Congress, Covington & Burling assigned a powerhouse team of lobbyists, including Roderick DeArment, former chief of staff to Senator Bob Dole; Martin Gold, former counsel to Senate Majority Leader Bill Frist; William Wichterman, former policy advisor to Frist; and Stuart Eizenstat, former ambassador to the European Union during the Clinton administration.[20]

In 2005, KBR hired lobbyist Joe Allbaugh, a former Bush campaign manager and FEMA director, and his firm The Allbaugh Company.[21] Ever since Congress appropriated $10.5 billion for hurricane disaster relief, Allbaugh has been seeking a piece of that pie for his clients, including KBR.[22] However, in an attempt at spin, Halliburton says that Allbaugh was a "consultant," not a lobbyist for KBR.[23] Apparently, Halliburton did not realize that Allbaugh registered with the Senate Office of Public Records, on March 15, 2005, in compliance with the Lobbying Disclosure Act of 1995, as a lobbyist for KBR.[24] In addition to The Allbaugh Company, Allbaugh started several other companies, including New Bridge Strategies. Founded in 2003 with the help of Mississippi Governor Haley Barbour, New Bridge Strategies helps companies obtain contracts in Iraq. Barbour also helped Allbaugh set up Blackwell Fairbanks, a company that represents the enormous defense contractor Lockheed Martin.[25]

Halliburton's investments in lobbying and campaign donations have paid dividends. In 2000, the company was the twentieth largest federal contractor, receiving $763 million in contracts. By 2005, they had climbed to sixth place, receiving almost $6 billion in work. This rapid climb contributed greatly to their bottom line, which underwent a 284 percent rise in profits during a single quarter in 2005.[26]

In addition to lobbying, war service industry contractors have been very active in donating money to political parties and candidates, mostly Republican. The Center for Public Integrity reported that 14 contractors who were awarded government contracts in both Iraq and Afghanistan donated a combined total of almost $23 million in political contributions since 1990; 13 of those contractors have employed former government officials or have other close ties to various government agencies and departments. The Center also reported that the second President George Bush received more money from these companies than any other candidate. Campaign cash and the political connections they help forge have given these contractors a high degree of influence.[27]

In the 2006 midterm elections, some war service industry contractors were apparently so desperate to keep a Republican majority in the House and Senate that they made donations to a Green Party Senate candidate in Pennsylvania in what some commentators described as trying to siphon off votes from Rick Santorum's Democratic challenger. According to Federal Election Commission filings, Blackwater's Erik Prince and his wife donated the legal maximum of $10,000 to the ultra-liberal Green Party of Luzerne County, Pennsylvania in the hopes of winning votes for senatorial candidate Carl Romanelli, who was running against both Santorum and Democratic candidate Bob Casey.[28] William Wichterman of Covington & Burling, a lobbyist for KBR and former policy advisor to U.S. Senate Majority Leader Bill Frist, also donated $1,000 to the Green Party of Luzerne County.[29] This attempt to influence the Pennsylvania election for the Senate failed, as Casey easily ousted Santorum as part of a Democratic takeover of the Senate.

But prior to November 2006, the war service industry's creative donations were largely to Republicans. Titan, for example, donated $182,000 to Republican committees and candidates, including the leadership political action committees of Lewis, Cunningham, Stevens, and Hunter. By contrast, Titan donated only $15,000 to Democrats.[30]

Political connections have also been very important for the war service industry. For example, Diligence LLC, a contractor that provides security for reconstruction projects in Iraq, was founded by William Webster, a former director of both the FBI and the CIA; the co-chairman is Joe Allbaugh. Before starting his company, Custer Battles founder Michael Battles received campaign contributions for his failed congressional race from Haley Barbour, a former Republican Party operative and the current governor of Mississippi, and Fred Malek, a former Nixon campaign dirty-tricks operative. What role, if any, these connections played in the awarding of contracts to his fledging company is currently unknown.

Access and influence with Congress and the executive branch of government have become necessary for contractors hoping to win large contracts with the military. To gain this access and influence, companies have invested heavily in hiring former government officials and former members of Congress. According to the non-profit gorvernment watchdog organization, Project on Government Oversight, this practice, known as the "revolving door," has "become such an accepted part of federal contracting in recent years that it is frequently difficult to determine where the government stops and the private sector begins."[31] The effectiveness of the revolving door has not been lost on the war service industry.

Prior to 1996, the Defense Department kept statistics on former civilian and military employees hired by contractors, in accordance with a law mandating it. But Congress repealed the law in 1996, ending all transparency in revolving door hiring practices. Since then, the frequency of Defense Department officials leaving to work for contractors has dramatically increased. The questions of ethics, loyalty to the public interest, and conflict of interest have been almost completely ignored in recent years. For contractors, the importance of access and influence has trumped all concern for the public good. Political connections to the Bush administration and the Republican side of Congress have been so pervasive in the war service industry that the Democratic takeover of Congress could create a whole different dynamic for the future of the industry.

The highest profile revolving door hire was Halliburton's hiring of Dick Cheney in 1995 as its CEO.[32] The Defense Department, under then Secretary of Defense Cheney, during the administration of President George H.W. Bush, awarded a $3.9 million contract in 1992 to Halliburton subsidiary KBR to study the feasibility of outsourcing combat support on the battlefield. KBR was subsequently contracted by the Pentagon to implement combat support operations under the LOGCAP contract.

In February 2005, Blackwater hired the former director of the CIA's Counterterrorism Center, Cofer Black, as its new vice chairman. Black has publicly announced that the company has a "brigade size" army ready to be hired for the world's "secondary battles." He feels that the government could "contract out stability." "We've war-gamed this with professionals," he said. "We can do this."[33]

In addition to hiring Black, Blackwater raised their Defense Department connections to another level with the hiring of former Pentagon Inspector General Joseph Schmitz as the chief operating officer and general counsel of The Prince Group, which owns Blackwater. Due to their military contracts in Iraq, Blackwater would have been under the purview of the inspector general during Schmitz's tenure in that position.

Schmitz is the son of the late John G. Schmitz, a former California state senator and member of the U.S. House of Representatives, who was also a prominent member of the John Birch Society, an ultra-conservative group that flowered during the Cold War. Joseph Schmitz has been the subject of Congressional scrutiny for allegedly slowing or blocking the investigations of officials in the current Bush administration while he was inspector general.[34]

Titan's staff of in-house lobbyists includes its chairman, Gene Ray, a former high-level Air Force official, John Dressendorfer, a former White House lobbyist under President Reagan, and Lawrence Delaney, a former acting undersecretary of the Air Force under the Clinton administration.[35]

In September 2006, *Harpers Magazine* reported on the "steady flow of CIA employees to Blackwater USA,." finding that the "pace of the movement to private firms has recently reached alarming proportions." Aggressive recruiting efforts by private security companies, considered "poaching" within CIA offices, have included approaching agency employees in the agency cafeteria or even in line for coffee. A former senior CIA official told *Harper's* that "there are many people inside who aspire to work for a private contractor because—overnight—they can at least double their earnings. It undermines morale and doesn't build a competent system. But the bigger story is that this is symptomatic of a new 'counterterrorism-industrial complex' that's popping up and that is starting to look a lot like Eisenhower's military-industrial complex. It's a multibillion dollar industry and it's beginning to drive policy."[36]

An investigation by the Project On Government Oversight identified 224 high-ranking government officials who moved through the revolving door to become lobbyists or high-level executives of government contractors. At least one-third of these officials occupied positions from which they could influence government contract decisions. The investigation further disclosed that at least two-thirds of the former members of Congress who have lobbied for the top 20 government contractors "served on Authorization or Appropriations Committees that approved programs or funds for their future employer or client while they served in Congress."[37]

Even though revolving door statutes exist, they are weak protection against abuse by high-level officials. A major legislative overhaul is needed to close the many loopholes in the current laws. Any such change, however, is likely to meet with strong resistance from the contractors, who count on highly connected former officials to help them gain access to government decision makers.

The war service industry is a major player in the influence-peddling game in Washington. But having thrown almost all their eggs in the Republican basket, they now face a potential change in fortune with the Democrats taking control of both the House and the Senate in January 2007. Whether the war service industry will continue to have sufficient political influence to affect military and foreign policy decisions, as well as defense-spending priorities, remains to be seen.

With the emergence of a Democratic-controlled Congress, hundreds of Republican staffers are bound to lose their jobs, and many lobbyists face the same fate. Lobbying firms will now be rushing to hire former Democratic staffers and lawmakers to continue to provide influence for their clients. Contractors will also be looking for Democrats to hire for their in-house lobbying departments.[38] Big-name Democratic lobbyists are now emerging from virtual exile during the last 12 years, expecting to be kings of the hill once again. The big question is whether Democratic lobbyists will wield as much influence as their Republican predecessors, who had such a significant effect on legislation. Incoming Speaker of the House Nancy Pelosi plans to push for laws limiting contact between lobbyists and lawmakers and cutting the lobbying connection to legislation. But, at the same time, lobbying firms are gearing up to fight against such laws.

Some law firms and lobbying shops have now started new "crisis management" businesses to help contractors during hearings.[39] The lobbying firm, The Carmen Group, has created a government investigations division while the law firm Holland & Knight has formed a "Congressional Investigations Response Team."[40] Former government lawyers and congressional committee staffers have been hired by these firms, at top dollar, to be consultants to contractors on how to defeat the kinds of investigations they once managed.[41] After the Democrats took over control of Congress in January 2007, and soon facing hearings, KBR hired the lobbying firm Akin Gump Hauer & Feld that has connections to Democratic lawmakers.[42]

Along with the changes in Congress, the recent naming of a new secretary of defense adds further uncertainty to the future of the influence game. With Rumsfeld, a supporter of privatization, now out, and Robert Gates, who is not part of the neoconservative circle, now the secretary of defense, it is not known what role contractors will play in future conflicts. How the changes in congressional and Pentagon power will affect the war service industry is difficult to predict, but it is unlikely to remain the same.

CHAPTER 20

DON QUIXOTE VS.
THE CHAIRMAN

From shortly after the beginning of the war until 2007, stories of alleged fraud and waste, ranging from KBR overcharges to smaller companies like Custer Battles using shell companies to defraud the government, emerged from Iraq on a fairly consistent basis. Unfortunately, these stories would get attention for a few days, there would be congressional speeches and statements promising to investigate and to make sure the troops were well served, the Pentagon would promise to do better, and then the subject would go away as soon as the next celebrity trial started.

Some of the more responsible members of Congress tried to insert language requiring more oversight into the supplemental money—almost $2 billion a week—the White House continued to request to fund the war. But their efforts have for the most part failed, and the members of Congress who are chafing about the money and the lack of oversight had been reluctant to make too much of it for fear of being labeled soft on defense or unwilling to support the troops. Such divisive labeling certainly loomed large in the last presidential election, and this has not been lost on the politicians of both parties.

There is one member of Congress, however, who has been doggedly persistent in his investigations of KBR, by far the biggest contractor in the war service industry today. Throughout the war, Henry Waxman has continued his quixotic struggle for transparency and accountability in the Iraq contracting. While he scrutinized many other companies, such as Blackwater and Parson, KBR has been his primary focus because of the sheer size of its contract and the problems its misconduct has created for the troops. Many soldiers and sources in the government have contacted him to describe the fraud and waste they are seeing. As the minority ranking member of the Government Reform Committee, he used his website and his staff to expose everything that he could on KBR in Iraq. His efforts got some press attention, but it was not lasting.

Until the 2006 midterm elections, he was in a politically impracticable and difficult position, pursuing a political powerhouse of a company with influential friends in the party controlling both houses of Congress and the White House. But Waxman continued to investigate many aspects of fraud by contractors in Iraq and built a stable of witnesses and documents to make his case. Once the majority chairman of the powerful committee that exposed the tobacco industry in the early 1990s, he chafed for the opportunity to explore all the fraud trails he had found. Because he had been in the minority since 1994, he could not call hearings on his own or issue subpoenas.

The nemesis in his crusade was the Republican chairman of the Government Reform Committee, Tom Davis from Virginia. Davis is an ironic foil to Waxman. He is an attractive, outspoken politician who represents a district in Northern Virginia situated right on the border with D.C. Some of the main businesses in his district are the consulting and government contract firms, often called Beltway Bandits, that ring the freeway around Washington. These companies greatly expanded as outsourcing as much of the government as possible became the fad, starting in the 1990s in the middle of the Clinton administration and exploding during the current Bush Administration. Davis himself was the chief counsel and vice president of one of the most successful and entrenched of the consulting companies, a company called PRC.

Davis is very dedicated to the contracting industry. According to the *Washington Post,* Angela B. Styles, former chief of the Office of Federal Procurement Policy, wrote an email stating: "The businesses in Mr. Davis [sic] district are primarily government contractors and he wants to make sure the $$ are free flowing without much regard to the fiscal consequences." A fiction writer could not have designed two better antagonists to sit next to each other on the same committee.

Waxman's first concern started with the RIO contract that was given to KBR to rebuild the Iraqi oil fields. As mentioned in Chapter 2, Waxman smelled smoke with the signing of this contract. When he asked for copies of all contracts that were given to KBR for the Iraq war, he immediately discovered that the KBR logistics contract few restrictions on the money to be spent. He continues to investigate the oil rebuilding contract but has now shifted much of his focus to the taxpayer-money-rich logistics contract. Concerned and suspicious that this company, a subsidiary of Halliburton, which was once run by Vice President Dick Cheney, might be getting special treatment, he is determine to oversee this contract and to find out if the vice president's office had any influence over its management.

KBR had had questionable cost and pricing problems with their Army logistics contracts in Bosnia and for their maintenance of the Army base at Fort Ord, California. On April 8, 2003, about the same time that Perry Jefferies, David List, and Adam Roe were entering Iraq, Waxman asked the Government Accountability Office (GAO) to look at various problems with KBR's contracts, such as possible special treatment, especially from the Vice President's office, and the wisdom of making the logistics contract open-ended.

By May 29, 2003, Waxman had seen an Army spreadsheet that showed the wide range of the logistics contract. He wanted to know more about this growing contract that was supposed to be for the feeding and the supplying of the troops. He found that it had been in place already during Operation Iraqi Freedom, nearly a year before the start of the actual war. He wrote acting Secretary of the Army Les Brownlee for more information on this contract and its task orders. He wanted to know what exactly this contract was for and whether the necessary oversight was in place. He wrote in his letter:

> Little is publicly known about Halliburton's work in Iraq under the LOGCAP contract. While there have been numerous articles about Halliburton's contract with the Army Corp of Engineers to repair and operate Iraq's oilfields, the Defense Department has released little information about Halliburton's activities in Iraq under the LOGCAP contract. This is ironic since the dollar values of the awards to Halliburton under the LOGCAP contract are nearly six times greater than those under the contract with the Corp. The Los Angeles Times did reveal earlier this month, however, that Halliburton has received at least $90 million for Iraq-related work under the LOGCAP contract.

These numbers seem small now that this logistics contract has reached the $18 billion mark. But what Waxman did not know at the time was that the contract was not only costing the taxpayers dearly but also allegedly contributing to the problems that allowed Perry Jefferies' unit to sit in the Dustbowl with few supplies.

On October 8, 2003, Waxman and Congresswoman Carolyn Maloney of New York introduced a bill, H.R. 3275, called the "Clean Contracting in Iraq Act." The bill included provisions to raise the oversight and transparency of contracting in Iraq and to introduce more competition into Iraq contracting by limiting sole-course contracts and using Iraq companies. With all his years of experience, Waxman must have known that this was a futile attempt at oversight in a Republican-controlled Congress in the middle of a war, but he laid down his marker anyway. The bill was referred to Davis' House Committee on Government Reform, where it died once the 108th Congress went out of session. Davis was not going to give Waxman a forum by considering this bill.

In February of 2004, Waxman had begun to hear allegations of fraud from unhappy Halliburton employees who had worked in Kuwait. According to a letter that he wrote to the director of the Defense Contract Audit Agency (DCAA), two employees had told him that price did not matter; as one employee put it, Halliburton's motto was "Don't worry about price. It's cost-plus." They also described wasteful spending on overpriced items, such as furniture and cell phones, and complained about inviting high quotes from vendors and using high-priced preferred vendors. This was just the tip of the iceberg compared to what Rick Lamberth had seen while working for KBR, but it was a clue that the normal checks and balances were not in place. Waxman wrote two more of his ubiquitous letters, this time to the DCAA and to the inspector general of the Department of Defense, asking them to investigate the problems.

By the end of February 2004, Waxman went to the belly of the beast. According to an article in the Wall Street Journal, Halliburton had an 18-page "Tiger Team" report produced by 80 of its managers and auditors. The conclusion of this report was that Halliburton's cost controls were "antiquated" and "weak." Waxman wrote directly to David Lesar, the CEO of Halliburton, and asked for the report. The letter was dated February 27, 2004, and he asked that the report be provided by March 5, 2004. It never arrived.

By March 2004, Davis had agreed to hold a full committee hearing on Iraq reconstruction contracts. Waxman wanted to look at those contracts but he also wanted to bring up his concerns about the logistics contract. Before the hearing, Waxman sent an eight-page memorandum to the Democratic members of the House Government Reform Committee to outline to them the problems he had found in his investigations of Halliburton and to summarize the government reports that backed up his concerns. Here is an excerpt dealing with his biggest concerns:

—DCAA's December 31 [2003] audit, known as a "Flash Report," found "significant" and "systemic" deficiencies in the way Halliburton estimates and validates costs. According to the DCAA audit, Halliburton repeatedly violated the Federal Acquisition Regulations and submitted a $2.7 billion proposal that "did not contain current, accurate, and complete data regarding subcontractor costs." For example, DCAA found that Halliburton "did not disclose the termination of two subcontracts . . .[that] were the basis for over $1 billion of projected food service costs."

—DCAA's January 13 [2004] memorandum to the Army Corp of Engineers concluded that Halliburton's deficiencies "bring into question [Halliburton's] ability to consistently produce well-supported proposals that are acceptable as a basis for negotiations of fair and reasonable prices," and it urged the Corps to "contact us to ascertain the status of [Halliburton's] estimating system prior to entering into future negotiations." Despite this explicit warning, the Corps awarded Halliburton a new $1.2 billion contract January 16. The Corps later claimed: "We have our own internal audit process [and] haven't turned up any wrongdoing or major problems."

—GAO reported that there is a $700 million discrepancy between the cost of the certified proposal that Halliburton submitted on October 8, 2003, for the largest task order under LOGCAP and the cost of a revised proposal that Halliburton submitted on December 23, 2003 for the very same task order.

—GAO reporter that the Defense Department exercises ineffective oversight over Halliburton's work in Iraq under the LOGCAP contract. According to the GAO, a military review board approved a six-month renewal contract with Halliburton worth $587 million in just ten minutes and based on only six pages of supporting documentation. In addition, "logistic support units" sent to the region to provide commanders with contracting advice included military reservists with no contract experience and no previous knowledge of LOGCAP.

—The Defense Energy Support Center prepared a breakdown of the costs it incurred to import gasoline from Kuwait to Iraq from August

to December 2003. According to the Center, its fuel costs for this period were $0.96 per gallon and its transportation costs were $0.36 per
gallon—for a total cost of $1.32 per gallon. In contrast, Halliburton
charged U.S. taxpayers $1.17 per gallon for fuel, $1.21 per gallon for
transportation, $0.24 per gallon for "markup" and $0.02 per gallon for
"other" expenses—for a total cost of $2.64 per gallon, twice as much as
the Defense Energy Support Center.

These new findings follow months of mounting evidence that Halliburton has routinely and systematically overcharged the U.S. government. In
December, DCAA reported that Halliburton submitted an unjustified
cost proposal for $67 million in food services and overcharged the gov-
ernment $61 million for gasoline imports.

At this March 11, 2004 hearing, Davis had the usual witnesses from
the government talk about reconstruction, such as Major General Carl
Strock from the Army Corp of Engineers, Dov Zakheim, the Department
of Defense comptroller, and Rear Admiral (retired) David Nash, the director of the Iraq Program Management Office of the CPA. He also invited General Paul Kern, the head of Army Material Command (AMC),
to talk about LOGCAP.

Although it seemed promising that Davis was holding a hearing with
witnesses who were in charge of various issues, it was clear from his opening statement that he was planning to counter Waxman's accusations. He
tried to set the stage to show that the Republicans were doing their oversight duties and that Waxman's case was largely a politically motivated attempt to embarrass the Bush administration. He said in his opening
statement:

> Large-scale procurements are complex and difficult to understand in and
> of themselves. When it comes to procurement, if you're not confused,
> you're not paying attention.
>
> Add in the urgency and inherent dangers of contracting in a war
> zone, and the challenge of acquiring urgently needed goods and services
> becomes quite daunting. Through this hearing we hope to separate fact
> from fiction, truth from rhetoric—and, in turn, help make sure we're co-
> ordinating contract processes in Iraq in a way that ensures success and
> safety.
>
> Fortunately our acquisition laws have been carefully crafted by Con-
> gress to provide enough flexibility for the government to quickly get the
> goods and services it needs in emergency situations. There are provisions

in the acquisition laws that allow for carefully circumscribed exceptions to our standard for full and open competition to provide for a more limited, less time consuming award of contracts for urgently needed supplies and services. I frankly cannot think of a situation that would better fit within these flexibilities than what we are now facing on the ground in Iraq. Sometimes we just don't have the time to take our time.

I find it ironic that those who are complaining that the government does not have sufficient people on the ground to oversee and administer the current contracts in Iraq would foster contracting strategies that would increase substantially the need for contract administration. For every complex problem, there's a simple solution that doesn't work.

I recognize that there have been mistakes. The contract oversight process is not always pretty, and decisions made under the pressure of combat are not always as lucid as those made under less threatening conditions.

I commend my Ranking Member and others who have raised some important questions pertaining to the reconstruction process. Today I hope we can differentiate between real issues worthy of serious inquiry and those with little or no basis in fact that are raised solely to create a whiff of scandal.

That there have been disagreements with contractors over payments should come as no surprise to anyone familiar with the administration of complex contracts in difficult circumstances. These difficulties should be viewed within the context of the wartime environment in Iraq.

Many of the disputes that have been made public show that the contract oversight process is working. This hearing is part and parcel of a functioning oversight process.

Make no mistake—I have no patience for fraud or abuse. I expect that any such instances that are proven will result in harsh punishment for the perpetrators. I also expect that, as the conditions on the ground improve, the next generation of contracts will be awarded and administered in accordance with our standard acquisition procedures. Emergency procedures are for emergencies only.

This is a monumental task, and there is no room for error. Nor is there room for partisan sniping aimed merely at undermining the overall reconstruction efforts. We're interested in the truth, not rhetorical calisthenics. We're interested in helping coordinate the many important contracts in place today or planned for the future. In short, we ARE interested in moving forward with a contracting framework that benefits our reconstruction goals.

We are NOT interested in simply repeating demagogic and disingenuous sound bites.

Despite this admonition, Waxman plowed ahead with his questions about Dick Cheney's possible influence over Halliburton contracts and about the problems in the KBR contracts. General Kern gave a boiler-plate explanation of the logistics contact, obviously staffed and channeled by the Army to assure the members of Congress were appeased by giving reassurances to both sides to both sides. He ends his statement by saying, "We are committed to supporting current operations and transformation simultaneously. Supporting our soldiers remains our number one priority and ensuring they get the very best quality of life and other logistics support is one way that the people of AMC do that. As I have described to you earlier, LOGCAP contracting is a process we need to constantly review and improve if we are to improve the Army's tooth to tail ratio. We will improve and continue to improve our management of this program."

Waxman was determined to get these officials under oath and on the record about any possible Cheney involvement with the Halliburton contracts. Davis headed him off at the pass and asked each official: "Have you or anyone in your office ever discussed with the Vice President or with his office the award of a contract for Iraqi reconstruction prior to any contract being awarded?" The group answered no. Waxman did not want to take that answer on faith.

In May 2004, the Defense Contract Audit Agency (DCAA), the auditing arm of the Department of Defense, issued a report on the deficient billing practices of KBR, especially with regard to their dining room facilities. The deficiencies forced KBR to submit all the billings to DCAA for review before getting paid. This was one of the factors that slowed KBR's billing process and led to their alleged work stoppage threats as revealed by Rick Lamberth. Later on, DCAA would challenge a large portion of these billings, only to have their suggestion of charges that the government should not pay, overturned by the Army.

Waxman sensed that Davis was showing some genuine interest in routing out possible fraud and waste from KBR and other contractors. The two men had a comparatively cordial relationship compared in the deeply divided House of Representatives, and they respected each other. Both knew that each could not help but engage in some partisan maneuvering in these hearings, but this was mild compared to the rocky years when Representative Dan Burton was chair and the committee became extremely contentious and partisan. But their cordial relationship was about to be strained as Waxman plowed ahead with his investigations.

Waxman got a whiff that his suspicions about Cheney's office's involvement with KBR contracts were right when *Time Magazine* ran a May 30, 2004 article quoting an internal DOD email stating that the Halliburton contract was "coordinated" with the vice president's office. On June 1, 2004, Waxman fired off another letter to Secretary of Defense Rumsfeld quoting from both the March hearings, at which Rumsfeld's principals had denied any involvement by Cheney, and the *Time* article, and asking Rumsfeld for information and documents. This was the one area that Davis wanted to avoid. But the DOD was about to spill the beans on the Cheney connection, and a group of whistleblowers from KBR had come forward to Waxman. By mid-June, these two events caused a big rift within the committee.

Waxman and his staff had been speaking to a group of KBR whistleblowers for several months. The group included David Wilson and James Warren, the two KBR truck drivers who were unhappy about the money motivation and the danger of KBR's truck convoys. They had gone public to the news media, and Waxman's staff called them in to hear more about their complaints. The accounts that they ultimately gave to the Committee, for the most part, matched the stories that they told in Chapter Nine. The other whistleblowers were Marie De Young, a KBR logistics specialist who had seen the company charge $45 per case of soda and $100 per 15-pound bag of washed laundry; Michael West, a KBR labor foreman who claimed that even though he and his crew spent weeks doing little work, they were instructed to charge 12 hours a day for 7 days a week; and Henry Bunting, a KBR procurement officer who told of a scheme to manipulate purchase orders so that KBR did not have to solicit multiple bids. A sixth individual, who declined to be named, was a KBR subcontractor executive who charged that KBR was paying greatly inflated prices to their subcontractors and passing the costs on to the government.

In late May of 2004, Waxman told Davis and his staff about these whistleblowers and asked that they be allowed to testify under oath before the committee. Davis' staff insisted the whistleblowers first come to the committee to be questioned extensively by the majority staff. Waxman accommodated this unusual request because he believed the former employees had important information to share. The committee planned a hearing for June 15.

On June 8, both the majority and minority committee staffs were briefed by a group from the DOD, including Michael Mobbs, a special advisor to Under Secretary of Defense for Policy Douglas Feith. Mobbs spilled the beans at that briefing, admitting that the vice president's office, especially Scooter Libby, the chief of staff at the time, was much more involved in the decisions regarding Halliburton's contracts than had previously been known. This was shocking to Waxman because of the assurances given by DOD officials under oath at the last hearing that the vice president's office had not been involved in the decision-making process.

On June 13, 2004, Waxman, not surprisingly, fired off a strong letter to Cheney asking about the discrepancies and requesting documents. As was his habit, Waxman also released the letter on his minority office website, so his discovery of a connection between the Vice President's Office and Halliburton in the contract negotiations soon became public. His summary of what he had been told by Mobbs was blunt:

> I have learned, however, that your chief of staff, I. Lewis "Scooter" Libby, was briefed in October 2002 about the proposal to issue the November 11 task order to Halliburton. This briefing was provided by a senior Defense Department official at a meeting of the "Deputies Committee," a committee comprised of the Deputy Secretary of Defense, the Deputy Secretary of State, the Deputy Director of the CIA, and equivalent leaders from other agencies. In addition to Mr. Libby, other White House officials were also present, including Deputy National Security Advisor Stephen Hadley, who chaired the meeting.
>
> Your staff was also informed prior to the award of the March 8, 2003, sole-source contract. Recent press accounts disclosed the existence of a Pentagon e-mail indicating that your office "coordinated" action on the sole-source contract in the days before it was awarded. I have since learned that the involvement of the Vice President's office was discussed at a March 5 meeting between Douglas Feith, the Under Secretary of Defense for Policy, and the author of the e-mail, Stephen Browning of the Army Corps of Engineers.

Davis now saw that Waxman, by writing the Vice President with such strong language and releasing the letter to the press, had thrown down the gauntlet to the feared Vice President Cheney. Davis pushed back by telling Waxman that his Halliburton whistleblowers could not testify at the June 15 hearing, only several days away, after all. Instead, there was only to be government witnesses at the hearing and Davis refused to invite Halliburton after Waxman asked they have a representative at the hearing. This was the break between the two men and the line in the sand was drawn.

Unsurprisingly, Waxman wrote a letter to Davis and released it to the press, along with written statements from the whistleblowers on what they had planned to tell the committee.

> Dear Mr. Chairman:
>
> I am writing to express my objections to your decision to prevent testimony of waste, fraud and abuse involving Halliburton from being presented at tomorrow's hearing on Iraq contracting—and to advise you that I and other members will be seeking subpoenas at the hearing in order to obtain this important testimony.
>
> Three weeks ago, my staff informed your staff of the identity of six individuals, five who worked directly for Halliburton and one who worked for a major Halliburton subcontractor. These individuals have firsthand knowledge of egregious examples of waste, fraud and abuse involving Halliburton's Iraq contracts. At the minority's expense, we brought four of these individuals to Washington for in-person interviews with your staff and arranged extended telephone interviews for the other two individuals. . . .
>
> . . . Despite the significance of the information that the six individuals offered to provide—and the corroboration offered by DCAA and GAO—you turned down my request that they testify under oath before the Committee. You also turned down my request that Halliburton be extended a written invitation to testify at the hearing. Moreover, you have not issued subpoenas to the Defense Department and USAID despite their persistent failure to provide relevant documents to the Committee.
>
> Our Committee is not fulfilling its obligation to protect the taxpayer from waste, fraud and abuse. For this reason, I and other members intend to use all procedural options available to the minority at tomorrow's hearing—including moving for the issuance of subpoenas and requesting a minority day of hearings—to ensure that the Committee received this essential information.

To avoid an embarrassing subpoena vote and a minority day of hearings, Davis finally agreed to allow the whistleblowers testify and asked Halliburton to attend a hearing on July 22, 2004.

The day before the hearings, Waxman released a report by the Government Accountability Office (GAO). According to Waxman's fact sheet on the report, GAO claimed, among other things, that the Army's execution of the LOGCAP contract had problems with "ineffective planning, inadequate cost control, insufficient training of contract management officials

and a pattern of recurring problems with controlling costs, meeting schedules, documenting purchases and overseeing contractors." This heightened
the tension for the hearing the next day.

Davis, in a move that was not usual decorum for a chairman, opened
the hearing with a statement attacking the whistleblowers even before they
could testify. Davis was in full damage control mode.

The usual congressional protocol is to let the whistleblowers have
their say and then bring up smooth DOD officials, Pentagon brass, and
representatives from the companies and rely on their calming public relations strategies to reassure the public that these companies have adequate
oversight.

But Davis made a strange move in this hearing. He was so incensed
about what the whistleblowers were about to say that he personally rebuffed the whistleblowers in his opening statement and did not wait for
the DOD or KBR to do the job. Michael West, who had cooperated with
the Committee with the help of the Project on Government Oversight
(POGO) never showed up for the hearing. West was planning to tell the
Committee that even though he and others had to make work 90 percent
of the time in order to stay busy, they were told to systematically charge
twelve hours a day, seven days a week, on their time cards. He told POGO
that working in Iraq "was no different from getting paid to sit on your
couch at home. We did not help the military, but rather the military helped
us." His chair at the hearing sat empty.

James Warren and David Wilson were two of the whistleblowers.
Warren could not believe that the Republican chairman was claiming that
they were disgruntled employees looking for money. "I voted Republican
the last few elections and now I am being attacked by a Republican chairman," he thought. Wilson remembers being so angry at what Davis said
that he felt himself rising in the chair only to have his attorney place a re-
straining hand on his shoulder from behind. Here are some excerpts from
Davis's statement:

> ...[B]efore we hear from the representatives of KBR we will first hear
> testimony from former employees who believe they personally witnessed
> waste and abuse. I'm afraid that it will become clear that these individuals
> are far from experts in government contracting and have, for various rea-
> sons, some personal bias against their former employer.
>   ...Although the minority has worked with these witnesses for a
> long time, in the case of Ms. Marie deYoung, the minority knew of her
> allegations eight months ago; they were brought to our attention only

Well, I want to thank the three of you for being here. You're doing a service, but you obviously are feeling the discomfort from the questions that I've been hearing asked of you. Now, you would think with the kind of questions you've had that you've made all this up. I guess that's what the Republicans are trying to suggest. It was interesting also from the question as she [Representative Blackburn (R-TN)] talked about specifics of what we're going to hear from the next panel, the Halliburton panelists. Well, this sounds like the Republicans had a private meeting with the Halliburton witnesses to go over what they're going to say. We weren't invited to that meeting, but we've invited and tried to work together with the staffs on both sides to interview other witnesses. But I want to go through some points because obviously you didn't make all this up. Since last December, government auditors have produced a series of reports that have found widespread, systemic problems with every aspect of Halliburton's work in Iraq, from accounting and billing practices to subcontractor management to exorbitant overcharging. And I'm just going to list a few of these. In December, the Defense Contract Audit Agency prepared a draft audit but found that Halliburton was overcharging for the gasoline it was importing from Kuwait. The draft report found $61 million in overcharges. DCAA concluded that Halliburton had not demonstrated that they did an adequate subcontract pricing evaluation prior to award of the Altanmia contract. On December 31, the auditor of DCAA issued a flash report concluding that Halliburton's cost estimating systems were deficient and that a $2.7 billion Halliburton proposal did not contain accurate current and complete data regarding subcontractor costs. DCAA concluded the estimating deficiency is not a one-time occurrence, it's systemic. That's the kind of thing you were talking about, Ms. de Young. In January, the DCAA review warned agencies throughout the Pentagon that they should not negotiate any further contracts with Halliburton until they check with DCAA to make sure these problems were addressed. In May, DCAA examined Halliburton's billing practices. This audit found systemic deficiencies in the way Halliburton prepares and submits its bills to the federal government. In June, the inspector general of the Coalition Provisional Authority issued an audit that found that Halliburton was overcharging for unauthorized and unnecessary expenses at this five-star hotel in Kuwait. That the inspector general of the Coalition Provisional Authority reporting on the same example that you've given us, Ms. de Young. And just yesterday, GAO completed its audit. And GAO found a pattern of recurring problems with almost every aspect of Halliburton's work on the LOGCAP contract to supply the troops with essential services. And GAO raised problems with cost control, subcontracts and a host of other areas. That's six audits by three different independent auditors, all of whom reached the same conclusions. Halliburton has been repeatedly overcharging and over-billing the U.S. taxpayers.

After the whistleblowers testified, Halliburton, as the parent company of KBR, made the usual noises about having safeguards in place and delivering on the contracted responsibilities and duties. Al Neffgen, the chief operating officer for government operations, Americas region at KBR, said the following in his statement:

> Supporting troops is an enormous logistics exercise. Every day we serve more than 475,000 meals to our troops, provide them more than 2.3 million gallons of water, wash almost 16,000 bundles of their laundry, collect nearly 10,000 cubit meters of trash. We did this with constant changes from the Army, the kinds of changes that are to be expected in a war zone. The LOGCAP contract scope of work called for KBR to be prepared to support 25,000 troops with an absolute maximum of 50,000. Within months, we were charged with supporting nearly 200,000 U.S. and coalition forces as well as 11,000 others, a total of 211,000 people. Under these conditions, no one should expect the assembling and complicated logistics would be the epitome of pristine precision. These unanticipated requirements did tax and stretch our systems, but we placed continuous pressure on ourselves to do better. We identify problems and fix them. We have an elaborate system to detect improprieties. And when they occurred, we acted. Let me give you two examples of where we identified and fixed problems. By late 2003, we were concerned about the overload of some of our procurement systems. We dispatched a special tiger team of seasoned procurement professionals that improved our systems. And when we discovered a billing irregularity that suggested a subcontractor may have improperly paid a kickback to a former employee, we investigated it, reported it to the federal authorities and provided the government a $6.3 million credit, far in excess of the alleged kickback amount. Despite all these challenges, KBR has constantly delivered on its promise to feed and house the soldiers and fuel and supply the military. In the end, that's our proudest accomplishment. Facing all these realities, KBR undoubtedly made mistakes. But where we identified mistakes we quickly moved to fix them. For example, earlier this year, a regular review showed some examples of splitting requisitions to keep them under $2,500. When it did happen, it was done to meet urgent Army need, not to avoid competition. When we found out about it, we put a stop to it. That's not the way we do business. The other area where we found fault with ourselves is in subcontract documentation. These issues came about

for a number of reasons, the huge ramp up of LOGCAP, the need to uti-lize more than 200 subcontractors and the speed needed to accomplish these jobs. Again, the goal was to provide service to the Army as quickly as possible. But it is an area where we could have done better, and we are doing so today. In addition to our self-criticism, we are well aware of the external criticism as typified by a few of our former employees. The com-pany has long had procedures to encourage such complaints and criti-cisms and to address them. We encourage any and all employees to promptly report any violations of our company's code of business con-duct either by going to a supervisor or using our confidential ethics hot-line and e-mail address for reporting any such concerns. We take any allegation seriously and fully investigate. We're sorry that a few of these former employees failed to use these procedures. In any event, we believe their criticisms are mistaken and misinformed. We welcome the oppor-tunity to speak to these facts on these and other issues.

David Wilson was very angry about how he and his fellow whistle-blowers were treated by Congressman Davis and his staff. He wanted to set the record straight and improve the situation for the soldiers and the KBR personnel in Iraq. He was not impressed with the power that the committee had, but he admits that he was a little intimated in taking on the company whose former CEO was now the vice president. But he was determined to get the information out. He still could not believe an Amer-ican company could be that irresponsible to the troops and the soldiers and get away with it.

Although Wilson and the other whistleblowers were angry and frus-trated, the politically experienced Waxman must have known that he had hit a major nerve. At least he was not being ignored. But the rancor of the hearings ended any bipartisan efforts between Waxman and Davis. From that point on, Waxman had to rely on his endless letters and releases to the press to get his message out.

But he forged on anyway. Until the end of 2006, he put out a report or press release on the problems with Iraq contracting at least once or twice a month.

He released an August 16, 2004 memorandum from the Defense Contract Audit Agency (DCAA) to the Army Field Support Command stating "(u)nsupported costs represented 42 percent of the total proposed value under the LOGCAP Task Orders identified in the schedule." The memorandum went on to say that KBR should have had supporting data by this time in the contract and DCAA concluded that "(i)t is clear to us

KBR will not provide an adequate proposal until there is a consequence." DCAA asked the Army only pay 85 percent of the money as specified in the contract with full payment only after their 'billings were approved. Much to Waxman's dismay, the Army later decided to pay KBR 100 percent of the contract regardless of the billing problems.

After Waxman publicly revealed the involvement of the Office of the Vice President in KBR contracting, Davis stopped any more Iraq contract hearings in the 108th Congress. When the 109th started in January 2005, Davis would not hold any Iraq contract hearings until September 28, 2006, two days before Congress adjourned before the midterm elections in November.

Waxman started doing joint hearings and projects with Senator Dorgan of the Democratic Policy Committee, the same committee that had Ben Carter testify about the water problems in Iraq. This became one of the only outlets for these two minority members of Congress and the Senate for their information since the Republican majority in both houses were not having regular oversight hearings. Waxman made a statement at the February 14, 2005 hearing where Frank Willis also testified about the excesses of the contractors under the CPA and the lack of oversight.

Waxman and Dorgan also teamed up in June 27, 2005 to produce a report that concluded that Halliburton' had a total of questioned and unsupported costs that exceeded $1.4 billion. The report showed that the LOGCAP contract alone had $1.2 billion in questioned and unsupported costs. Later, on February 27, 2006, Waxman wrote a letter to Davis bemoaning the fact that the Army Corps of Engineers gave KBR $250 million in cost reimbursements, profits and bonuses for the RIO oil contract, even though the DOD auditors had claimed that these costs were unreasonable and unsupported.

In July 2006, the Army announced it was going to break up the LOGCAP contract when they negotiated the next phrase, LOGCAP IV. They planned to break up the contract and have three contractors do the work with a curious deal to hire another contractor to monitor and oversee the other contractors' work—a job usually done by the DOD. Waxman jumped in with a July 5, 2006 letter to Secretary Rumsfeld applauding the DOD for finally breaking out the contract but putting in his concerns about other potential problems such as the potential conflict of interest of the contractor overseeing the new LOGCAP contract.

In September 2006, Waxman joined up twice with other Democrats in the House of Representatives to introduce two new bills. One was a

Clean Contracting Act to introduce more transparency and competition with government contracting and the other bill was a joint effort with the other Democrats on the House Government Reform Committee to put more "honesty and accountability" in government. The bill included bans on secret meetings with lobbyists, taking politics out of government science, and protecting federal whistleblowers. This legislation did not have a chance in the Republican Congress but, once again, Waxman was laying down his marker for future action.

Many in Congress, the press, and the companies saw the diminutive Waxman as an unrealistic Don Quoxite character who was almost alone in taking on the war service industry's contracting practices during a war. But he proved to be right, even without any political power and they had to stop discounting his efforts. Much of what we know about the excesses of this industry was due to his lonely, but determined efforts.

The whole dynamics of the Waxman' crusade and his relationship with Rep. Davis changed November 7, 2006, when the midterm elections put the Democrats back in control of the House of Representatives. For the first time since 1994, Waxman gained a chairmanship and subpoena power that could wielded against the contractors in January 2007. Rep. Tom Davis was now in the minority and had to go along with more in depth investigations of Iraq contacting.

Although Waxman wants to get to the bottom of the LOGCAP and other KBR contract, he plans to take a broader view and wants to examine the flaws of private contractors in Iraq as a whole. Surprisingly, in the 16 years that Waxman was chairman until 1994, even with numerous investigations including Big Tobacco, he never had to resort to using his committee's subpoena power to get what he wanted for his investigations. He was shocked when the Republicans took over the committee and issued many subpoenas and would not work in a bipartisan manner.

Although Waxman realizes in this new world of politics that he might have to use subpoenas in his new investigations, he told the National Journal in September 2006, that he did not want to continue the partisan politics:

> I have never accepted the way that Republicans operated, of doing things solely on a non-partisan basis. I would want to do hearings, look for solutions, and act on a bipartisan basis. You can get a list of all the bills that I have passed into law. I can't think of a single one where we passed it solely on a partisan vote. If we control the agenda, maybe we can get support for it.

. . .I am offended how partisan the Republicans have been. I think that it's destroyed a lot of what's important in this institution—that people develop expertise on issues, and operate in a civil and bipartisan way. Republicans have been told that they had to march in lockstep, and they weren't interested in anything that the Democrats had to say. As chairman, I would want Republicans to join us and to get their input. I would certainly reach out to Republicans who want to work on policy. Partisanship is counterproductive for this institution.

Waxman also told the Associated Press shortly after the election that he was not interested in payback. *"A lot of people have said to me, 'Are you going to now go out and go on a wild payback time?' Well, payback is unworthy,"* he said. *"Doing oversight doesn't mean issuing subpoenas. It means trying to get information."*

Congressman Waxman now has his chairmanship and has begun the long and exacting process of investigating the contacting chaos from the past years in the Iraq war. But it is clear that the war service industry now has a congressional overseer with clout and subpoena power to back it up. This will be one of the first times the industry will have an unsympathetic chairman looking over their shoulders and it will be interesting to see if the hopes of bipartisan oversight will last. Perhaps the war service industry, with its influence born in the Republican Party, will reach out for willing Democrats with promises of influence and jobs. But Waxman, with his seat permanently secured in California and no need for campaign funds, will continue to dig for information with letters that now have clout and the threat of subpoenas to follow any reluctance to cooperate.

CHAPTER 21

LEGAL PRAYER

Even though Robert Isakson made it back safely from Iraq in 2003, he wasn't through with Custer Battles. "In my opinion, they were cheating the government and taxpayers and just being rewarded with more contracts." As a former FBI Agent, Isakson understood fraud, and Custer Battles trumped everything he had seen.

In 2004, Isakson got together with William Baldwin, a former Custer Battles employee. Baldwin had already taken his suspicions of possible fraud to officials in the CPA. The DOD finally decided to suspend Custer Battles from further government contracts in late 2004, a year after Willis and McVaney had first tried to rein them in. In fact, the government contended that Custer Battles was inflating some bills by as much as two-thirds because someone in the company had left behind a company spreadsheet in a meeting with the government. Yet the government continued to give Custer Battles contracts for almost a year after they had this incriminating information.

Isakson and Baldwin were disgusted that Custer Battles had made so much money before the suspension that they decided to file a *qui tam* False Claims Act lawsuit. This federal law allows anyone who directly witnesses fraud to file a lawsuit against the guilty party on behalf of the federal government. The Department of Justice (DOJ) has a set time to review the lawsuit, filed in secret, in order to decide whether to join the case. If the Justice Department turns down the case, the whistleblowers are allowed to take it through the courts themselves on behalf of the federal government, receiving a percentage of any funds they might recover for the government. If the Justice Department accepts the case and recovers money, the whistleblowers are entitled to a smaller percentage.

Isakson and Baldwin hired attorney Alan Grayson, a tall Florida lawyer given to wearing cowboy boots in court, who filed a lawsuit, under seal, alleging that Custer Battles defrauded the government through its contracts with the Coalition Provisional Authority (CPA) and the U.S. Agency for International Development (USAID) by as much as $50 million. The allegations include fabricating "forged leases" for forklifts that had been abandoned by Baghdad Airway and repainted by company employees, artificially inflated costs, and claiming payment for services not actually performed and equipment not actually provided. Some of the fictitious costs were generated from shell companies set up by Custer Battles in the Cayman Islands.

The case ran into legal challenges when the federal government declined to enter it and it was unsealed and served to Custer Battles. The court then ruled that only some of the charges could be tried. Although the Justice Department never explained why they were not pursing the case, the reason given to Grayson was that the Justice Department did not consider the CPA a government agency; therefore, they lacked the authority to go after fraudulently spent money, even though it was taxpayer money. This interpretation stunned many people, because it meant that even if contractors were found to have defrauded the CPA, the federal government would still be powerless to prosecute them or to retrieve the ill-gotten gains.

But Isakson and Baldwin refused to fold up their tent and go home. They were determined to take this case through the courts themselves.

Isakson and Baldwin still would not back down—the fight was on. If the DOJ interpretation were allowed to stand, it would hover like a black cloud over all future *qui tam* cases involving fraudulent contractors in Iraq.

Appearing in a Virginia courtroom in December 2004, Grayson argued that the CPA, which was running Iraq at the time, was largely controlled by the United States and was clearly understood to be a "government entity" by the U.S. Congress when it approved the $87 billion funding package in November 2003 for reconstruction and military spending in Iraq. John Boese, Custer Battles's attorney and one of nation's leading lawyers in defending companies in *qui tam* cases, countered that the funds used by the CPA were Iraqi not U.S. funds. "The fact that CPA was in temporary possession of the money and distributed it does not form a basis for a false claim." In addition, Boese argued that, since none of the money the CPA paid Custer Battles came from U.S. taxpayers the False Claims Act did not apply. It was later found that some U.S. Treasury funds were used. He pleaded for the case's dismissal, certain that the DOJ would not weigh in on behalf of Isakson and Baldwin. His partner, Richard Sauber, a former high-powered DOJ attorney, felt so sure that the DOJ would stay out of the case that he reportedly said to the media that "I'll bet you $50 that they will not show up."

After hearing the arguments in his courtroom, Federal Judge T. S. Ellis of the U.S. Eastern District in Virginia said "I've got to make a difficult decision. This case can be decided, but only on undisputed facts." Judge Ellis is a Harvard-educated lawyer appointed to the bench by President Reagan in 1987. He had a difficult time keeping the lawyers focused on the core issues and even had to snap at them a few times to get them back on track.

But the DOJ, acting under building pressure from press exposure, eventually did weigh in with an advisory opinion, arguing that the CPA did indeed fall under the False Claims Act statute. The court decided, on April 1, 2005, that fraud claims arising from contracts issued in Iraq could be litigated in federal courts in the United States, thus clearing the way for DOJ to pursue not only the Custer Battles allegations, but cases of potential fraud in Iraq worth hundreds of millions of dollars.

Without the government's help, Grayson convinced a jury that Isakson and Baldwin were right. The jury found in their favor and awarded around $10 million dollars in damages and compensation to the government. Custer and Battles finally had to face up to the law, even though they claimed that they did not have the money to pay the judgment. This was one of the first successful efforts to hold the war service industry accountable.

This lawsuit was a test case to see if the federal government could begin to recover money fraudulently obtained by the new war service industry. Custer Battles hired some of the top political attorneys in Washington, and the Justice Department did not intervene, hoping the case would just go away. But Isakson and Grayson stuck it out and rocked the Justice Department with their win. It is said by Justice Department sources that there are currently 30 sealed *qui tam* cases on Iraq that could be affected by the outcome of the Custer Battles case.

Unfortunately, a federal district court judge laid aside the verdict in August 2006. He acknowledged that there was ample evidence of fraud in the case, but disagreed with the DOJ's assertion that the CPA was a federal government entity, considering it an international legal entity even though it was created, staffed, and largely financed by the U.S. government. This meant that much of the fraud that occurred during the frantic Wild West days of the CPA (which was disbanded after the government was turned over to the Iraqis) could not be prosecuted.

The case remains in the district court and will be appealed.

Meanwhile, Isakson and Grayson were not done with Custer Battles yet. They filed another *qui tam* lawsuit against former acting Navy Secretary Hansford Johnson, Custer Battles, former acting Navy Undersecretary Douglas Coombs, and six companies connected to Custer Battles. The lawsuit, which was filed under seal but leaked to the Associated Press in July 2006, claimed that Custer Battles tried to get around their suspension by the DOD.

According to the complaint, after leaving government service, Johnson and Coombs formed a company called Windmill International Ltd., which acquired a Romanian company called Danubia. Danubia then allegedly bought the remains of Custer Battles, including its equipment. The suit stated that Rob Roy Trumble, the former operating officer for Custer Battles, started two companies, called Emergent Business Services and Tar Heel Training, at the same address as Custer Battles's Rhode Island office, attempting to use them to get around the Custer Battles suspension. According to the Associated Press story, the complaint contended that Custer Battles tried to get around the suspension in the following ways:

—It transferred Iraq operations to Danubia Global. "This would be a change in name only, since all Custer Battles Iraq operations managers . . . would retain the same responsibilities and perform the same functions," the suit says.

—In the United States, Custer Battles continued recruitment, benefits administration and travel arrangements through Emergent and Tar Heel—the new companies formed at Custer Battles' office.

"Again, this would be change in name only since Custer Battles managers performing these functions, including defendant Trumble, would retain the same responsibilities and perform the same functions," the suit said.

While serving as the acting undersecretary of the Navy, Coombs made many trips to Iraq to work with military advisors and contractors. The lawsuit, which is officially still not public, is in the hands of the Justice Department, which is deciding whether to join the case and launch another round of investigations into Custer Battles.

In another bizarre twist in an already bizarre story, Michael Battles' German-born wife, Jacqueline Battles, was arrested in September 2006 by the German government for allegedly running a money laundering operation. Battles had allegedly been sending money to his wife in Germany, where she deposited the funds in various accounts set up in her maiden name of Vihernik. The German government found the transactions "suspicious." They ordered her detained after confirming that about $1 million and suspecting that $1 million more had been transferred illegally. As of the fall of 2006, she had not been charged, but was told to remain in Germany, where she is being watched by an electronic monitor.

The Associated Press wrote a story in November 2006 quoting the concerns of the U.S. prosecutor over the actions of Mrs. Battles:

> German authorities allege that though Mrs. Battles was not part of her husband's firm, she "received minimum 1,571,111.06 euros ($2,005,837.49) from her husband," according to a letter in July from lead prosecutor David Kirkpatrick to Grayson requesting evidence.
>
> "The way the money was transferred shows that (Mrs. Battles) is informed about the suspicious background of those transactions," Kirkpatrick wrote. "Obviously she was trying to channel the money through accounts in a number of countries for the purpose of concealing the origin of those amounts."

As these lawsuits and investigations make their way through the federal government and the courts, the saga of Custer Battles goes on. If the lawsuits succeed, we will have a much better understanding of how two ex-military men could game the Iraq contract system in such a major way. If the Congress and the media are unable or unwilling to do the necessary oversight on the war, these *qui tam* lawsuits will be the last resort to investigate and fix the problems with the war contracting. The Custer Battles story is symbolic of all that was wrong about allowing contractors to operate with so little oversight in a battlefield situation.

CHAPTER 22

SLUMLORD OF IRAQ

Washington, D.C., October 2005.

Neal Higgins, the counselor and investigator for the U.S. Senate Democratic Policy Committee, was reading items on the Internet when he spotted an article about the contamination of water at Camp Ar Ramadi, as described by former KBR employee Ben Carter. Outraged at the potential damage the contaminated water could have done to the troops, Higgins felt it was an issue the committee, given its oversight mission, needed to pursue in its hearings on contracting abuses in Iraq.

President Harry Truman signed legislation in 1947 creating majority and minority party policy committees in the Senate. During the almost 60 years since it was created, the Democratic Policy Committee has served Senate Democrats in ways such as providing research and legislative support and producing reports on important policy issues. At the start of the 109th Congress, the policy committees' mission was expanded to include conducting oversight investigations and holding public hearings to ensure accountability in government. Unlike regular congressional committees, the policy committees do not have subpoena power, and their hearings are rarely attended by members of the other party.

Starting on November 3, 2003, the Democratic Policy Committee held the first of its series of hearings on contracting abuses in Iraq. Led by committee chairman, Senator Byron Dorgan, it opened the hearing by ask-ing how the $18.6 billion of U.S. money being flown to Iraq for contracting purposes was going to be spent.

The hearings continued on February 13, 2004, when the committee focused its attention on Halliburton and its practices in Iraq. Dorgan, in his opening statement, questioned the administration's decision to award large contracts without the benefit of a competitive bidding process.

The third hearing in the series on contracting abuses in Iraq was held on September 10, 2004, and again focused on Halliburton and allegations of wasteful practices. This was followed on February 14, 2005 by a hearing on allegations of "rampant mismanagement, waste, and abuse by the Coali-tion Provisional Authority in Iraq." On June 27, 2005 and September 16, 2005, the committee brought attention to the Army Corps of Engineers contracting practices and more allegations regarding Halliburton's per-formance on the LOGCAP contract.

After reading about the water contamination information, Higgins tracked down Ben Carter's contact information and called him and Ken May, a former co-worker of Carter's at Ar Ramadi. Carter and May had written to Halliburton to complain about being forced out of their jobs after creating a stink about the unsafe water conditions in Iraq. Higgins was troubled to hear that they were also pursuing a worker's compensation claim against the company. He could already hear the Republicans' re-sponse to this information, which they would no doubt use to substantiate their portraits of Halliburton's critics as disgruntled employees hoping to get some money out of the company. But he knew that Carter and May were still upset at what they had been put through at Ar Ramadi and felt the story they had to tell about water contamination on the base was too important to ignore.

After talking with both Carter and May, Higgins felt that their knowl-edge of the issue was of limited duration since they were on site in Iraq for only a short time. It was a drawback that he had to rectify before going to Dorgan. So, Higgins contacted a source he knew, a former employee of KBR who did not want to go public but was in possession of some impor-tant knowledge about the company. The source backed up Carter's allega-tions, and Higgins now felt confident that the issue should be exposed in a hearing so the soldiers in Iraq could be made aware of the problem.

Higgins went to work to get information on the LOGCAP contract. He first requested Task Orders 59 and 89 of the contract from the Defense Department's Congressional Liaison Office. The stonewalling started almost immediately. The Liaison Office responded by saying that the Office of the Secretary of Defense was in the process of redefining what they could and could not release to Congress, and in the meantime they could not turn over the compact disc containing the task orders. Thus, everything now had to go through the Secretary of Defense's office. Higgins was frustrated. The information was only three miles away and he couldn't get it. Cooperation with the Pentagon had come to a halt.

Despite this missing information on the contract, Higgins pressed on to hold a hearing and formally expose the water contamination problem, lining up both Carter and May to testify.

Washington, D.C., January 23, 2006.

On a cool, wintry, afternoon in Washington D.C., in late January 2006, Senator Dorgan convened an oversight hearing in the Dirksen Senate Office Building on whether Halliburton had failed to provide clean water to the troops in Iraq. Sitting in front of Senator Dorgan and Senator Dayton, a member of the Armed Services Committee, were Carter, May, and Eric Olsen, a water-quality expert.

Dorgan explained to the audience that non-potable water that did not meet testing standards had "dangerous implications for soldiers and others—we feel a responsibility to have a hearing of this type."

Carter could not believe where he was. The room was crowded. It looked just like it did on TV. He was very nervous. He was actually going to get this problem out to the public and the soldiers who could be, and may already have been, affected by the bad water. He saw Higgins sitting behind the senators grinning at him. He had been up until 3:00 A.M. working on his statement and was exhausted. Carter read his statement, his voice cracking. After the testimony was completed, he felt vindicated when Senator Dorgan concluded the hearing by saying: "There are enough dangers in the country of Iraq for American troops without having to subject them to the dangers of unsafe or contaminated water by a contractor that didn't do the job they were supposed to have done."

The hearing went well, and Carter was feeling good. He felt this public exposure at a congressional hearing would be an insurance policy for him against any possible reprisal from Halliburton. It may have been merely paranoia on his part, but the sentiment is not uncommon among whistle-blowers. Some employers have a subtle but effective way of playing with whistleblowers' minds, trying to make them appear crazy and paranoid.

Carter wondered whether he was being watched and his phone was tapped. He felt he was seeing and hearing things that were not there. "You start having nightmares and imagining terrible things happening to you and your family," he said. Similar concerns have caused some whistleblowers to spiral downward, losing their careers, families, everything. Carter sensed he was beginning to slide down that path, but he caught himself before descending too far and eventually felt like he was back on track. At least he hoped so.

The committee's work didn't stop with the hearing. The next day, letters were sent out under Dorgan's signature to Secretary Rumsfeld and the Pentagon's Inspector General's Office, calling for an investigation into the matter. Dorgan also sent a letter to David Lesar, CEO of Halliburton, to investigate the "failure of KBR . . .to provide safe non-potable water to U.S. troops in Iraq."

Halliburton was non-responsive to Dorgan's request. They knew that he did not have subpoena power. They may have been feeling some heat from the publicity generated by January 23 hearing, however, because they soon issued a statement denying that the water was contaminated and asserting that there had been no reports of illnesses on the base. The Pentagon referred the issue to the inspector general, but in an apparent attempt to downplay the investigation, said that "the allegations appear to have no merit."[1] However, the inspector general didn't bite on Rumsfeld's not-so-subtle suggestion that there be a no-merit finding. Taking the matter seriously, the inspector general's new office in Qatar took it on as one of its first two investigations. It took a number of months, but in September 2006, the inspector general started a full audit of all potable and non-potable water at all military sites in Iraq to determine its safety. The compact disc containing the contract information finally showed up at Higgins' office the day after the January hearing—timed, Higgins felt, to avoid public embarrassment.

Higgins kept up his probe into the issue. He wanted more information, especially the Granger report that Carter had told him about. He also wanted to hold another hearing and went to work with that goal in mind. While preparing for a new hearing, Higgins received a call from the mother of an Army doctor serving in Iraq. The mother got Higgins' immediate attention when she said that her daughter had experienced the same problems with contaminated water that Carter had seen in Iraq. Higgins requested that she ask her daughter to provide him with the information, and the mother said she would try. Then, on March 31, 2006, Higgins received an email from Captain Michelle Callahan, U.S. Army, 101st Sustainment Brigade Surgeon. The information it contained was explosive.

Callahan reported to Higgins that her situation at Q-West (Qayyarah Airfield West), a U.S. military base located in northern Iraq, was almost identical to the issue at Ar Ramadi. In January 2006, she became concerned when there was a sudden increase of soldiers requiring treatment for bacterial infections. Callahan had noticed the shower water was cloudy and had a foul odor. Thinking that there may be a connection between the water and the soldier's illnesses, she asked the environmental science officer to test the water. The tests disclosed the water showed no evidence of chlorine and was positive for coliform bacteria—it was contaminated. Callahan immediately had the water treated, but wanted to know why the water had been contaminated.

The environmental science officer had heard from a newly hired KBR water quality technician that the water may have been "concentrate reject" from the water purifier. Callahan decided to investigate. The environmental science officer "went to the water treatment site and followed the lines from the ROWPU concentrate drain to water trucks filling up with this water. He then followed this truck and observed it pumping the water into the water storage tank at PAD 206." She learned that KBR was filling the water storage tanks with highly contaminated waste water from the water purifier.

After this discovery, the environmental science officer held a meeting with the KBR site manager and the contractor's water quality technician, water purifier operator and other KBR managers. After telling the group of his discovery that KBR was using reject concentrate water to fill the water storage tanks, the KBR water purifier operator said "that it has always been done this way and there is not a problem with it," Callahan told Higgins. The Army officer explained it was against Army Regulations to use reject concentrate from the water purifier for personal hygiene. But, the KBR operator argued "that since the raw water from the Tigris is first filtered through carbon prior to going into the ROWPU that it is acceptable for hygiene," Callahan alleged. This argument was rejected. Callahan explained that, "charcoal filtration only removes particulate [mater] and binds some chemicals. All the bacteria and chemicals that make it [though] the charcoal are concentrated to twice the level as in the Raw water. This is the water with which the soldiers at Q-West have been showering, shaving, and brushing their teeth.".[2]

Higgins now had damning information that not only gave Carter and May credibility, but also showed that the contractor, eight months after the

Ar Ramadi incident, was allegedly still providing contaminated water to the troops at another military base. Halliburton also had failed to notify their own employees of proper procedures after the Ar Ramadi incident and seemed to resist attempts to rectify the problem. Higgins also received a "Point Paper" from the Defense Contract Management Agency, which administers contracts for the Pentagon. The agency had investigated the contaminated water issue at the Q-West site and found questionable water-supply practices for non-potable water on the part of KBR. They issued a Corrective Action Request prohibiting the use of wastewater for human contact. Evidence suggested that the contractor had been using outmoded and no-longer-valid procedures for obtainment and treatment of water used for showering.[3]

Not long before the second hearing, scheduled for April 2006, Higgins was able to obtain a copy of the Granger report through a source. He now had another key element to add to the hearings. A KBR internal investigative report by a high-level company official in Iraq, notifying them that the water was contaminated and potentially posed serious dangers to both the troops and contractor personnel, had surfaced.

Even though Dorgan had requested this very report in his letter to Lesar, it wasn't Halliburton that had produced it, according to Higgins. Instead, at 8:00 P.M. on the night before the April 7 hearing, Halliburton sent Higgins a package containing a different internal report, this one contradicting the Granger report and essentially exonerating the contractor of wrongdoing. But, Higgins found that KBR prepared the new report, citing corrective actions taken, in February 2006. This was the same period of time Captain Callahan allegedly discovered that KBR had been hauling wastewater into tanks at Q-West to be used by the troops.[4]

The next day, when the Granger report was to be revealed at the hearing, Senator Dorgan's staff received an email message from Stuart Eizenstat, the former chief domestic policy adviser for President Carter and deputy treasury secretary under President Clinton who was now representing Halliburton. The message claimed that the Granger report did not represent the company's official position; rather, it was purely the opinion of its authors. The hearing exposed the contradictions between the two reports and brought to light Callahan's revelation of KBR's continued use of wastewater for non-potable use.

At the hearing, Dr. Matthew Harrison, a retired Army Dental Corps captain who had been assigned to Ar Ramadi, testified that he had developed a gastrointestinal disorder within his first two months at the base. He suspects that his symptoms, which continued well after his retirement, were the result of exposure to contaminated water.[5]

Jeffrey K. Griffiths, a professor of public health and medicine at Tufts University School of Medicine, testified that soldiers would have been better off using water straight from the Euphrates River. In addition, he said that "the source water used for our soldiers at Ar-Ramadi was basically diluted sewage; highly polluted and completely unacceptable by any standard for being used without robust treatment. In what appears to be a profound misunderstanding of the way a reverse osmosis unit works, concentrated untreated polluted water was provided to our soldiers for hygienic purposes that is highly likely to make them sick."[6]

It may take months, if not years, to accurately diagnose gastrointestinal illnesses contracted by soldiers as a result of exposure to contaminated water. The exotic parasites and pathogens common in Iraq are not common in the United States. Specific knowledge and very specific tests will be needed to identify soldiers suffering from these diseases. The problem, which is difficult to quantify, is a matter of great concern to Higgins .

The question of whether soldiers were affected by contaminated water still needs to be answered. Several soldiers told compelling stories of dealing with foul and untested water and suffering from extreme gastrointestinal problems extending well beyond their tours in Iraq. As one soldier put it, "Halliburton has become the slumlord of Iraq. Only a slumlord wouldn't notify its tenants of a problem if it meant they had to spend more money and resources to fix them."[7]

In response to the contracting abuses in Iraq exposed by former KBR employees in testimony before his committee, Dorgan introduced a bill in June 2006, called the "Honest Leadership and Accountability in Contracting Act of 2006," by attaching it to the defense authorization bill. Dorgan's bill was intended to improve oversight of military contracts "by eliminating fraud and abuse and improving competition in contracting and procurement." Unfortunately, the bill was rejected by a roll call vote, with every Senate Republican voting against it. Senator John Warner (R-VA), the chairman of the Armed Services Committee, explained his vote by saying that "the organization is now in place to try to monitor the situations the senator has enumerated."[8]

Despite this rejection, Dorgan continued to hold hearings on contracting practices in Iraq. The standing committees, still under the control of the Republicans, were not going to conduct oversight on contracting in Iraq. On September 18, 2006, the Democratic Policy Committee heard testimony from three former KBR employees, including two truck drivers who were part of the fuel convoy that saw several of its other drivers killed, injured, or kidnapped in the April 2004 ambush. With the new Democrat controlled senate beginning in January 2007, the Democratic Policy Committee has set the template for hearings on defense contracting. Senator Dorgan said that the oversight responsibility of Congress has "been long ignored with the majority party here and obviously, that's going to change."[9]

CHAPTER 23

THE EMPIRE STRIKES BACK

Ft. Belvoir, Virginia, June 2005.

Back from a one year tour in Iraq as a LOGCAP planner, Major Rick Lamberth reported to the LOGCAP Support Unit ready to provide the command his experiences and lessons learned at Camp Speicher. He was concerned about what he saw as KBR's poor performance, cost overruns, negative impact on the troops and the unnecessary high costs to the taxpayer. But, much to his surprise, the support unit command did not seem to be interested in what he had to say. No debriefing and no meetings were requested. He had anticipated answering questions about his experiences. This was not a surprise to Lambeth, given the poor communications and lack of support within the LOGCAP command. LOGCAP planners were forced to depend on KBR for support that, for some planners, was inadequate.[1]

The command awarded Lamberth the Bronze Star for exceptional meritorious service as a LOGCAP support officer in Iraq, gave him outstanding performance marks for this work, and then sent him off to work on a LOGCAP project with the LOGCAP Planning Cell – an effort to plan for future contingency operations. Lamberth felt he could have provided valuable information about LOGCAP operations on the ground in

Iraq, especially to those who were scheduled to deploy there. He felt the support unit command wanted only to impress the generals and high-level civilians in the Pentagon that they had everything under control with no serious problems on the contract. He believed it was nothing more than a public relations campaign of positive information.

While in Iraq, Lamberth had provided his command at Ft. Belvoir with a weekly situation report—known as a "sitrep." A copy of this weekly report also was sent to the LOGCAP staff and Defense Contract Management Agency representative located at Camp Victory at the Baghdad International Airport. Lamberth did not mince words in his report. He often questioned KBR's business practices and performance that he was actually observing at Camp Speicher. Also, he implied that DCMA personnel were not enforcing parts of the statement of work for the LOGCAP contract. Integrity was important to Lamberth and he was not about to compromise his values to report something that was not true.

However, about three to four months into his reporting, Lamberth was contacted by a DCMA representative in Baghdad who was upset with what Lamberth was writing in his reports about his agency, and KBR. He wanted Lamberth to stop sending the reports. But, Lamberth told the representative he was reporting the facts from his observations and through canvassing both Army officials and KBR employees at Camp Speicher and would continue to send reports unless ordered to stop by his superiors. Lamberth's direct supervisor was satisfied with the reports and asked him to continue sending them.

Lamberth was frustrated with what seemed a desire by the LOGCAP command to ignore what he considered to be the contract abuses and cost overruns on the part of KBR and its negative affect on the troops and taxpayer. He felt that they just wanted to sweep the possible problems under the rug so they didn't have to deal with it and jeopardize their careers. He then decided the best way to bring attention to the problems with LOG-CAP in Iraq was to disclose this information to someone in Congress to help stop the problem. Military personnel have severe restrictions against talking about the military publicly but, according to the law, talking to an appropriate member of Congress is considered a protected disclosure outside the normal channels. Having tried to unsuccessfully work within the Army system to bring attention to the issues, it was time to go outside that system to those who could do something about it.

Lamberth realized that it was a big career risk to go outside the Army, but his concern for the troops and the taxpayer overrode his concerns. He thought that if he could get a member of Congress to keep his name confidential, he just might be able to pull it off. He had heard about Representative Waxman's investigations on the LOGCAP contract as the ranking minority member of the House Governmental Reform Committee. On June 28, 2005, Lamberth met with a member of Representative Henry Waxman's staff at Joe Theismann's Restaurant, a popular upscale restaurant located across from the King Street metro stop in Old Town Alexandria.

Approaching the meeting, Lamberth felt alone and somewhat skeptical because he didn't know the congressional staffer and wasn't sure what to expect. He felt uncomfortable talking to a civilian about Army business. He was committing one of the great sins of the military, and the Executive Branch, for that matter – airing the government's dirty laundry to a congressional and potentially public source. Later on, he was told of Admiral Rickover's famous quote about whistleblowing, "If you must sin, sin against God, not against the bureaucracy. God may forgive you, but the bureaucracy never will."

It wasn't long before he felt more comfortable talking to the staffer, but he was cautious and struggled at times to best recount what he saw as an employee with KBR in Kuwait, and an Army officer in Iraq overseeing the contractor. After the meeting, Lamberth left the restaurant feeling a lot better about the experience, more confident, and more positive that something was going to be done to address the contract abuses he claimed to have witnessed.

However, his protected disclosure was about to be revealed internally within the LOGCAP Support Unit. About two or three months later, Lamberth decided he wanted to try and persuade some of his colleagues to also come forward to back-up his congressional disclosure. In doing so, he approached a few of his fellow officers in the LOGCAP Support Unit, and told them, in confidence, that he had made the disclosure. Lamberth said they had stories of their own to tell of the abuses by KBR on LOGCAP, but were afraid to come forward for fear of reprisal by the Army. It was not long, as Lamberth soon found out, his confidential conversations were broken when the information of his disclosure was passed up the chain of command by someone.

Two weeks later, a senior officer confronted Lamberth about his disclosure and trying to get others in the unit to come forward. He warned him not to make any additional disclosures because it could have an adverse impact on his career.

Shortly thereafter, Lamberth met with another staff officer who echoed the senior officer by telling Lamberth his career could be ruined if he continued to cooperate with the congressional committee. Lamberth decided he would have a hard time continuing to be part of LOGCAP and would try and transfer to another unit.

Before that could happen, a staff officer asked Lamberth if he would volunteer to go to Afghanistan for a four month tour as a LOGCAP planner. Another officer was supposed to go, but had refused for personal reasons. Lamberth at the time was attending graduate school, and had enrolled to attend the Army's Intermediate Level Education course. He didn't want to disrupt his educational goals, but he made the decision to go for the short tour. He thought it was his duty to do so.

But, before he left for Afghanistan, Lamberth was pressured to extend his tour from four months to one year. He was not going to accept an extension. After just spending a year in Iraq and now trying to get his master's degree, Lamberth wanted to get on with his life. His expectation was to spend four months in Afghanistan, return to the U.S., and then transfer to another unit. He was promised by an officer senior to Lamberth that his request to continue in the unit would be withdrawn and his request to transfer to another unit would be in place by the time he returned from Afghanistan. Lamberth did not want to return to a unit that could derail his career because he had become a protected whistleblower.

Lamberth left for his Afghanistan tour on January 2, 2006. After spending about a week and a half at Ft. Bliss, Texas, he arrived in Afghanistan where he was assigned to a small military base in the Kabul area. It was a much smaller operation than what he experienced in Iraq and he found that everything moved much slower. He saw some of the same problems with the LOGCAP contract that he had seen in Iraq, but on a smaller scale.

By March, one of Lamberth's superiors in Afghanistan, began to demand he extend his tour another eight months. Lamberth says the superior accused him of trying to leave Afghanistan early despite the fact that he had orders specifying his tour would end in April 2006. The Army senior personnel officer in Afghanistan, Chief Warrant Officer Barrin McClendon, backed up Lamberth by writing an email to the supervising officer confirming his four month tour was in full compliance with regulations. Lamberth prevailed, and was released on schedule at the end of April 2006.

Shortly before leaving Afghanistan, Lamberth found out that his request to transfer to another unit was not processed as promised. He called a senior officer who told Lamberth the orders would be signed releasing him from the unit. According to Lamberth, the senior officer made it known to him he was not wanted in the unit because of his congressional disclosure.

After returning from Afghanistan at the end of April 2006, Lamberth again found that his release orders had not been processed. Once again a staff officer with the LOGCAP Support unit promised the orders would be finalized and he could start drilling with a new unit immediately. Acting under that assurance, Lamberth was accepted into another reserve unit, a Theater Support Command unit, and started drilling with them.

Lamberth said he soon found out that his release and transfer paperwork was never sent forward to be implemented and that prevented him from continuing to drill with his new unit. In early June 2006, Lamberth was offered a tour with another unit, this time within the Army Corps of Engineers. He accepted the offer and on June 26, he started duty with his new unit in Washington D.C.

Lamberth heaved a sigh of relief. He was out of LOGCAP and the toxic environment that prevailed in that unit. He had a new challenge now with the Corps of Engineers that he felt would soon lead to a promotion to Lieutenant Colonel. He could also continue his studies for a master's degree without worrying about a deployment to the Middle East. However, according to Lamberth, retaliation would soon rear its ugly head and threaten his 25-year career with the Army.

On August 8, 2006, Lamberth was contacted by another staff officer with the LOGCAP Support unit who advised him charges were going to be brought against him, but declined to explain what those charges were. What he did know was that he did nothing wrong. He immediately called a Judge Advocate General (JAG) legal assistance officer at Ft. Belvoir who told Lamberth not to make any written statement.

According to Lamberth, he met with a staff officer, acting as an investigative officer at Ft. Belvoir who read him his rights, but, again, would not explain what the charges were except to say it had to do with an illegal transfer regarding a temporary transfer packet with the Corps of Engineers. Despite his requests, the LOGCAP officer refused to elaborate on what he was being charged with. Instead, the officer asked Lamberth if he wanted to provide a written statement. A written statement about what, he thought? About what the weather was that day? If the charges were not going to be explained, how could he respond with a written statement, or respond in any other way? He told the officer there was no way he could provide a written statement without knowledge of what he was being charged with. Lamberth claimed he told the officer he did nothing wrong and was being set up. The meeting ended and Lamberth was dumbfounded, shocked, and depressed. He had no way to refute the charges since the details of the specific charges were unknown to him.

Lamberth felt the charges had been trumped up to retaliate for his congressional disclosure. He was confident he had done nothing wrong. He says that all he was trying to do was tell the truth about the problems he experienced in Iraq with LOGCAP. He speculates that the LOGCAP Support Unit leadership felt threatened by that information and was taking steps to "kill the messenger." It was the classic response to a whistleblower by expending all their energy to discredit him, Lamberth believed, instead of simply trying to solve the problems that were negatively affecting the troops. He continued to try and find out more about the charges. He attempted to call and email senior officers at the unit several times without success. None of them would return his calls or emails.

Lamberth decided not to sit around and wait for the LOGCAP Support Unit's next move. He contacted Representative Waxman's staff member he had made his disclosures to and told him of the charges. He also contacted the Defense Inspector General's office's military retaliation section and requested assistance. He began to gather paperwork and create rebuttal documents for the Committee and started working on the formal appeal to the DOD Inspector General's office. He also retained an attorney who has an expertise in military law.

In early December 2006, Lamberth was told by a supervising officer at the Corps of Engineers that he was going to receive an official reprimand and that it was in the mail. Lamberth knew that such a reprimand would spell the end of his career with the Army. He would never be promoted with this type of reprimand in his personnel file yet he was still in the dark about the charges.

What was the LOGCAP support unit command afraid of, Lamberth thought? If the charges were supposedly true, then why don't they provide him the courtesy of properly defending himself? He had heard through the grapevine from his former colleagues at LOGCAP that there was some sort of investigation conducted. A former colleague at the Theater Support Command Unit told Lamberth he was questioned by an investigative officer, but did not understand by the questioning what they were investigating. All he could do now was fret and wait for the bomb to drop.

Lamberth received the reprimand on December 24, Christmas Eve, even though it was dated December 15. According to the reprimand, Lamberth was being charged with allegedly making "four false official statements concerning your military status and units of assignment" and it was more fully explained in the official investigative report. Specifically, the reprimand accused Lamberth of "indicating" he had served a 365 day tour in Afghanistan on June 26, 2006; of "indicating" he belonged to the Individual Ready Reserve and not assigned to a unit on July 10, 2006; of submitting a request to be released from his tour of duty in Afghanistan on April 12, 2006 due to a personal hardship and that he was enrolled in an Army leadership course; and "indicating" he had completed a 730 day tour in Southwest Asia on July 10, 2006.

Lamberth was given 30 days to respond. But how was he going to adequately respond because he was never given the investigative report that had details behind the allegations? How was he supposed to have "indicated" the things alleged, he wondered? Mental telepathy? He twice requested the investigative report from the LOGCAP unit, but was denied access to it, he says. Without the report, he had no idea how they came up with the charges. The specific dates and charges didn't make sense to him. Lamberth contends he never "indicated" to anyone he had ever served a 365 day tour in Afghanistan or a 730 day tour in Southwest Asia. He had been released from his tour in Afghanistan in April 2006 because that was what his orders legally specified and he was enrolled in an Army leadership course at the time.

After a 25-year spotless career with the Army, it all came down to this. Lamberth was being charged with being dishonest. How ironic, he thought. He had been trying to tell about the potential dishonesty with the contracting process. He claims he had been lied to by officers, told he was a "snitch," and threatened with reprisal.

Lamberth had now entered into the bizarre and unreal world of whistleblowing. It is even more difficult because he was an Army officer talking about serious problems with an increasingly unpopular company during an increasingly unpopular war. He feels that the Army bureaucracy believed they could avoid an inconvenient investigation if they could discredit Lamberth with a reprimand and make him the issue instead of their lack of oversight and discipline on the LOGCAP contract.

Lamberth's die is cast. He is resolute to fight the reprimand to get his good name back and dedicated to continue to work with Representative Waxman's staff to expose and fix the glaring problems and inadequacies that he saw in the LOGCAP contract. He believes that he owes it to his fellow soldiers. He hopes that the system will work for him and he can continue the career in the Army that he loves. Based on past history of military whistleblowing and Admiral Rickover's insightful quote, the odds are greatly stacked against him.

CHAPTER 24

YOU GO TO
WAR WITH THE
SECRETARY OF
DEFENSE YOU HAVE

In early December 2004, Secretary of Defense Donald Rumsfeld was at Camp Buehring in the Kuwaiti desert, talking to troops about to be deployed into Iraq. By then, equipment shortages and lack of armor on the Army's vehicles were concerns among the soldiers. One soldier, Army Specialist Thomas Wilson of the 278th Regimental Combat Team, mustered enough courage to ask the secretary a tough question. "Why do we soldiers have to dig through local landfills for pieces of scrap metal and compromised ballistic glass to uparmor our vehicles?" he asked.

The question brought cheers of encouragement from the other soldiers, but Rumsfeld's answer was abrupt. "As you know, you have to go to war with the Army you have, not the Army you want," he replied.

Two of the generals tasked with planning the logistics of this war were Lieutenant General Paul Kern, commanding general of the Army Material

Command (AMC) from 2001–2004, and Major General Wade "Hamp" McManus Jr., commanding general for the U.S. Army Field Support Group in Rock Island, Illinois, from 2000–2004. Both of these men had to deal with the enormous problem of ramping up quickly for the war in Iraq with the Army they had.

According to Brigadier General Mark Scheid, who was appointed chief of logistics war plans the day before September 11, 2001, planning for the war in Iraq started shortly after the invasion of Afghanistan, and it was all very secretive. Eventually, Scheid said, he had to bring in others, including the AMC. Although the AMC is the main logistics branch of the Army and is responsible for the LOGCAP contract under the command of Mc-Manus, it has traditionally been the poor sister in funding to the more prestigious branches of the Army, such as the Procurement Division, which spends large amounts of money on shiny new weapons, and the Special Forces, which takes on glamorous secret missions. Army logistics has never been a sexy command, but in real, non-theoretical "hot" wars, it can make or break the success of the Army's combat mission.

Kern was thrust into the job of quickly preparing for Iraq war. In measured and calm tones, he told us about the myriad problems he faced. First, Secretary Rumsfeld had put a cap on the number of troops to be deployed in Iraq, limiting not just combat soldiers but also the number of soldiers that would be available for logistic purposes. Rumsfeld had replaced General Eric Shinseki as the Army chief of staff after the General told Congress that it would take hundreds of thousands of soldiers to control postwar Iraq. The significance of this action was not lost on the general officer corps, who became reluctant to voice their own opinions about the Defense Department's plans; however, as many of the generals who served in the planning in Iraq retire, they have begun speaking publicly about how strapped they were for manpower, including Army personnel for logistic services.

From about 1996 or 1997 until 2002 during the Balkan experience, funding for the LOGCAP contract was maintained at around $60 million or less. Once U.S. forces engaged in Afghanistan in late 2001, however, the Army's personnel needs exceeded current levels, and the decision was made to use LOGCAP to make up the gap as the military hurriedly prepared for war in Iraq. At that point, Kern realized that LOGCAP was going to grow much faster than before, and in radically new directions. Kern started seeing new requests for the LOGCAP contract on a daily basis. They tried to match the requests for logistics versus funding available.

According to Kern, the LOGCAP Support Unit, an Army Reserve unit out of Ft. Belvoir, Virginia, comprised only 50 reservists. Once they were deployed into Iraq, the Reserve unit quickly started running out of personnel and time needed to keep up with the workload, forcing AMC to rapidly expand the unit. This rapid growth under the LOGCAP contract strained AMC's ability to keep up with the tracking of the work. McManus noted that many of the decisions made for Iraq were based on accounting assumptions from past LOGCAP operations, assumptions that did not hold true for this much larger task.

The day-to-day task of ramping up the logistics fell to McManus. As enthusiastic and talkative as Kern is calm, McManus had a can-do attitude even though he knew he was facing great odds. He now had to turn to LOGCAP to fill the manpower needs created by the downsizing of the military force structure over the last decade and by Rumsfeld's troop cap. McManus claims that, when there is a cap on troops, there is a cap on capability. If your deployment is heavy with fighting forces and light on logistics forces, you will soon begin to encounter problems.

Needing to support a large number of combat soldiers with a relatively small logistic force, the generals turned to LOGCAP as the only tool at their disposal. They had to use that capability because more and more of the Army's tasks had been outsourced in the years preceding the Iraq war. According to testimony given to the House Government Reform Committee by Al Neffgen, KBR's chief operating officer for government operations, Americas Region, "the LOGCAP contract scope of work called for KBR to be prepared to support 25,000 troops, [to] an absolute maximum 50,000." Now McManus had to ramp it up in order to cover up to 200,000 people at war. He scrambled every day to make the most of his resources work, but the war moved more quickly than he could.

According to McManus, there was no real planning for what would happen after the war, and he was just working day-to-day. Much to his alarm, some of the bases in Iraq ended up at one point with just one day's worth of food on hand. McManus said that the first year of the Iraq war was the most challenging for LOGCAP and his group at Rock Island. He didn't believe that anyone had envisioned the operation taking on the scope and scale it has over the last four years. With a non-contiguous battlefield (that is, one without front lines) in Iraq, the logistics operation encountered considerable difficulties in its efforts to supply the soldiers. LOGCAP had never been used before in that type of battlefield. There were problems every where they turned, the biggest, according to

McManus, being the the difficulty of getting the right repair parts to the right units in an extremely fluid and dangerous situation.

At the beginning of the Iraq war, McManus had a basic idea of what it would take to supply the troops. But once the military took Baghdad and occupied the ground, the logistic difficulties really kicked in. In the harsh and demanding environment, the challenge was getting supplies to the bases in order to make daily living more comfortable for the troops. McManus believed that the problems didn't come from a shortage of supplies, but from the difficulty of effectively distributing them to forward units. Eventually he was pushing so many parts into Kuwait and then Iraq that he lost track of where many of them were going, and the paper-trail coordination between the Army and KBR became a mess.

According to McManus, the effort to push supplies to the forward bases was made more frustrating by the need to find some way to move KBR convoys through a very dangerous country. Some military units, especially at remote bases, were going without hot meals and had to manage food inventory down to just days. They were eating MREs and sleeping on the ground. Convoy difficulties made things so tight that even the main bases sometimes found themselves with just a day's worth of food left. Making matters worse, there was no backup option for if, hypothetically, KBR was unable or unwilling to complete their convoy missions. Kern was concerned that all military units were committed to combat operations, leaving none to step in if and when the contractor failed.

On top of the severe stress of having to, for the most part, rely on the contractor to supply the troops, McManus was also responsible for supplying all the personnel at the CPA facilities in the Green Zone. This duty came as a surprise to Kern, who felt that his AMC command was already overtaxed by the LOGCAP process. McManus remembered his exasperation at one of the silliest problems he ever had to face as a two-star general. CPA officials were having trouble getting their underwear washed every day in Baghdad and they were irate because they couldn't find Iraqi employees willing to wash their laundry. McManus tried to explain to them it was a cultural thing; it was why the Iraqis wore long gowns. They don't believe in washing other people's underwear. He felt like telling them go to J. C. Penney's next time to buy a six-pack of underwear. McManus had bigger issues to deal with—keeping convoys moving to supply the troops and trying to get a handle on skyrocketing costs. He contrasted the ridiculousness of the CPA request to the urgency of trying to get food to the bases.

McManus thought the Army would be in Iraq for two years—three at the most. Acccording to Kern, everybody initially thought that the war would be over and the Army sent home in a relatively short time. Kern believes that the idea contingency contracting, such as the LOGCAP contact, is based on the expectation that wars wil be short; Iraq, of course, has not fulfilled that expectation.

The DOD had not planned for logistics, or anything else, for that matter, beyond just winning the war, handing the country over to the Iraqis, and getting out. In fact, according to the *Daily Press* of Newport News, Virginia, General Scheid claimed that when he and other Army planners tried to plan for postwar needs, they were told by Secretary Rumsfeld that the next person to bring up the issue of postwar troops would be fired.

Despite these problems, both generals thought that, in some ways, LOGCAP actually worked. McManus believes it helped to improve the soldiers' quality of life, a very important task for the Army. Kern believes that when operations began in Iraq, LOGCAP worked reasonably well given the significant, and ultimately unmanageable, numbers of troops involved.

In different interviews, both men agreed on several lessons learned. The pace and fluidity of the war and the necessity of keeping up a constant flow of support materials to the troops made the policies used in peacetime contracting inappropriate in Iraq. The process needs to be expedited in the future, there need to be new rules to limit skyrocketing costs. The Army bureaucracy should be streamlined so that contractors are paid faster for work accomplished. Even though Kern thinks that these are important changes that need to be made, he also acknowledges that the reality of the bureaucracy and peacetime contracting rules will probably necessitate some compromises.

KBR stopped being paid directly mainly because the DCAA could not trust their billing records. The DCAA felt the need to scrub the KBR numbers before bills were sent to the Army for payment. This reinstated the classic tension between the need to pay contractor bills on time and the importance of oversight to prevent fraud, waste, and abuse.

During the war and occupation in Iraq, a lot of paperwork traveled around the country in Humvees, trucks, and other modes of transportation, a system Kern thinks should be automated and he tried to improve the system in many "knock-down-drag-out" meetings. He says he did not have enough auditors and personnel to oversee the contractors once they got past the first couple of months and LOGCAP underwent its explosive expansion. It was difficult to keep oversight and management personnel in-country, and the LOGCAP Support Unit, an Army Reserve unit, quickly ran out of people to cycle though and had to try to restaff itself with new reservists. The DCMA had to increase the number of personnel to handle the day-to-day duties of contract administration, but the growth was so swift that it became difficult to keep up with the billings.

McManus also believes there was not enough oversight—especially early in the deployment—because the scope and scale of the war effort was so dramatic. He says he tried to implement the right structure to manage LOGCAP, but it was a difficult issue to resolve on the fly while the war relentlessly continued on.

In hindsight, Kern feels that he should have done several things differently, such as establishing a better funding process by putting monies in categories where they could be quickly retrieved when needed; taking funding from the normal budget process at the start of war; and standardizing common types of tasks in contingency operations and assigning priorities to each type.

McManus wants the many issues that surfaced in Iraq addressed for the future if LOGCAP is going to work for combat support services. He believes the government needs to recognize the risk companies face in providing supplies in a war zone and address the problems that have arisen during the Iraq war. He sees a delicate balance between the need both to protect and provide support to the soldiers and to recognize industry limitations in a war zone. The DOD needs to utilize the huge quantity of data accumulated from audits by DCAA, GAO, and DCMA to determine how to handle similar requirements in the future. "[The] question one has to ask," he says, "is have we asked our companies to do things we shouldn't have? Are we pushing them too far to deliver?"

McManus was concerned the various tasks on the LOGCAP contract were open ended with no limit on the money to spend and grew exponentially until it became a monetary tsunami. The requirements for logistics never stopped coming and won't stop coming until the system is changed to properly accommodate them.

McManus also believes that, if the Army is going to use contractors in combat operations, then they also have to plan to oversee their work. The problem he faced was that auditors and overseers were drawn from within DOD and were therefore counted against the troop cap he had to work with.

The supplemental money appropriated by Congress to the Army for logistics was, as Kern describes it, "colorless," meaning it could be allocated at the discretion of the Army. It could be used for traditional logistics needed to fight the war, such as body armor, night vision goggles, boots, etc., or to fund the LOGCAP contract. The LOGCAP contract continuously exceeded its funding limits in Iraq and ate up much of the supplemental money. Kern says he does not know if supplemental money intended for traditional logistics was instead diverted to LOGCAP to cover overruns, but his "gut says that it was." He says that if a supplemental bill isn't passed in time, money is just taken out of the Army's operations and maintenance (O&M) budget to pay the bills on LOGCAP.

The Army had to make choices when the supplemental money was not there. Funds for LOGCAP operations in Afghanistan and Iraq were usually taken out of the operating costs for the Continental United States. McManus emphasizes that the funding for combat equipment has nothing to do with logistics support. They are two very different commands, and the decision to buy ballistic vests or soft-serve ice cream was not made by one individual. He also thinks that communication about particular needs during the war effort was not good because each command had a difficult enough time just trying to keep up with the chaos and shortages on the ground.

McManus realizes that KBR had to front large amounts of money to keep the contract going because of a combination of problems, both with KBR and the Army. KBR's billing process was slow, but so was the Army bureaucracy's processing of the bills. Because of the "at risk" capital expended by KBR, they had a right under the Defense Federal Acquisition Regulations to cease operations. While McManus had no direct knowledge of work stoppages by KBR, he recognized that such threats may have happened. KBR was under enormous pressures to recoup "at risk" capital.

McManus is sympathetic to KBR. He says costs of LOGCAP were skyrocketing, and that "was terrible for KBR." They were operating with "at risk" money—almost $1 billion at one point. No other company could have gone into Iraq and coped any better with the funding challenges KBR had to face, he believes.

Kern explains the problem in another way. He says that funding for LOGCAP was allocated by the Army civilian management, known as G8, on an incremental or quarterly basis. Funding to KBR depended on the availability, or limits, of supplemental money. He says you "can't spend money unless you have money." The Army had to have the money in its account to fund the contractor

Kern admits that, under the Defense Federal Acquisition Regulations, contractors "will not be obligated to continue work" if the funds to pay them are not available because Congress has not kept up with the supplemental appropriations. Kern insists that the Army needed a company like KBR behind LOGCAP because the cash flow requirements to sustain operations were so considerable; there was no way, he believes, that a smaller company could have handled them.

Both men truly do not think that KBR would have stopped work, despite their contractual right to do so. McManus believes that despite the enormous amount of "at risk" money used by KBR, no one thought they would actually stop operations in Iraq. He thinks that KBR's "ethos" would not have allowed them to stop operations. McManus remembers raising the issue of stoppage to his superiors when he realized how much money KBR was cashflowing. He knew that KBR had a legal right to stop operations and it was a "piece of tactical logistics never seen before."

When asked whether KBR threatened to cease operations at meetings in Kuwait and Iraq, McManus said, "I'm sure it did happen, [but] it didn't get to my level." Kern does not know about specifics of meetings where KBR allegedly threatened to stop work, but he is able to imagine a few ways serious conflicts have arisen. KBR could have failed to submit their invoices on time, their own billing process unable to keep up with the work. The not-to-exceed ceilings on task orders could have been overrun, or there could have been uncertainty regarding what type of work the government would and would not pay for. Kern believes that KBR does have to shoulder some of the blame because they had so many problems with their internal billing.

Having survived careers in the military bureaucracy, both of these generals are realists. Both believe the war service industry contractors are now a permanent fixture in the Army. But they are concerned that the contractors and their employees have the right to refuse work or walk off the job. If KBR walked off the battlefield, Kern says, the Army would have to divert combat forces to handle the supplies. If combat resources or enough vehicles were not available to move supplies, the Army would be stuck. McManus says that, in his experience, war involves constantly making risky decisions. The risk of contractors not performing is something that gets passed down the chain of command or ignored in the pressure to get supplies to the troops. When you make a decision to do something, you have to live with it; it is just a "crap sandwich somebody has to eat."

Both generals are of the opinion, much like Ray Kimball, that contractors are better suited to peacekeeping scenarios, such as Bosnia, than to war or peace enforcement situations in which bombs are exploding, bullets are flying, and an insurgency eliminates the idea of secure territory. McManus says that, when you are not being shot at, logistics are a whole lot easier, as in Bosnia, where things moved quickly and uniformly. McManus believes that combat operations change the whole dynamic.

When you have peace for 10 years, Kern says, then hiring contractors to support the troops starts to look attractive. The rationale is that you only pay contractors when you need them, whereas with military personnel, you pay them no matter what. But war changes everything, and the Army should think again about the consequences of contractors on the battlefield.

Although both generals think that contractors are probably here to stay, when pressed, they admit that in a wartime situation they would rather have Army personnel handling the logistics than contractor personnel. It is, they explain, a matter of command and control. McManus said if he had to do it over and was in position to make the decision, he would use only soldiers on the battlefield—"that's why we have an army. That's what it's for." He sees it as much simpler to have military personnel handle the logistics, ensuring clarity in command and control and in the deployment of assets.

Kern agrees, saying that he "would have preferred using military over contractors. More control. You train them and know what you have. You haven't recruited, trained, and equipped contractors. You don't have NCO's with them all the time. You don't know their families."

The Government Accountability Office lends weight to this concern. On September 22, 2006, they released a letter report to a subcommittee of the House Committee on Government Reform describing the difficulty of screening contractor employees. They concluded:

DOD and contractors have difficulty conducting comprehensive background screenings for U.S. and foreign nationals because of a lack of resources and inaccurate, missing, or inaccessible data. . . .Recognizing the limitations of data, military officials we interviewed who were responsible for security at installations in Iraq and elsewhere told us that they take steps to mitigate the risks contractors, particularly non-U.S. contractors pose. For example, officials from most of the units we spoke with told us that contractor employees are routinely searched as they enter and leave the installation, while the majority of the units we spoke with told us that they interviewed some contractor employees before granting them access to the base.

These findings are consistent with with the experience of Adam Roe, the Army truck driver who says he was instructed by base commanders to keep track of KBR's foreign national truck drivers whenever they had a layover at a forward operating base.

In a U.S. Army War College research project called "Increasing Combat Support and Combat Service Support Units in the U.S. Military," Lieutentant Colonel Paul M. Burnham, U.S. Army Reserve, addresses the problem of having to rely on contractors as a result of the military's deactivation of many of its support services units. Because "contractor support cannot perform equally to military units in high intensity conflict,." he asserts that the military "must reinvest in additional CS [Combat Support] and CSS [Combat Services Support] units to support the full spectrum of operational requirements of high intensity conflict." In addition, Burnham proposes eliminating or minimizing "large logistics contracts to support the U.S. Military in high intensity conflict areas."

A dramatic and tragic incident with a KBR convoy, in addition to the 2004 ambush discussed in Chapter 9, underscored the problem of using civilians in the battlefield. In September 2005, KBR truck driver Preston Wheeler was in the target of an ambush that wounded him and killed three of his fellow KBR truck drivers. What made this ambush unique was that Wheeler videotaped the incident, and it was shown on network television a year later.

The tape shows that the military escorts took a wrong turn and ended up bringing the whole convoy into a dead end. On the way back, they were attacked by insurgents. It appears from the tape that the Army escort left the area and that the KBR truck drivers were unable to help themselves. Two of the drivers were dragged from the truck and executed in front of Wheeler and his camera. He kept rolling the tape despite being wounded in the arm.

Wheeler claims he was abandoned by the Army, who returned to fight the insurgents 45 minutes later. The Army denied that accusation and said they were following correct Army procedures. It may be impossible to know who was right in this chaotic situation, but Ray Kimball believes it would have had a better outcome if the truck drivers had been soldiers. "Would it have gone down differently if it was a purely military convoy? Absolutely, because the other drivers would have brought fire to bear and tried to push through as well," he said after viewing the convoy tape. "Once again, here was a situation where civilian truck drivers were in a combat, peace-enforcement type of system and were not able to defend themselves."

Most military men who have dealt with the stress of combat understand the extreme importance of cohesiveness and trust in Army units. In the heat and fear of war, men fight for their unit and their buddies. They are willing to stay together and fight against their own self-interest because they have bonded with in the others in their unit. Many soldiers who are wounded and sent home feel this bond so strongly they yearn to rejoin their unit back on the battlefield, even before they are healthy enough to do so. McManus and Kern know that the logistics teams need that same motivation, especially now in insurgency-type conflicts, where even non-combat units face serious danger away from the protected bases.

Deputy Under Secretary of Defense for Logistics and Materiel Readiness Jack Bell has a different view of the contractors' performance in the Iraq and Afghanistan combat theaters. He was a COO for various airlines before serving as the first chief of staff of the State Department's Afghanistan Reconstruction Group (ARG) in Kabul, Afghanistan, and then as the deputy under secretary of the Army for four months in August 2005. He thinks that KBR fulfilled their commitment and that there has been no significant problem with contractors refusing to serve in the theater of battle. He has read the GAO and IG reports on this issue but still holds that contractors worked fine on the battlefield. He declined to comment on the potential problems raised by contractors' right to walk off the job because he did not want to talk about "hypothetical" problems.

The idea that soldiers were unhappy with the lack of supplies and equipment during the war was dismissed by Bell, saying that "soldiers complaining on the battlefield is actually a sign of good morale as far as we are concerned."

Any billing problems with KBR have been solved, he believes, with the government getting refunds from the company for any inappropriate charges. He stressed that contractors on the battlefield were working, but is always concerned about the risk to contractors on the battlefield.

The Army has assured him, he says, that any shortages were resolved quickly. "To our knowledge, none of our warfighters suffered long-term adverse consequences due to the failure to provide them the equipment or supplies they needed to conduct the war fight," he said during our interview with him. He added that the Army Materiel Command and the Army Field Support Command assured him that any problems did not matter in the long run.

When he was informed of this statement from Under Secretary Bell, Representative Henry Waxman gave this strong rebuke:

> Any service member who has been to Iraq will tell you that it's idiotic to claim there have not been significant consequences from the pervasive equipment and supply shortages. Months after the invasion, 40,000 troops lacked protective Kevlar plates for body armor vests. The Army division patrolling the Sunni triangle had only nine portable radio jammers to protect against IEDs, and the 2nd brigade of this division had only one. Forty-six of the 1st Armored Division's 140 Bradley fighting vehicles were "dead-lined," and 80 of its Humvees were taken out of service because of a lack of spare parts. Visiting congressional staff were pulled aside and begged for more night vision goggles. At the same time, Halliburton was allowed to bill the taxpayer for thousands of meals it never served, charge $45 for a case of soda, and rack up millions of dollars in unjustified "overhead" and "award" fees. Lives have been lost because of the inexcusable supply shortages.

It is hard to understand what the DOD would count as "long-term consequences" and if that category excludes injury, health problems from poor food and contaminated water, dehydration from lack of water, heat exhaustion because of unfixed air conditioners, or many of the other problems described by the soldiers we interviewed.

Although Generals McManus and Kern both appeared frustrated by their experiences in Iraq, they feel they did their best with a bad situation. McManus admits that soldiers did have to make due without the necessary equipment and says the Iraq war is about as imperfect a war as you can support. He thinks the Army should not have forced the troops to rely so much on their own resourcefulness to do the amazing things they accomplished in such difficult conditions.

Upset about being unable to make changes from within the system to protect the soldiers, McManus says that speaking up had its price: "Damned if you do, damned if you don't. If you raise stink in uniform you kind of disappear. If you retire and say something, they say you should have said something when you were on active duty and you're not credible now."

⌒

General Kern also had the unhappy task of being the military's internal investigator into the abuses at the Abu Ghraib prison that came to light in

June 2004. He now teaches at West Point and is a member of the Cohen Group, a consulting and influence group headed by former Secretary of Defense William Cohen. McManus now works for Northrop Grumman Corporation's vice president for strategic logistics, Tactical Systems Division, a subcontractor on some KBR contracts.

There have been numerous reports from the GAO, the Congress, and the press about the readiness problem the Army and the National Guard currently face, and many worry that the Army is falling to its lowest readiness state in many years. But Donald Rumsfeld said this to a group of military and civilian personnel in a September 2006 speech: "I'm convinced that with the distance of a few years, we'll all be able to look back at this time and see that, while a number of things that have been accomplished have been controversial . . .we are becoming a stronger, better equipped, a more flexible and considerably more capable force."

Generals Kern and McManus had to go to war with the secretary of defense they had.

CHAPTER 25

THE WAR SERVICE INDUSTRY— WHAT NOW?

The war service industry may be here to stay. In the wake of 9/11, the war on terrorism, and the wars in Afghanistan and Iraq, this fledgling industry has grown rapidly and is now firmly rooted in the system. More contractors have worked in Iraq than in any other conflict in American history.[1] The question now is what form the industry will take in future conflicts; its answer will have profound implications for our troops and their ability to fight effectively and survive.

Outsourcing combat logistics support and certain security duties was sold on the premise that private enterprise could do the job more efficiently and cheaply than the military by freeing up more troops to be trigger pullers. That was the theory. In reality, however, privatization has had a negative impact on the troops in war zones. There are numerous anecdotal stories of supplies not getting to the troops or unmonitored security operators running roughshod over Iraqi civilians. But, at the same time, there is evidence that these problems are systemic, much of it attributed to insufficient government oversight over these contractors.

The fundamental danger of outsourcing the critically important supply chain lies in the contractor's ability to quit the battlefield, to decide not to perform because of the dangers involved. There is no constitutional basis for compelling a contractor to perform on a contract. In short, military commanders cannot rely on contractors to be there when it counts. They might turn out to be unable or unwilling to transport supplies in a particular hostile environment, or they might decide to cease operations altogether. In a 2005 U.S. Army War College Strategy Research Project on using contractors for combat support, Lieutenant Colonel Paul Burnham reported that "the issue (willingness of contractors to deploy) surfaced during OIF (Operation Iraqi Freedom) when contractors refused to work when the situation became very hostile, causing the involuntary extension of several U.S. Army transportation units during OIF to mitigate the problem . . .As stated in a June 2003 GAO report, 'contractor employees could become unavailable due to enemy activity or accidents.' This unavailability was a real problem in OIF."[2]

The Army did not plan for the possibility of contractors refusing to perform, even though the Department of Defense inspector general had warned them of the possibility as far back as 1991.[3] The attitude of Army brass was that contractors would do their job; they simply would not cease operations or quit the battlefield. But there was no precedent to support that attitude—it was nothing more than wishful thinking.

There has been an effort by the Congress to close a loophole by applying the UCMJ to contractor conduct in a war zone. During the passage of the Pentagon's fiscal year 2007 budget legislation (P.L. 109–364), Senator Lindsey Graham (R-SC), added a change to the applicability of the UCMJ to include "contingency operations". This change went unnoticed until picked up by the media in January 2007. The change technically would bring contractors under the UCMJ during a contingency operation such as the conflict in Iraq. Before, contractors would only be under the UCMJ when a war was declared by Congress. The last time that happened was in World War II.

Because of the change to the UCMJ, there has been much speculation in the media, and over the internet, about how, or if, this change would actually be applied to contractors. Would it be used only for serious felonies committed by contractors in the theater of war? Or, would it be used for contract performance violations such as refusing a direct order to perform on the contract? Will this be the tool needed to bring contractor performance under the command and control of military commanders? Does it eliminate the "just say no" factor? Without specific interpretation of this new law or precedents created from case law, it could be interpreted in many ways and used for violations of the UCMJ that are "far less serious than the crimes that Congress envisioned when drafting the bill."[4]

But, according to attorney Scott Horton, an adjunct professor of law at Columbia University, chairman of the International Law Committee at the New York City Bar Association, and a member of Council on Foreign Relations, there is a constitutional question of prosecuting contractors under the UCMJ. He said, the "UCMJ always had provisions in it permitting the prosecution of what were historically called 'camp followers,' and today would be called military contractors. Back during the Vietnam war, this provision was held to apply only in times of 'declared war,' which effectively rendered it moot, since the US doesn't declare war any more. Why did the court do this? Because if applied, this provision would face an immediate constitutional dilemma. That's Reid v. Covert, 354 U.S. 1 (1975), holding that the 5th and 6th amendments protect U.S. citizens abroad, so that the 5th amendment right to a grand jury and the 6th amendment right to a jury trial (neither present in the UCMJ) preclude military prosecutions. With the limitation about 'declared wars' removed, the underlying question of constitutionality remains."[5]

In addition, Horton said, "Now Congress attempted to deal with this problem by enacting the Military Extraterritorial Jurisdiction Act (MEJA) which does provide a long-arm for criminal prosecution of military contractors abroad. The problem in its essence is not absence of a statutory basis for prosecutions, but a failure of prosecutorial will. For instance, of the cases referred to the ED (Eastern District) VA (Virginia) for review and prosecution, not a single case has been commenced. DOJ (Department of Justice) is exercising discretion not to prosecute . . . If a military prosecutor were to attempt to bring a case, he'd face the constitutional issue right up front, and it's reasonably clear that the action would be a long shot. I don't see such cases being brought."[6]

Horton suggested that the only way the UCMJ could be applied to contractors is if a contractor is also a reservist and is activated by the military, thus placing the contractor under the UCMJ as an active duty soldier for the purpose of prosecution.[7]

Eugene R. Fidell, president of the National Institute of Military Justice, echoed Horton by saying "Ultimately, if this power is used, it will create a substantial issue that would likely reach the Supreme Court, and it will put us at odds with contemporary international standards."[8] Adding to the problem of prosecuting civilians in military courts, Fidell said there has been a history of civilian convictions in military courts being thrown out by U.S. courts.[9]

However, Horton felt that there may be reasons the Supreme Court would be willing to overrule (or more likely distinguish) those cases today. Those reasons include the fact that military justice has trended toward a convergence with civilian criminal justice system norms and principles; the establishment of the Court of Appeals for the Armed Forces with discretionary appeals to the Supreme Court; contractors on the battlefield are performing many duties which historically have been performed by soldiers in past wars; therefore contractors are taking "the king's shilling, and so should be subject to the king's justice."[10]

It may take many years to sort out how this law will be, or can be, applied to contractors on the battlefield. It is unlikely to affect how contractors perform in the near future.

Whether or not contractors will ultimately be subject to military law, it remains the contractors' emphasis on profit over all else clashes sharply with the priorities of the Army. Capitalism simply does not mesh with the way the Army operates on the battlefield. Business and the military operate on different value systems and rules of employment. Army personnel take a strict oath and give up some of their rights in order to fight effectively as a unit. The contractor and its employees, no matter how patriotic they may feel, have their own self-interest as their number one priority.

However, the dangers to contractor employees on the battlefield are real. According to the Department of Labor, 641 contractors had died in Iraq by October 2006, including Americans and foreign nationals. At the same time, the organization, icasualties.org, which tracks contractor casualties in Iraq, listed 140 American contractor deaths, most involving private security employees and American truck drivers.[11]

If a contractor refuses to perform, the issue is normally handled through the contractual remedies available to the Army. This means that combat commanders lose command and control of the supply chain wherever contractors are being relied on to perform under hostile conditions. They cannot relieve the contractor of their duties, as they can with failing military officers. When the contactor fails to supply the troops, the job then falls to the unprepared and overextended troops themselves.

Soldiers have had to take over some of the contractors' duties out of necessity, such as driving supply trucks, guarding foreign national contractor employees on base, repairing equipment the contractor was supposed to have fixed, and providing force protection to supply convoys. In addition, when contractors are kidnapped, troops are diverted from their regular duties to find them. Thus, the concept of freeing up troops to be trigger pullers does not seem to have been fully realized. If the Army is going to continue to rely on the war service industry to get supplies to the troops on the battlefield, they will face the possibility of having to divert a sizeable number of soldiers to oversee the contractors or take over their duties when they fail to perform.

Leaving soldiers out in the remote sites without adequate food, water, ammunition, repair parts, and other combat equipment, unfairly exposes them to even more risk than they already have to face in a war. Taking short cuts that deprive the troops of safe water is not acceptable. If, as alleged, KBR allowed highly contaminated wastewater to be used unknowingly by the troops, it potentially exposed them to the risk of serious illnesses and even death. Such incidents could degrade the combat readiness of the Army to fight and win.

KBR has been moving increasingly toward replacing American workers with foreign nationals—mainly Nepalis, Pakistani, and Filipino workers hired through subcontractors. This shift creates additional problems for the Army, especially in the area of base security. How are these foreign nationals vetted? Are they vetted at all? How easy would it be for insurgents to infiltrate these workers or bribe them to plant IEDs on base? Who's watching them? Another potential problem is theft of supplies, especially combat equipment from the warehouses, to be sold on the black market, possibly to insurgents, leaving the troops short on critical equipment and exposing them to attack.

The Army also faces new problems related to some subcontractors' use of foreign nationals—human trafficking and worker abuse. Defense Department investigators have found evidence of a practice, widespread among contractors and subcontractors in Iraq, of "holding and withholding employee passports to, among other things, prevent employees 'jumping' to other employers." This practice is in direct violation of human trafficking laws.[12] Complaints have also surfaced of foreign nationals being subjected to poor sanitation, squalid living conditions, and poor medical care.[13] On April 19, 2006, the Joint Contracting Command—Iraq/Afghanistan issued a memorandum to all contractors ordering them to cease the practice of withholding passports and requiring a minimum of 50 feet of acceptable square footage of personal living space per worker.[14] It is inevitable, as more foreign nationals are brought in to work in Iraq, that problems of abuse will continue to surface, requiring the military to pay even more attention to the contractors. With little oversight personnel in the theater, this responsibility will ultimately fall to already overburdened soldiers.

Many of the contractor problems in Iraq have largely gone unnoticed by the Pentagon, mainly due to a lack of competent oversight personnel on site. Given the size, complexity, and rapid expansion of the LOGCAP contract, the Department of Defense has not provided enough personnel to conduct an adequate surveillance of the contract.[15] Even the Department's inspector general did not have any personnel in Iraq until mid-2006. With little oversight, the war service industry has been largely unregulated. There are no controls over whom they hire or with whom they can subcontract. The Pentagon has had to deal with this new contractor phenomenon while trying to manage a war at the same time. The oversight rules, regulations, and plans needed for this industry have not caught up to the accelerated spending seen in Iraq contracting. This has, unfortunately, allowed the war service industry to become riddled fraud and waste. Since Defense Department auditors usually evaluate future contract costs based on the historical costs of the original contract, the fraud and waste of the original contract becomes the new baseline for cost in future contracts.

Administrative contracting and LOGCAP personnel on the ground in Iraq have been too overwhelmed by their regular duties to provide any type of performance monitoring of the contractor. Their time on the job has often been taken up with putting out unexpected management fires and fighting with contractor managers. In the United States, the Defense Department often assigns complete staffs of administrators to work on site at large contractors to manage contracts and look after the interests of the government. In Iraq, most military sites had only one or two contract managers and one LOGCAP official to handle the load.

Failing to monitor contracts is also failing the troops. It allows contractors to do what they want, without having to worry much about government interference. In September 2006, GAO Comptroller General David Walker testified before the House Appropriations Committee's Defense Subcommittee that the Pentagon's overworked acquisitions staff has been mismanaging contractors, resulting in lost time and money and shortchanging the war fighting capabilities of the troops.[16] Jeffery R. Smith, a former CIA general counsel who now works at the law firm Arnold & Porter and represents military contractors, told *Business Week* in July 2006 that, without more oversight, the worst companies will become a permanent part of the war service industry. "What has happened in Iraq is just disgraceful. Iraq has attracted patriots and crooks—and there are probably some crooked patriots. We're going to be cleaning that up for years to come, I fear."[17]

With the Pentagon playing such a limited role, oversight responsibility has fallen on the Congress and the power of the *qui tam* provisions of the Federal False Claims Act. Until January 2007, congressional oversight depended almost entirely on the limited powers of Representative Henry Waxman, the ranking Democrat on the House Committee on Government Reform, and Senator Byron Dorgan, chairman of the Senate Democratic Policy Committee. Their efforts have helped expose some of the contract abuses in Iraq, but there was only so much they could do from their position in the minority party. With Waxman now taking over chairmanship of the Government Reform Committee and the Democratic Policy Committee gaining in power as a consequence of the Democrats' electoral victory, congressional oversight should increase significantly.

The *qui tam* provision of the Federal False Claims Act, also known as the whistleblowers law, gives whistleblowers with direct knowledge of contractor fraud the means to bring a lawsuit, on behalf of the government, against the contractor. When such a lawsuit is filed, the Department of Justice is mandated by law to investigate the allegations. If the suit is successful, the whistleblower receives a percentage of any money recovered by the government. Although such lawsuits are filed under seal, it is likely that many involving contractors in Iraq have already been filed and are currently being investigated. *Qui tam* is a powerful tool to bring accountability to the contracting process. These lawsuits are often the last resort for the taxpayer.

Even with its limited oversight activity, the Defense Contract Audit Agency (DCAA) still identified $2.1 billion in questioned costs and $1.4 billion in unsupported costs in Iraq contracts between February 2003 and February 2006.[18] These findings are normally provided to contracting officers for their negotiations with the contractors. But, because of contractor and political pressures, contracting officers may find it very difficult to justify cost reductions on contracts based on DCAA's findings.

Despite KBR's widely reported performance problems and questionable costs, the Army, instead of disciplining the contractor by withholding its award fee, awarded it $72 million in performance bonuses in 2005, giving it top ratings of "excellent" and "very good." It would have been interesting to see ratings from the military commanders and troops on the ground who had to depend on KBR,[19] especially those allegedly subjected to the contractors' occasional threats to stop work in the war zone.

The prediction that privatization would save money has not been proven true. The Pentagon has been unable to provide any information—positive or negative—on the cost effectiveness of using contractors instead of troops for combat support. In fact, the record keeping in this war has been so chaotic that until the late fall of 2006, the Pentagon had no accurate census of how many contractors and contracts they had in Iraq.

The GAO, along with the Congressional Budget Office and Congressional Research Service, maintained that Pentagon data on the costs of war "cannot be trusted."[20] What we do know is that, as of 2006, the United States has appropriated more than $300 billion for the war in Iraq, with another $127 billion to $160 billion more being sought by the Pentagon for 2007.[21] Before the war, the White House estimated the total cost would be about $50 billion. With the "blank check" funding of supplemental appropriations, the possibility of inflated labor costs, and billions in unsupported and questioned costs, it may take years, even decades, to sort out the actual costs of using contractors versus troops for combat support.

The runaway costs of the LOGCAP contract have contributed to a funding problem for the Army that has affected their ability to repair or replace necessary combat equipment for the troops. Army Chief of Staff General Peter J. Schoomaker testified before Congress in 2006 that the costs of repairing or replacing war equipment had reached $12 billion to $13 billion a year.[22] An internal Army document provided to the *New York Times* in 2006 says that "the Army needs $66.1 billion to make up for all of its equipment shortfalls."[23] Many soldiers have no access during their training to such important fighting equipment as M-4 rifles and the long-range surveillance systems used to spot insurgents laying down IEDs.[24] Army officials had to cut $3 billion in 2005 and 2006 from programs for weapons that are in heavy use in Iraq.[25] With LOGCAP costs eating up much of the supplemental money, money originally allocated for combat equipment may also have been eroded. Equipment shortages have been widely reported in the media, as have the complaints of soldiers. The Army could afford to pay the LOGCAP costs for such perks as soft-serve ice cream, recreational facilities, pastry chefs, and more, but somehow couldn't afford night vision goggles, body armor, or air conditioning units for the troops.

General Kern believes the Army had to pay their contractors in Iraq by shifting money from other budgets, such as purchasing combat equipment, to pay for LOGCAP.[26] So, what has been done to get the troops the equipment they desperately need? Military families have had to raise money to buy air conditioners and other very basic supplies for their overheated sons and daughters in the military. The entertainer Cher helped organize an effort to buy upgraded helmets to better protect the troops.[27] Soldiers have been asking relatives and friends to help them obtain supplies of coagulating bandages and agents to stop arterial bleeding, which they were supposed to get for front-line battles but never received.[28] Some soldiers, like Bobby Yen, have had their parents buy upgraded body armor from catalogs.

The use of private security firms on the battlefield has also created difficulties for the military relating to command and control. These contractors have been operating in the war zone with little coordination from the military, which sometimes doesn't even know where the contractors are operating. Several security operators have been arrested and jailed in Iraq for the allegedly shooting at Marines.[29] Will Hough has said he witnessed colleagues shooting at Iraqi civilians and running their cars off the road (allegations that the contractor has disputed). Other former security operators voiced similar charges. Two former employees of the security contractor firm Triple Canopy filed a lawsuit in 2006 claiming that their supervisor deliberately shot at Iraqi vehicles and civilians (The company and the supervisor have denied any wrong doing).[30] Many security employees operate in Iraq with little training, little supervision, and no rules governing their actions. When they run loose on the battlefield, it affects the mission of the military and sometimes puts troops in harm's way. The abuses of security contractors enrage the Iraqi civilian population, and the troops end up taking the brunt of this anger.

Ideally, if the war service industry is to continue, it should be limited to providing services on secure, fortified installations with sufficient oversight to monitor performance and costs. The policy of privatizing the supply chain on the battlefield introduces a loss of command and control on the part of combat commanders who depend on supplies in order to complete their missions successfully. These commanders can't rely on contractors to be there when it counts, yet, because they can't relieve them of command on the battlefield, they have little power to quickly solve problems in the life-and-death reality of combat. Off base, the military should take back responsibility for the supply chain in war zones. Private security firms should also be limited to guarding reconstruction projects and maybe providing security on military facilities, not escorting convoys or providing other services that would have them running loose on the battlefield.

The Pentagon's response to these suggestions might be that there are not enough military personnel to fully man the supply chain in a war. That may be true if the number of troops available is artificially limited, as was the case in Iraq, but the experience of past wars, such as the first Gulf War, shows that it is possible to deploy enough support troops to fully operate the supply chain.

If the Pentagon insists on maintaining the policy of outsourcing the supply chain, creativity will be needed to make it work. For example, General Paul Kern, the former commander of the Army Material Command, floated an idea in the Pentagon of contracting with special trucking companies manned by Army reservists. He suggested that, as a condition of a contract, the trucking companies would be manned and run in peacetime mainly by reservists. Then, when troops are deployed to a war zone, these companies could be activated as Army reserve soldiers and placed under the control of combat commanders, subject to the Uniform Code of Military Justice.[31]

This concept does have precedents. The Air Force has had a program called the Civil Reserve Air Fleet, known as CRAF, since the Korean War. CRAF gave incentives to passenger- and cargo-based U.S. airlines if for making a certain percentage of their commercial aircraft available to be called up during a time of war. In the Gulf War, two thirds of the troops and one quarter of the cargo were moved by CRAF flights. The only difference in Kern's plan is that the trucking units, and perhaps other units such as food catering, would mainly be staffed with reservists who could be ready to fight when needed.

The Pentagon is not an institution known for its creative thinking. Thus, it is not surprising, especially that Rumsfeld was secretary of defense at the time, that General Kern's idea did not receive a full hearing within the Pentagon bureaucracy. But in the future, the Pentagon civilian and military decision makers will need to be both more creative and more realistic about how the supply chain affects troops in a war zone.

Examining "numerous facets of Halliburton's contract with the U.S. military," the GAO found in July 2004 " . . .significant problems in almost every area, including ineffective planning, inadequate cost control, insufficient training of contract management officials, and a pattern of recurring problems with controlling costs, meeting schedules, documenting purchases, and overseeing subcontractors."[32] The combination of limited oversight and ineffective contract management on the part of the Pentagon and the "significant problems" in KBR's execution of the contract has resulted in a deterioration of the troops' combat capabilities, not to mention skyrocketing costs to the taxpayer.

If the war service industry is here to stay, how will we feed the contractor beast after Iraq and Afghanistan, in the absence of any hot war or occupation? Will the industry and those who benefit from it try to influence our politics and foreign policy, perhaps pushing the country into some new war or occupation to keep the money flowing? How can costs be controlled and oversight provided to make sure contractors fulfill their commitments? This question will remain especially pressing so long as the Pentagon is unable to raise oversight staffing levels to meet the demands of LOGCAP and other contracts for operations in Iraq. How should the Pentagon deal with the possibility of contractors suddenly deciding to quit the battlefield and leaving our troops in the lurch? Making contractors subject to the UCMJ most likely will not override a contractor employee's constitutional rights to quit their job or fail to perform contractually. These and other questions need to be answered so that the disheartening and disastrous stories you have read in this book are not repeated. Our troops were betrayed by the policy of privatization in Iraq. They deserve better from their government.

AFTERWORD

All of the contractor personnel and the troops profiled in this book were deeply affected by what they saw and experienced in Iraq. Many of them are working in various ways back in the United States to try to improve conditions for the soldiers who are still there. As the level of disillusionment with the war rises, more and more soldiers and contractor employees are coming forward with disturbing tales of a failed system. Here is what has happened to some of our interview subjects once they left the war and the war service industry.

— Rick Lamberth has settled in the Northern Virginia area and currently works for a defense contractor as a logistician. He is fighting to regain his reputation after a reprimand was issued to him in December 2006. Lamberth is still a Major in the Army reserves and drills on weekends with an Army Corps of Engineers unit.

— Perry Jefferies, Ray Kimball, and Bobby Yen all joined Iraq and Afghanistan Veterans of America (IAVA) and regularly contribute blogs to its website about the major issues of the war and their effects on veterans. They also occasionally tour colleges to talk about the war. Perry Jefferies works at the blood bank at Fort Hood and often sees soldiers recently returned from Iraq. Bobby Yen lives in Los Angeles and works as a computer programmer. Ray Kimball was promoted to major and now teaches at West Point.

— Robert Isakson is still running his disaster relief company and is waiting for the appeal on his original lawsuit to work its way through the courts. Though Custer Battles as a company is defunct, Isakson and Grayson filed a new *qui tam* suit alleging that Custer Battles used political connections in the DOD to set up a new sham company to get contracts from the DOD in Iraq. That company, called Danubia, bought Custer Battles's equipment and has hired much of their personnel.

—David List is scheduled to be deployed back to Iraq, and Adam Roe is working for a private contractor near Fort Hood, Texas. Roe still tries to help his fellow soldiers cope with their experiences in Iraq.

—Ben Carter is back in the United States and, ironically, suffers chronic gastrointestinal problems that may be related to the water he drank in Iraq. He has settled in Montana and has filed a claim to KBR for workman's compensation and trying to put his life back together. He continues to work with the Congress and the DOD inspector general, who has opened an investigation into the bad water supplied by KBR across Iraq.

—David Wilson is still driving a truck around the country and still fuming about how KBR treated him and other truck drivers. James Warren is back driving a truck around the country with his wife.

—Will Hough is working hard to improve his health and regain his career as a personal trainer. He worries about the young vets coming home from this war without sufficient support from their government.

—Congressmen Waxman and Davis are still jousting over Iraq investigation, though. they have switched roles now that Waxman has become the chair of the committee. With the chairmanship and its power to issue subpoenas, Waxman is determined to do the oversight on KBR and other contractors that he prevented from doing for the past five years. As disillusionment with the war grows, increasing numbers of soldiers and contractor personnel are sharing stories of contractor fraud, waste, and ineffectiveness with the committee's expanded staff.

APPENDIX

What follows is expanded information on the LOGCAP contract, oversight, contingency contracting concepts, and other information addressed in this book.

Origins of Outsourcing

Substantial reductions in troop strength occurred after the end of the cold war, especially within logistics and support units. Between the Gulf and Iraq wars, the U.S. Army saw a 40 percent reduction in manpower. These reductions created a dependence on outsourcing logistics support, especially combat support, and certain security duties, during world-wide conflicts, now called contingency (a term used for an "event") operations. When combat units storm onto a battlefield, logistics support still has to be there. To make up for the gap between combat units and logistics units created from force reductions, the DOD made the decision to outsource those previous military support functions to contractors. Outsourcing support for contingency operations thus begat a new form of DOD procurement called "contingency contracting" and the emergence of a new industry—the war service industry, to support contingency troop mobilization and operations.

Contingency Operations

Contingency operations, as defined by globalsecurity.org, are military actions deployed in support of national policy short of war. These operations are usually undertaken when "vital national interests are at stake and when direct and indirect diplomacy or other forms of influence have been exhausted or need to be supplemented by either a show of force or a direct military action."

Funding Contingency Operations

DOD components do not normally budget for contingency operations. Such funding is accomplished initially through the use of appropriated funds until emergency supplemental money is appropriated by the Congress. Supplemental funding has been the most frequent means of financing contingency military operations including contracting.

Contingency Contracting

Contingency contracting is direct contracting support to tactical and operational forces engaged in the full spectrum of armed conflict and military operations (both domestic and overseas), including war, other military operations, and disaster or emergency relief. Contingency contracting support has evolved from purchases not greater than the simplified threshold to defense procurement services for military operations such as in Iraq.

LOGCAP

The Logistics Civil Augmentation Program, known by the acronym "LOGCAP," is an initiative by the U.S. Army to use civilian contractors to provide certain services such as supplies, construction of base facilities, feeding and maintaining base infrastructure in wartime and other contingency operations in support of U.S. military forces. It was designed to provide timely support for unplanned, short-notice contingency operations.

History and Development of the LOGCAP contract

During Vietnam and Gulf War I, the military relied on contractors primarily to maintain and operate sophisticated weapon systems such as guided missiles and other tech-heavy, computer-operated, systems. Usually, they were manufacturing representatives who gave the military its own technical support, but, with few exceptions, remained out of harm's way. Contractors did not replace military tasks in those wars but merely provided skills the military lacked.

Privatizing military functions in modern warfare was a post Vietnam War idea that gained traction after the end of the "Cold War." The Pentagon downsized the military, in the late 1980s, in response to Congressional demands as part of the "peace dividend." Most of the cuts occurred in the support areas, such as a 60 percent reduction in the AMC, creating a large gap in the military's ability to support troops engaged in the post cold war spread of conflicts. At the same time, the rest of the DOD budget, especially for expensive weapon systems and aircraft, has had a healthy growth in the past seven years. The DOD wanted to hold on to many of its glamorous weapons systems in development so support and logistics became an easy target for cuts. The gap formed as a result of the budget disparity, created a reliance on private contractors to make up for the lack of support and logistics soldiers. The Pentagon believed that channeling corporate efficiency to the military would lead to cost savings and free up troops as "trigger pullers."

To implement this reliance, the Pentagon created the Logistics Civil Augmentation Program (LOGCAP) in December 1985 in response to the Defense Appropriations Law, enacted in 1983–84, that directed DOD set up a contingency contract for support of military mobilization deployment actions. The Pentagon hierarchy intended that LOGCAP provide rapid, responsive and flexible support to the Army. This contract would be a non-traditional method of logistics integrated into an Army steeped in tradition. Not surprisingly, LOGCAP caused resistance among Army brass. Military commanders, at the time, expressed considerable distrust of a contractor's ability to supply troops on the battlefield because they would be too slow, unreliable, and uncontrollable.

In an effort to reduce these concerns, the Department of the Army decided to decentralize the LOGCAP process to active numbered Armies—each would develop, award, and administer their own LOGCAP contracts. For many reasons, the decentralization concept did not work well and, by 1990, in response to continued concern by military commanders of contractors on the battlefield, the Army limited LOGCAP chiefly to administrative support in non-hostile environments. In doing so, the Army decided to centralize LOGCAP and establish it as an umbrella support contract awarded to one contractor. Operation Desert Storm (ODS), in 1990–91, provided an opportunity for LOGCAP planners to conduct field-testing of LOGCAP that could be used for future events. After ODS, the Army felt LOGCAP would work for future contingency operations and decided to move forward with implementing the contract.

❧

In 1992, when Dick Cheney was Secretary of Defense under President George H.W. Bush, the DOD awarded a $3.9 million contract (later raised to $9 million) to Halliburton's subsidiary, KBR (was also known as Kellogg, Brown and Root). The contract was awarded to study how private military contractors could provide support to soldiers on the battlefield around the world. KBR's classified report convinced the DOD it was possible to award one umbrella contract to a contractor to provide all the support services necessary in a conflict. As a result, the Pentagon created a "super contract" that became known as LOGCAP Umbrella Support Contract (also dubbed "the mother of all service contracts").

The Army awarded the first LOGCAP contract (LOGCAP I) to Brown & Root (now KBR) in August 1992 that provided support to contingency operations in Haiti, Somalia and the Balkans. In 1995, Cheney became the CEO of Halliburton. Under Cheney's leadership, Halliburton moved up from 73rd to 18th on the Pentagon's list of top contractors.

However, in 1997, KBR lost the contract when the Army awarded LOGCAP (LOGCAP II) to DynCorp Services to continue operations in the Balkans. But in January 2001, Cheney became Vice President of the United States and, in December 2001, KBR managed to regain award of LOGCAP III. For the war in Afghanistan and Iraq, the Army decided to use LOGCAP III to provide logistics support to its troops. Primarily due to a sharp increase of contracting connected to the war in Iraq and Afghanistan, Halliburton has increased its receipt of contracting dollars by 600 percent between 2000 and 2005 making it the fastest growing defense contractor during that period of time.

∽

In 2003, the Pentagon, under Secretary of Defense Donald Rumsfeld, started a plan to increase its long-term reliance on contractors. The plan, called the "Third Wave," was overseen by then Army Secretary Thomas White. It called for replacing up to 214,000 military and civilian positions that would go to private contractors. Although White put the plan on the back burner for a while, it gained new life. News reports, at the time, suggested there would be a replacement of 20,000 support military personnel with private contractors by October 2005, with a target of 300,000 more within the decade. However, Secretary White, in a memorandum dated March 8, 2002, warned the Army "lacked the basic information needed to manage effectively its expanding force of private contractors." In addition, he wrote "Currently, Army planners and programmers lack visibility at the Departmental level into the labor and costs associated with the contract workforce and of the organizations and missions supported by them." Little did he know how true his admonition would become in Iraq.

LOGCAP Funding

LOGCAP funding has depended primarily on supplemental funding appropriated by Congress. In the absence of supplemental funding, DoD components finance contingency operations and contracting through existing appropriations—usually taken from the Component's Operations and Maintenance budget, that the Army calls "cash flowing." When supplemental appropriations is passed, the money, normally "colorless" in that is a "blank check" to be used as determined by the Army, is allocated to the Office of Management and Budget (OMB). OMB, in turn, apportions the money to the Under Secretary of Defense (Comptroller) who then apportions the money down to the military services. In the case of the Army, to the Army Resource Manager, or G8.

Supplemental money is allocated to the Army, by OMB, incrementally, usually on a quarterly basis. If the incremental money is used up before the end of a quarter or new supplemental funding is delayed, a cash flowing problem is created and money has to be shifted from the regular O&M budget. Such "cash flowing" causes a strain on the Army's budget that could, for example, affect their ability to purchase needed combat equipment in order to fund LOGCAP.

Contract Oversight

With almost two billion dollars a week being spent on the war in Iraq and Afghanistan, spending on government oversight has declined. The DOD has experienced massive budget and staff cutbacks in contract oversight personnel. In the 1990s, Legislation was passed by Congress under "acquisition reform" and pushed by the defense industry, to cut back on the number of DOD contracting and oversight personnel. Downsizing continued under then Vice President Al Gore's "Reinvention of Government" initiatives. The Defense Contract Management Agency (DCMA), the agency that manages DOD contracts, had its staffing levels cut more than 55 percent over the last eleven years. The Defense Contract Audit Agency (DCAA), the agency that audits DOD contracts, saw its staffing levels cut more than 40 percent. With depleted oversight staffing levels, DOD was not prepared to perform even adequate control and oversight of the rapidly expanding task orders of the LOGCAP contract in Iraq, Kuwait, or Afghanistan. Even prior to September 11th, DOD oversight staffing levels made it difficult to keep up with overseeing normal levels of traditional forms of procurement. Despite skyrocketing procurements since September 11th, oversight staffing levels have not kept pace causing a serious inability to manage contracts, especially cost reimbursable contracts.

By the time the Iraq war was underway, there were not enough auditors, contracting officials, inspectors, or investigators, to monitor over 50,000 contractor personnel and the multitude of subcontracting layers created by prime contractors. The GAO warned in 2004, "DOD did not have sufficient numbers of trained personnel in place to provide effective oversight of its logistics support contractors." The Army activated and deployed Reserve units responsible for supporting the LOGCAP contract, but many of the personnel had little knowledge of the contract. DOD generally has been unable to determine whether LOGCAP work is actually being done competently and efficiently or that costs are allowable. Even the DoD Inspector General, the primary oversight agency within the DoD, has had no personnel in Iraq due to budget constraints. More recently, they have set up an office in Qatar, but with limited personnel. Such a lack of oversight in Iraq and Afghanistan encourages fraud, waste and abuse—a lawless land for contractors to operate. Some contractors have been honest enough to avoid the temptations, but others have run wild with greed.

In addition to anemic levels of oversight personnel available in Iraq to monitor performance on the LOGCAP contract, there has been little to no effort to oversee, manage, or supervise the thousands of security operators running loose throughout Iraq.

Exposure of fraud, waste and abuse in Iraq contracting has been left to whistleblowers and Democrats in Congress. Despite aggressive efforts on the part of contractors to discredit whistleblowers, they are still emerging to reveal serious performance problems that have affected both the troops and the taxpayer.

When war in Iraq became imminent, Secretary of Defense, Donald Rumsfeld, insisted on a light, rapid combat force for what was anticipated as a short-term effort—implementation of Rumsfeld's "10–30–30" plan—deploying to theater in 10 days, defeating enemy within 30 days, and ready for redeployment elsewhere in another 30 days. In order to pull off Rumsfeld's plan, the Army was forced to turn the contractor faucet on full blast to keep supplies moving to the troops advancing to Baghdad. It would be the first true test of the Army's dependence on contractors under battlefield conditions.

The Congressional Research Service estimated, in April 2006, operations, maintenance and procurement costs have risen from $50 billion in 2004 to $88 billion in 2006. The Army's budget has been strained by Iraq and Afghanistan to the degree that it is considering requesting an additional $23 billion to its fiscal year 2008 budget. The Army alone obligated more than $103 billion in procurement expenses in 2005. LOGCAP expenses are rising to the $18 billion level. With KBR billings on average, $450 million per month, how much are these obligations affecting the Army's ability to buy necessary combat equipment for their troops?

Oversight Agencies

The DOD has a number of contracting officials and agencies responsible for various aspects of contract and contractor oversight. The Contracting Officer (CO), or Procuring Contracting Officer (PCO), serves as the sole authority to bind the Government through the obligation of funds in the pre-award process. They have the authority to enter into, administer or terminate contracts and make related determinations and findings. The PCO has the responsibility for ensuring performance of all necessary actions for effective contracting, ensuring compliance with the terms of the contract, and safeguarding the interests of the U.S. in its contractual relationships.

The Administrative Contracting Officer (ACO) acts at the direction of the PCO, or in the capacity as a Defense Contract Management Command employee, to monitor the daily performance of contractors. The ACO administers contracts, often at a contractor's location, on behalf of the DOD and acts as the official spokesman for the DOD with respect to claims and disputes between the DOD and the contractor. The ACO also assures contractor compliance with cost, delivery, technical, quality and other terms of the contract.

The Defense Contract Audit Agency (DCAA) supports the PCO in auditing both pre-award and post-award contracts. The DCAA also audits the contractor's accounting and internal controls systems. Also, DCAA determines the accuracy and reasonableness of a contractor's cost representations.

The Department of Defense Inspector General (DODIG) conducts audits, investigations, inspections and evaluations of DOD contracts, personnel, programs and operations. It is also responsible for developing oversight policy for DOD functions. The Defense Criminal Investigative Service (DCIS) is the criminal investigative arm of the DODIG that investigates allegations of contractor fraud among other responsibilities.

Cost Reimbursable Contracts

LOGCAP was awarded as a cost-reimbursable contract. Under this type of contract, contractors decide how much a service will cost to perform. These contracts are also known as "cost-plus" contracts because the contractor's profit comes from fees paid by the government beyond the cost of the service. Cost-plus-percentage of cost contracts were used extensively in World War I with unfortunate results to the government. The incentive with this form of cost contract, for the contractor, was to increase costs in order to increase profits. Because of substantial fraud and abuse by contractors, this type of contract was made illegal after World War II and replaced with cost-plus-fixed fee (CPFF) and award fee (CPAF) types of contracts.

CPFF contracts include reimbursement for incurred costs plus a fixed fee arrangement while CPAF contracts include an award fee, based on a subjective evaluation by DOD, on top of a base fee. LOGCAP is a CPAF contract with a base fee of one percent and an award fee of two percent. They usually include a ceiling, or not-to-exceed cost that the contractor may not exceed except at their own risk or approval by the government. The biggest concern of the CPFF contract lies in the reasonableness of the costs incurred by the contractor. As such, these types of contracts require a significant level of oversight, or audit, to validate a contractor's incurred costs.

Cost Plus contracts were used on a very limited basis during the cold war era, usually reserved for work that is very urgent or research and development efforts which area hard to decide how much work is required. The contract type of choice for the Pentagon during this era was the Fixed Price contract that put more risk on the Contractor. With the emergence of contingency contracting, the Pentagon has gone back to the use of Cost Plus contracts because of the urgency of the services and the unknown costs of specific operations such as in Afghanistan and Iraq. There is almost no risk for the contractor under cost-plus contracts and no financial incentive to work efficiently or to seek ways to save money.

Contract Definitization

The definitization of a contract is the agreement on, or determination of, contract terms, specifications, and price, which converts an undefinitized contract action (UCA) to a definitive contract. An undefinitized contract action is any contract action for which the contract terms, specifications, or price are not agreed upon before performance is begun under the action. An UCA is used when the negotiation of a definitive contract action is not possible in sufficient time to meet Government requirements and the Government interest demands that the contractor be given a binding commitment so that contract performance can begin immediately. Each UCA must include a not-to-exceed price. Government liability, under an UCA, is normally restricted to a maximum of 50 percent of the not-to-exceed price.

In the rush to war in Iraq, task orders under the LOGCAP contract were hastily negotiated and agreed upon under an UCA based on the fact that Government requirements had not been fully determined. Under LOGCAP III, the contractor agreed to begin negotiating promptly with the Contracting Officer the terms of a definitive contract. The definitive contract would replace the not-to-exceed price with a negotiated price in no event to exceed the not-to-exceed price. Timelines are established in the contract for definitization that is normally spelled out in the number of days for submission of proposal, beginning of negotiations, and a target date for final definitization.

Reimbursement Rate

Under the LOGCAP III contract, FAR clause 52.216–26 (Payments of Allowable Costs Before Definitization), the Government will promptly reimburse the contractor for all allowable costs under this contract at the following rates:

(1) One hundred percent of approved costs representing financing payments to subcontractors under fixed-price subcontracts; provided, that the Government's payments to the contractor will not exceed 80 percent of the allowable costs of those subcontractors.

(2) One hundred percent of approved costs representing cost-reimbursement subcontracts; provided, that the Government's payments to the contractor shall not exceed 85 percent of the allowable costs of those subcontractors.

(3) Eighty-five percent of all other approved costs.

The determination of allowable costs will be made by the Contracting Officer in accordance with applicable cost principles of the FAR. The total reimbursement made shall not exceed 85 percent of the maximum amount of the Government's liability.

Allowable costs

Allowable costs includes recorded costs that result, at the time of the request for reimbursement, from payment by cash, check, or other form of actual payment for items or services purchased directly for the contract. Also, cost of contract performance in the ordinary course of business and costs incurred for supplies and services purchased directly for the contract and associated financing payments to subcontractors.

Allowable costs include direct labor, direct travel, other direct in-house costs; and properly allocable and allowable indirect costs as shown on the records maintained by the contractor for purposes of obtaining reimbursement under Government contracts. Also allowable are the amount of financing payments that the contractor has paid by cash, check, or other forms of payment, to subcontractors.

Incurred Labor Costs

Incurred labor costs, especially for cost reimbursable contracts, usually are the most significant costs charged to the contract. It is normally used to comprise the base, or the largest element of the base, used for allocating indirect costs. Historical labor costs are often used to estimate labor for follow-on contracts. Thus, if a contractor inflates labor costs, the ramifications can be enormous to the Government for a current contract and as a basis for follow-on contracts. Contractor personnel have complete control over the documents of original entry such as timecards and the responsibility for accuracy is diffused throughout the contractor's organization. Consequently, the risks associated with the accurate recording, distribution, and payment of labor is almost always significant to the Government.

U.S. Department of Defense LOGO Clause

The Defense Federal Acquisition Regulation Supplement § 252.232–7007, Limitation of Government's Obligation (LOGO) clause states "the contractor will not be obligated to continue work . . .beyond that point." "That point" occurs when the Pentagon runs out of appropriated funds for a given period of time and must wait for additional funding. The military can not spend money beyond the amount appropriated. This can happen during a contingency operation with incremental funding. On April 12, 2006, DOD issued a final ruling changing the language to "the Contractor is not authorized to continue work . . .beyond that point."

For LOGCAP III, the Army inserted clause § 52.232–19, Availability of Funds for the Next Fiscal Year: "The Government's obligation for performance under this contract . . .is contingent upon the availability of appropriated funds from which payment for contract purposes can be made. No legal liability on the part of the Government for any payment may arise for performance under this contract . . .until funds are made available to the Contracting Officer for performance and until the Contractor receives notice of availability . . ."

Defense Contract Audit Agency Audit of KBR's Billing System

DCAA Audit Report No. 3311–2002K11010001, May 13, 2004, found that KBR's billing system was inadequate in part. They found deficiencies in the contractor's billing system that were not prepared in accordance with applicable laws and regulations and contract terms. They also found system deficiencies "resulting in material invoicing misstatements that are not prevented, detected and/or corrected in a timely manner." Findings included:

Not following its written billing procedures when processing vouchers. Billing rates were not adjusted to actual rates in a timely fashion and the Administrative Contracting Officer was notified of refunds and overpayments.

KBR did not have adequate controls over subcontract billings. Policies and procedures were inadequate for notifying the government of potential significant subcontract problems. KBR also did not monitor the ongoing physical progress of subcontracts or the related costs and billings.

As a result of their findings, the audit agency directed that KBR was not authorized for direct billing and will be required to continue to provide all billings to DCAA for provisional approval prior to submission for payment.

LOGCAP III

LOGCAP III (Army Contract No. DAAA09–02-D–007) was awarded to KBR in December 2001. It is an indefinite-delivery/indefinite-quantity cost-plus award-fee and an "on-call" provider service contract with actual costs dependent on specific requirements. LOGCAP III is an umbrella contract with task orders issued to specifically address performance requirements and contract terms for a particular event or requirement. Task orders are negotiated independently and contain their own statement of work and "Not to Exceed" dollar limits. The "Not to Exceed" amounts have been determined largely on cost estimates provided by the Contractor.

The contract provides a "Partnering" provision stating . . ."The primary objective of the process is providing the American soldier with the highest quality supplies/services on time and at a reasonable price. Partnering (between the Army and KBR) requires the parties to look beyond the strict bounds of the contract in order to formulate actions that promote their common goals and objectives. It is a relationship that is based upon open and continuous communications, mutual trust, and respect, and the replacement of the 'us vs. them' mentality of the past with a 'win-win' philosophy for the future. Partnering also promotes synergy, creative thinking, pride in performance, and the creation of a shared vision for success."

Force Structure Planning

Force structure is defined as the numbers and types of units that comprise the force, their size, and their composition (i.e., divisions and brigades). Force structure planning is normally submitted as a plan for deployment of certain combat and support units strategically to meet possible conflicts and other challenges.

Time-Phased Force & Deployment List

Time-Phased Force & Deployment List (TPFDL) is referred to in the military by the acronym "tip-fiddle" or "tip-fid" for short. TPFDL is the military plan for the deployment of individuals and units into battle, the order of their deployment and the deployment of logistical support. It is a major planning document for how troops and logistics are going to move into a war zone.

The Army depended on the coordinated deployment of troops and logistics to handle all the tasks necessary to fight and support a war and the TPFDL was the means to achieve this very important function. According to the GAO, TPFDL was replaced with a deployment plan called "Request for Forces." This new plan segregated the initial deployment plan into over 50 separate deployment orders.

DoD's priority was for combat forces to move into the theater of operations first while logistics unit commanders had to justify the flow of their units and equipment into the theater – often with little success. Each deployment order required its own transportation feasibility analysis that caused an imbalance in the types of personnel needed in the theater to handle logistics requirements. Two major support commands were either deleted from the deployment plan or shifted back in the deployment timeline. As a result, logistics personnel could not effectively support the increasing numbers of combat troops moving into the theater.

Total Asset Visibility

Total Asset Visibility (TAV) was developed by the Pentagon as part of its "Revolution in Military Logistics" to support deployable supply and maintenance information systems using automatic identification technologies. It is a fully-automated system to provide complete, integrated visibility over logistical assets. This is done by using optical memory cards, bar coding, and radio frequency tags and readers for rapid data capture. Users gain access to the system through personal computers set up to give commanders in the field visibility of critical logistics. The goal of this system is to contribute to reduced inventories and receipt-processing time; improved visibility of in-theater truck convoy and rail movements; and increased throughput of shipments.

Theater Transportation Mission

The Theater transportation mission is set up to facilitate transportation requirements wholly within a theater of operations. It involves movement control and terminal operations that provides transportation support to the theater, to carry out linkages to strategic transportation, and to support reception and forward movement of supplies.

Theater Distribution Center

The Theater Distribution Center (TDC) is a supply center within a theater of operations that receives cargo from seaports and air debarkation points for processing. In Kuwait, the TDC is located near Camp Doha. Cargo moves from the TDC into Iraq or to other facilities in Kuwait.

NOTES

Introduction

1. Interview of Gen. Paul J. Kern.
2. Bob Woodward, *State of Denial: Bush at War, Part III*, New York: Simon & Schuster, 2006, p. 74.
3. GAO Report No. 03–695, Military Operations, "*Contractors Provide Vital Services to Deployed Forces, but are not Adequately Addressed in DOD Plans,*" June 2003, pp. 2–3.
4. Department of Defense Inspector General Audit Report No. 91–105, "*Civilian Contractor Overseas Support During Hostilities,*" June 26, 1991, p. 1.
5. Interview of Gen. Paul J. Kern.
6. Johnathan Weisman, "*Projected Iraq War Costs Soar,*" Washington Post, April 27, 2006.
7. Renae Merle, "*Census Counts 100,000 Contractors in Iraq,*" Washington Post, December 5, 2006.
8. Ibid.
9. Ann Scott Tyson, "*U.S. Army Battling to Save Equipment,*" Washington Post, December 5, 2006.
10. David Morse, "*Rumsfeld's McArmy Goes to War,*" Salon.com, September 18, 2003.

Chapter 1

The information in this chapter is based upon interviews of Rick Lamberth, background interviews with five knowledgeable sources, and government records.

1. GlobalSecurity.org, "Camp Arifjan."
2. David Phinney, "Halliburton Bribery Scandal Deepens," CorpWatch.org, March 29, 2005.
3. Laura Peterson, "Outsourcing Government: Service Contracting has Risen Dramatically in Last Decade," The Center for Public Integrity, October 30, 2003
4. GAO Report No. 04–854, Military Operations, "DOD's Extensive Use of Logistics Support Contracts Requires Strengthened Oversight," July 2004.
5. Michael R. Gordon and General Bernard E. Trainor, Cobra II, The Inside Story of the Invasion and Occupation of Iraq, New York: Pantheon Books, 2006, p. 99.
6. GAO Report No. 04–854, p. 18
7. Ibid.
8. Ibid.
9. "Dollars, Not Sense: Government Contracting under the Bush Administration," U.S. House Committee on Government Reform – Minority Staff, June 2006, P. 41.
10. Henry S. Bunting, Statement to the U.S. House of Representatives Committee on Government Reform, June 14, 2004.

Chapter 2

1. Based on interview with Representative Henry Waxman and several interviews with his staff from the Minority office of the House of Representatives Government Reform Committee, as well as a staff member on Representative Tom Davis's Majority office.

Much of Waxman's work in this area is documented at the Government Reform Committee website.

2.   Faye Fiore, "For Better or Worse, He's on it." Los Angles Times, 7/17/06.

3.   Tumulty, Karen, The Scariest Guy in Town, Time Magazine, 11/27/06.

Chapter 3

The information in this chapter is based on interviews with Maj. Raymond Kimball, U.S. Army.

1.   Ian Garrick Mason, "Supply and Command," Boston Globe, April 25, 2004.

2.   Cecilia Butler and Sandra Latsko, "Army Total Asset Visibility," U.S. Army Logistics Management College, January-February 1999. Article can be found at WWW.almc.army.mil/alog/issues/JanFeb99/ms404.htm.

3.   Mason, "Supply and Command."

4.   Ibid.

5.   Gordon and Trainor, Cobra II, pp. 96–101.

6.   Ibid

7.   Ibid

8.   Ibid

9.   Ibid

10.   David Zucchino, "Army Admits Invasion Plagued by Snafus," Los Angeles Times, July 3, 2004.

11.   Gordon and Trainor, Cobra II, p. 214.

12.   GAO Report No. 04–305R, "Defense Logistics: Preliminary Observations on the Effectiveness of Logistics Activities during Operation Iraqi Freedom," December 18, 2003, p. 3.

13.   Zucchino, "Army Admits Invasion Plagued by Snafus.

Chapter 4: Breaking Down

The information in this chapter is based on interviews of Rick Lamberth, background interviews with five knowledgeable sources, and review of government reports obtained by authors through research.

1.   Gordon and Trainor, Cobra II, p. 67.

2.   Zucchino, "Army Admits Invasion Plagued by Snafus,"

3.   GAO Report No. 05–275, Defense Logistics, "Actions Needed to Improve Availability of Critical Items," April 2005, p. 42.

4.   Ibid

5.   Ibid

6.   Ibid

7.   Ibid., p. 44

8.   Ibid., p. 43

9.   GAO Report No. 04–305R, p. 1–2.

10.   GAO Report No. 04–854, p. 4.

11.   GAO Report No. 05–275, p. 44.

12.   Ibid., pp. 23–24.

13.   Interview of Gen. Paul Kern.

14.   Ibid

15.   Ibid

16.   DCAA Audit Report No. 3311–2002K11010001, "Audit of KBR Billing System Internal Controls," May 13, 2004, p. 1.

17.   Paul F. Khoury, "Government Contracts Issue Update," Wiley, Rein & Fielding, LLP, Newsletters, Summer 2006.

18.   GAO Report No. 04–854, p. 25.

52.   Interview of Lt. Gen. Paul Kern.

Chapter 5

1.   Based on several interviews with Perry Jefferies, Adam Roe and four sources knowledgeable with Jefferies' unit.
2.   Government Accountability Office, GAO–04–305R, Defense Logistics: Preliminary Observations on the Effectiveness of Logistics Activities during Operation Iraqi Freedom, 12/18/03. www.gao.gov

Chapter 6

1.   Based on several interviews with Perry Jefferies, Adam Roe and four sources knowledgeable with Jefferies' unit.

Chapter 7

1.   Based on interviews with Perry Jefferies, Adam Roe, and three members of the military knowledgeable with David List and the unit.

Chapter 8

1.   Based on interviews with David Wilson, James Warren, and other truck drivers who worked in Iraq. This is also based on the statements and testimony before House Government Reform Committee

Chapter 9

1.   Based on interviews with David Wilson, James Warren, and other truck drivers who they worked in Iraq and their statements and testimony before the House Government Reform Committee.
2.   U.S. Army Report of Commander's Inquiry of the 724th Transportation Company Hostile Engagement, August 2, 2004. Report can be found at http://www.publicintegrity.org/docs/privatewarriors/PW_Internal_Army_report_KBR.pd
3.   Glantz, James, Truckers Testify That Halliburton Put Lives At Risk, New York Times, 9/19/06
4.   Witte, Griff, Ex-Workers Testify About Halliburton, Washington Post, 9/19/06
5.   Larvenz, Sean A., Statement before the Senate Democratic Policy Committee Hearing, 9/18/06
6.   Edward Sanchez, Statement before the Senate Democratic Policy Committee Hearing, 9/18/06
7.   Witte, Griff, Judge Dismisses Halliburton Suit, Washington Post, 9/23/06
8.   Rood, Justin, Halliburton to Employee: TPM Muckracker, 9/18/06. Story can be found at http://www.tpmmuckraker.com/archives/001548.php
9.   T. Christian Miller, Blood Money: Wasted Billions, Lost Lives, and Corporate Greed in Iraq, New York, Little, Brown and Company, 2006, pp. 161–162

Chapter 10

       The information in this chapter is based on interviews of Bobby Yen
1.   Rajiv Chandrasekaran, "Ties to GOP Trumped Know-How Among Staff Sent to Rebuild Iraq," Washington Post. Adapted from "Imperial Life in the Emerald City."
2.   John Crawford, The Last True Story I'll Ever Tell: An Accidental Soldier's Account of the War in Iraq, New York: Riverhead Books, p. 24.

Chapter 11

1. Based on interviews with Robert Isakson, other Custer Battles employees, Frank Willis, and other anonymous sources. Various documents also provided. Documents and emails quoted in this chapter are from the author's own copies.
2. Federal Election Commission records, www.fec.gov, case number ID: C00367284
3. Congressional Research Service, CRS Report for Congress, Order Code RL32370, The Coalition Provisional Authority (CPA): Origin Characteristics and Institutional Authorities, April 29, 2004
4. CPA reports, emails and other documents provided to author.

Chapter 12

1. Based on interviews with Robert Isakson, his attorneys and other anonymous sources. Also based on trial transcripts from DRC, et.al v CusterBattles, et.al, U.S. District Court, Eastern District of Virginia, case number 1:04CV1499.
2. T. Christian Miller, "Blood Money," pp. 182.
3. Witte, Griff, Invoices Detail Fairfax Firm's Billing for Iraq Work, Washington Post, 5/11/05.
4. Berman, Ari, Off the Meter, A $35,000 Cab Ride in Baghdad, The Nation, 5/2/05.

Chapter 13

1. Based on interviews from Perry Jefferies, Adam Roe and three other sources who served with Jefferies' unit.
2. Global Security, information on Camp Caldwell and Kirkush, http://www.globalsecurity.org/intell/world/iraq/kirkush.htm
3. Berenson, Alex, The Struggle for Iraq: Security Force; Iraqis' New Army Gets Slow Start, New York Times, 9/21/03
4. Daniszewski, John, New Iraqi Army Makes Its Debut, Los Angeles Times, 9/16/03. Author also interviewed Daniszewski and he confirmed that he did not know about the American soldiers on the other side of the camp.
5. Shanker, Thom, The Struggle for Iraq: The Military; General Says Training of Iraqi Troops Suffer from Poor Planning and Staffing. New York Times, 2/11/06.

Chapter 14: Corporate Cowboys in a War Zone

The information in this chapter is based on court records of lawsuit, Nordan, et al. v. Blackwater Security Consulting, et al., interviews with attorney Marc P. Miles, Callahan & Blaine, Santa Ana, California, and numerous articles and reports on the incident and its aftermath obtained by authors through research.

1. Jennifer King, "Celebrating the Life of Navy Seal, Actor & Athlete, Scott Helvenston – A Fallen Hero in Iraq," The Rugged Elegance Inspiration Network, News and Events, April 3, 2004.
2. Jay Price, Joseph Neff, and Charles Crain, "Chapter 5: 'Scotty Bod' grows up," Newsobserver.com, Raleigh, North Carolina, July 30, 2004.
3. King, "Celebrating the Life of Nave Seal, Actor & Athlete, Scott Helvenston – A Fallen Hero in Ira."
4. Price, Neff, and Crain, "Chapter 5: 'Scotty Bod' grows up."
5. Ibid
6. Jeremy Scahill, "Blood is Thicker than Blackwater," The Nation, May 8, 2006.
7. Joanne Kimberlin and Bill Sizemore, "Blackwater: Inside America's Private Army, Part 1," The Virginian-Pilot, PilotOnline.com, July 23, 2006.
8. Price, "Chapter 4: A business gets started," Newsobserver.com, July 29, 2004.

9. Ibid
10. Scahill, "Blood is Thicker than Blackwater."
11. Robert Young Pelton, Licensed to Kill: Hired Guns in the War on Terror, New York: Crown Publishers, 2006, p. 122.
12. Ibid., p. 126.
13. Scahill, "Blood is Thicker than Blackwater."
14. Ibid
15. Ibid
16. Ibid
17. Price and Neff, "Chapter 3: A Private, Driven Man."
18. Price, Neff, and Crain, "Chapter 1: Mutilation Seen Around the World."
19. Price and Neff, "Chapter 2: Army Molds a Future."
20. Price, Neff, and Crain, "Chapter 6: Fury Boils to the Surface."
21. Larry Diamond, Squandered Victory, The American Occupation and the Bungled effort to bring Democracy to Iraq, New York: Times Books, p. 233
22. Price, Neff, and Crain, "Chapter 6: Fury Boils to the Surface."
23. Scahill, "Blood is Thicker than Blackwater."
24. David Barstow, "Security Firm Says its Workers were Lured into Iraqi Ambush," New York Times, April 9, 2004.
25. Woodward, "State of Denial: Bush at War, Part III, p. 359.
26. Scahill, "Blood is Thicker than Blackwater."
27. Woodward, "State of Denial: Bush at War, Part III,p. 359–360.
28. Price, "Contractors in Iraq make cost balloon. Extensive paramilitary work earns profit on several levels, Newsobserver, October 26, 004.
29. Ibid
30. Scahill, "Mercenary Jackpot: US Pays Blackwater $320 Million in Secretive Global 'Security' Program," The Nation, August 11, 2006.
31. Neff, "Army Disavows Blackwater Work," Newsobserver, September 29, 2006.
32. Juan Cole, Quote in TomDispatch.com, "Deconstructing Iraq: Year Three Begins," March 19, 2005.
33. Frontline interview with Peter Singer, "Private Warriors," June 21, 2005.
34. Iraq Coalition Casualties: Contractors. Can be found at http//icasualties.org/oif/Civ.aspx.
35. Kristin Collins, "Families sue aviation contractor over soldiers' deaths," Newsobserver. com, June 14, 2005.
36. Journalnow.com, "N.C. security company faces largest death toll in Iraq," Associated Press, April 22, 2005.
37. Scahill, "Blood is Thicker than Blackwater."
38. Ibid
39. Scahill and Garrett Ordower, "From Whitewater to Blackwater," The Nation, October 26, 2006.
40. Ibid
41. Sizemore, "Book, films, take a hard look at N.C. security outfit Blackwater," Virginian-Pilot, Pilot Online, September 23, 2006.
42. Scahill, "Blood is Thicker than Blackwater."
43. Ibid.

Chapter 15

1. Based on interviews with Will Hough and other contractors who served as private security guards in Iraq, including two who served with Hough.
2. Iraq and Afghanistan Veterans of America (IAVA) blog site. www.iava.org
3. Farrell, Joelle, 'Risking My Life for Kitty Litter,' New Hampshire Concord Monitor, 10/03/06.
4. Job Notice from Blackwater, Inc. 4/18/05

5.   Myers, Lisa, Four Men Say They Witnessed Brutality, NBC News, 2/17/05.
6.   Otto, Phil, Team Shark Rocks, soldier of Fortune Magazine, 12/04

Chapter 16: The Other Side of the Force

The information in this chapter is based on interviews with Rick Lamberth, background interviews of five knowledgeable sources, and numerous articles, government reports, and congressional testimony obtained by authors through research.

1.   LOGCAP III, Task Order 89, Statement of Work, Part E.1.2 states: "The contractor shall provide all equipment, operators, and services to transport all classes of supply, with the exception of Class VIII blood, pharmaceuticals, refrigerated materials or other special handling requirements, from the above locations to logistic support areas within the Iraqi Zone at a distance NTE 400 km from each location."
2.   Ibid
3.   Michael Howard, "Turkish Truck Firms Quit Iraq," Guardian Unlimited, August 3, 2004.
4.   Turkish Hostages Released," Turkish Daily News, August 5, 2004.
5.   "KBR won't repair equipment," Stars & Stripes, European and Mideast Editions, Letters to the Editor, August 29, 2005 and September 4, 2005.
6.   Ibid., September 4, 2005.
7.   The Office of the Special Inspector General for Iraq Reconstruction Report No. 06–035, "Interim Audit Report on Inappropriate Use of Proprietary Data Markings by the Logistics Civil Augmentation Program (LOGCAP) Contractor," October 26, 2006, disclosed that KBR routinely marks almost all of its information it is specifically required to maintain for the government, as "proprietary data" including information on its daily dining facility headcount. The Inspector General felt the routine use of proprietary markings by KBR "is an abuse of FAR (Federal Acquisition Regulations) procedures, inhibits transparency of government activities and the use of taxpayer funds, and places unnecessary requirements on the government to both protect from public disclosure information received from KBR and to challenge inappropriate proprietary markings."
8.   Rory Mayberry, Testimony before Senate Democratic Policy Committee, June 27, 2005.
9.   Robert Michael West, Statement for the U.S. House of Representatives Government Reform Committee, June 6, 2004.

Chapter 17

The information in this chapter is based on interviews of Ben Carter and Harold Orr, as well as numerous emails and documents generated from the water contamination incident at Ar Ramadi. Also authors obtained congressional hearing transcripts and records regarding testimony on the incident.

1.   Drew Brown, "Injuries, illnesses take more soldiers from battlefields than enemy fire," Knight Ridder Newspapers, January 4, 2006. Article can be found at www.twincities.com/mld/twincities/news/politics/13548965.htm
2.   Greg Lamotte, "Background Report – Iraq/Water," Voice of America, July 23, 2004.
3.   Scott Thornton, et al., "Gastroenterities in US Marines during Operation Iraqi Freedom," Naval Environmental & Preventative Medicine, 2005. Study information can be found at www.journals.uchicago.edu/CID/journal/issues/v40n4/34300/34300.text.html.
4.   Wil Granger, KBR Report of Findings & Root Causes, Water Mission B4 Ar Ramadi, May 13, 2005.
5.   Email from Melissa Norcross to Jim Donahue, dated September 8, 2005.

Chapter 18

1.   Based on interviews with Adam Roe, other Army truck drivers and KBR employees, including a current KBR manager in Iraq.

Chapter 19

1. Scahill, "Exile on K Street," The Nation, February 20, 2006.
2. Joseph Neff and Jay Price, "Chapter 7: Strong Words Mask Inaction," Newsobserver.com, Raleigh, North Carolina, August 1, 2004.
3. Jeremy Scahill, "Blackwater Down," The Nation, October 10, 2005.
4. Ibid
5. Scahill, "Exile on K Street."
6. Elizabeth Brown, "More than 2,000 Spin Through Revolving Door," The Center for Public Integrity, April 7, 2005.
7. Alex Knott, "Industry of Influence Nets More Than $10 Billion," The Center for Public Integrity, April 7, 2005.
8. Robert Schlesinger, "The Private Contractor – GOP Gravy Train," Salon, Thinkingpeace.com. Article found at www.thinkingpeace.com/pages/arts2/arts29.html.
9. Ibid
10. Ibid
11. Scahill, "Exile on K Street."
12. Schlesinger, "The Private Contractor – GOP Gravy Train."
13. Tony Capaccio, "Titan Logs Most Contractor Deaths," Bloomberg News, March 25, 2005. Article posted on The Denver Post website.
14. Jeffrey H. Birnbaum, "Livingston's Sweet Lobbying Setup," Washingtonpost.com, October 17, 2005.
15. CACI First Quarter Results Reported October 26, 2005.
16. Alex Knott, "The Pentagon's Stealth Rainmaker," The Center for Public Integrity, September 29, 2004.
17. Jim Donahue, "Halliburton Gave $4 Million to Politicians and Received 600 Percent Gain on Contracts Since 2000, Halliburtonwatch says," U.S. Newswire, September 26, 2006.
18. "Halliburton Spent $770,000 Lobbying Washington in First Half of 2004, a 400% Increase from 2003," Halliburtonwatch.org, October 2, 2004.
19. "About Halliburton, Lobbyists," Halliburtonwatch.org, undated.
20. "Halliburton Spent $770,000 Lobbying Washington in First Hal of 2004, a 400% Increase from 2003."
21. Jonathan E. Kaplan, "Former FEMA Chief Allbaugh in the Middle," The Hill, September 8, 2005.
22. "What's Allbaugh Doing for Halliburton?" Think Progress, September 6, 2005.
23. "Former FEMA Head and Halliburton Lobbyist Visits Louisiana for Deals," Halliburtonwatch.org, September 8, 2005.
24. Lobbying Registration filings available at www.sopr.senate.gov.
25. Kaplan, "Former FEMA Chief Allbaugh in the Middle."
26. Donahue, "Halliburton Gave $4 Million to Politicians and Received 600 Percent Gain on Contracts Since 2000, Halliburtonwatch Says."
27. Maud Beelman, "Winning Contractors: U.S. Contractors Reap the Windfalls of Post-war Reconstruction," The Center for Public Integrity, October 30, 2003
28. Will Bunch, "Iraq Mercenaries Supporting Political Mercenaries: More on the Appalling Sell-out of the Pennsylvania Green Party," Attywood Daily News, October 18, 2006. Article found at www.attyood.com/2006/10/iraq_mercenaries_supporting_po.html.
29. Bunch, "Santorum, The Green Party and some very strange bedfellows," Attywood Daily News, October 18, 2006. Article found at www.attyood.com/2006/10/iraq_mercenaries_supporting_po.html
30. Schlessinger, "The Private Contractor – GOP Gravy Train."
31. "The Politics of Contracting," Project on Government Oversight, June 29, 2004.
32. Laura Peterson, "Kellogg, Brown & Root (Halliburton)," The Center for Public Integrity, 2006.

33. Kelly Kennedy, "Blackwater's Army for Hire?" Defense News, March 2006.
34. "Blackwater's Top Brass," The Virginian-Pilot, Pilot Online, July 24, 2006.
35. Schlessinger, "The Private Contractor_GOP Gravy Train."
36. Ken Silverstein, "Meet the Counterterrorism-Industrial Complex," Harper's Magazine, September 19, 2006.
37. "The Politics of Contracting," Project on Government Oversight.
38. Kate Ackley, "Out of Work GOP Aides Face Tough Road Ahead," Roll Call, November 9, 2006.
39. Jeffrey H. Birmbaum, "Former Aides to Congress Switch Sides for Upcoming Probes," Washington Post, December 11, 2001.
40. Ibid.
41. Ibid.
42. Jess Patch, "Halliburton Unit Hires Lobby Firm to Help with Democrats," *Politico.com*, January 30, 2007.

Chapter 20

1. Based on interviews with Representative Henry Waxman, Committee staff, and other anonymous sources.
2. O'Harrow, Robert; Higham, Scott, Wife, Friend Tie Congressman to Consulting Firm, Washington Post, 7/28/06
3. All documents and government reports listed or written by Representative Henry Waxman can be found at the Government Reform Committee website.
4. Cohen, Richard E., Key Democrat discusses priorities for government oversight, National Journal, 9/14/06
5. Werner, Erica, Waxman Set to Probe Areas of Bush Government, Associated Press, 11/10/06

Chapter 21

1. This chapter is based on legal documents filed on the Custer Battles qui tam action, U.S. ex rel Isakson v Custer Battles, and interviews with attorneys involved in the case, interview with Robert Isakson and numerous news articles, some are listed below.
2. Hirsh, Michael, Follow the Money, Newsweek, 4/4/06
3. Eckholm, Eric, On Technical Grounds, Judge Set Aside Verdict of Billion Fraud in Iraq Rebuilding, New York Times, 10/19/06.
4. Dreazen, Yochi J., Probe Targets Ex-Navy Official for Link to Disgraced Contractor, Wall Street Journal, 5/5/06.
5. Hastings, Deborah, Ex-Pentagon Officials Accused of Fraud, Conspiracy, Associated Press, 7/22/06.
6. Rising, David, Germany Working with US Authorities in Probe of R.I. Contractor, Associated Press, 11/10/06

Chapter 22

Based on interviews of Neal Higgins and Ben Carter as well as transcripts and records obtained from Senate Democratic Policy Committee hearings.
1. Senator Byron L. Dorgan, opening statement before the Senate Democratic Policy Committee hearing, Washington D.C., April 7, 2006.
2. Email from Capt. Michelle A. Callahan, U.S. Army, to Neal Higgins, "Q-West Water Contamination," March 31, 2006.
3. Defense Contract Management Agency Point Paper, "Water Quality Issue at Base Q-West, Iraq," April 17, 2006.
4. Jerry D. Allen, P.E., "KBR, Final Report, Water Quality at Ar Ramadi, February 2006.

5. Statement of Dr. Matthew Harrison for the Senate Democratic Policy Committee, April 7, 2006.

6. Statement of Jeffrey K. Griffith before the Senate Democratic Policy Committee, April 7, 2006.

7. Iraq and Afghanistan Veterans of America Blog response posted by Marissa Sousa, "Halliburton=Slumlord," January 25, 2006.

8. Bob Geiger, "GOP Kills Bill to Police Halliburton," Alternet.org, June 20, 2006. Article found at www.alternet.org/story/37849.

9. WSJV, FOXNews.com, South Bend, Indiana, "Democratic Majority to Work on Focuses," January 6, 2007.

Chapter 23

Based on interviews with Rick Lamberth. Also research of emails and documents in the possession of Lamberth.

1. LOGCAP Support Unit, Det. 48-Iraq, After Action Report and Lessons Learned, Operation Iraqi Freedom, June 2005.

Chapter 24

1. This chapter is based on interviews with Lieutenant General Paul Kern, Major General Wade "Hamp" McManus Jr., and Deputy Under Secretary of Defense for Logistics and Materiel Readiness, Jack Bell.

2. Burns, Robert, Disgruntled Troops Complain to Rumsfeld, Associated Press, 12/04.

3. Heinatz, Stephanie, Army Official: Rumsfeld Forbade Talk of Postwar, Daily Press, Newport News, VA, 9/9/06.

4. Neffgen, Alfred V., Statement by Alfred V. Neffgen, Chief Operating Officer, KBR Government Operations, Americas Region, Before the Committee on Government Reform, U.S. House of Representatives, 7/22/04

5. Government Accountability Office, Military Operations, GAO–06–999R, 9/22/06, GAO reports can be found at www.gao.gov .

6. Lt. Col. Paul Burnham U.S. Army Reserves, Increasing Combat Support and Combat Service Support Units in the U. S. Military, United States Army War College, 3/18/05.

7. Brian Ross and Rhonda Schwartz, U.S. Troops Abandon Me, Says Convoy Driver, ABC News, 9/27/06.

8. Woods, Sgt. Sara, Defense Department Becoming Stronger, More Capable, Rumsfeld Says, American Foreign Press Service, 9/22/06

Chapter 25

1. Griff Witte, *"Contractors Rarely Held Responsible for Misdeeds in Iraq,"* Washington Post, November 4, 2006.

2. Paul Burnham, Lt. Col., USAR, *"Increasing Combat Support and Combat Services Support Units in the U.S. Military,"* U.S. Army War College Strategy Research Project, March 18, 2005, p. 6.

3. Department of Defense Office of Inspector General Audit Report No. 91–105, *"Civilian Contractor Overseas Support During Hostilities,"* June 26, 1991, p. 1.

4. Farah Stockman, *"Contractors in war zones lose immunity: Bill provision allows military prosecutions,"* The Boston Globe, January 7, 2007.

5. Interview of Scott Horton.

6. Ibid.

7. Ibid.

8. Stockman, *"Contractors in war zones lose immunity."*

9. Ibid.

10. Interview of Scott Horton.

11. Farah Stockman, "*U.S. Contractors in Iraq face peril, neglect,*" Boston Globe, October 16, 2006.

12. David Phinney, "*A U.S. Fortress Rises in Baghdad: Asian Workers Trafficked to Build World's Largest Embassy,*" Corpwatch.org, October 17, 2006.

13. Ibid.

14. Ibid.

15. GAO Report No. 04–854, Military Operations, "*DOD's Extensive Use of Logistics Support Contracts Requires Strengthened Oversight,*" July 2004.

16. Statement of David M. Walker, Comptroller General of the United States Before the Subcommittee on Defense, Subcommittee on Appropriations, House of Representatives, "*DOD Acquisitions: Contracting for Better Outcomes,*" September 7, 2006.

17. Business Week Online, *When Outsourcing Turns Outrageous,* Business Week, July 31, 2006

18. GAO Report No. 06–1132, Iraq Contract Costs, "*DOD Consideration of Defense Contract Audit Agency Findings,*" September 2006.

19. Sue Pleming, "*Army Gives Halliburton $72m Bonus,*" Reuters, May 11, 2005.

20. Lionel Beehner, "*The Cost of the Iraq War,*" Council on Foreign Relations, November 8, 2006.

21. Richard Wolf, "$127B *War Request on the Way,*" USA Today, November 17, 2006.

22. Lolita C. Baldor, "*Equipment Shortages Stunt Combat Readiness,*" ArmyTimes.com, July 27, 2006.

23. Thom Shanker and Michael R. Gordon, "*Strained, Army Looks to Guard for more Relief,*" The New York Times, September 22, 2006.

24. Gregg Jaffe, "*Despite a $168B Budget, Army Faces Cash Crunch,*" The Wall Street Journal, December 12, 2006.

25. Ibid.

26. Author interview of Gen. Paul Kern, U.S. Army, Retired.

27. "*Cher and Operation Helmet Join Forces to Help American Soldiers,*" Warner Bros. Records, June 12, 2006.

28. Martin C. Evans, "*Lifesaving Kits for GIs in Short Supply,*" Newsday, June 8, 2006.

29. T. Christian Miller, "*Bloodmoney in Iraq,*" Tom Paine, Common Sense, Tompaine.com, September 13, 2006.

30. C.J. Chivers, "*Contractor's Boss in Iraq Snot at Civilians, Workers' Suit Says,*" The New York Times, November 17, 2006.

31. Interview with Gen Kern.

32. Minority Staff Committee on Government Reform, U.S. House of Representatives Fact Sheet, "*GAO Issues Report on Halliburton's Troop Support Contract in Iraq,*" July 21, 2004.

BIBLIOGRAPHY

Books

1. Bob Woodward, *"State of Denial: Bush at War, Part III,"* New York: Simon & Schuster, 2006.
2. T. Christian Miller, *"Blood Money: Wasted Billions, Lost Lives, and Corporate Greed in Iraq,"* New York: Little, Brown and Company, 2006.
3. Larry Diamond, *"Squandered Victory: The American Occupation and the Bungled Effort to Bring Democracy to Iraq,"* New York: Times Books, Henry Holt and Company, 2005.
4. Michael R. Gordon and General Bernard E. Trainor, *"Cobra II: The Inside Story of the Invasion and Occupation of Iraq,"* New York: Pantheon Books, 2006.
5. Robert Young Pelton, *"Licensed to Kill: Hired Guns in the War on Terror,"* New York: Crown Publishers, 2006.
6. John Crawford, *"The Last True Story I'll Ever Tell: An Accidental Soldier's Account of the War in Iraq,"* New York: Riverhead Books, 2005.
7. Rajiv Chandrasekaran, *"Imperial Life in the Emerald City: Inside Iraq's Green Zone,"* New York: Alfred A. Knoff, 2006.
8. P.W. Singer, *"Corporate Warriors: The Rise of the Privatized Military Industry,"* Ithaca: Cornell University Press, 2003.
9. Paul Rieckhoff, *"Chasing Ghosts: A Soldier's Fight for America from Baghdad to Washington,"* New York: New American Library, 2006.
10. Pratap Chatterjee, *"Iraq, Inc. A Profitable Occupation,"* New York: Seven Stories Press, 2004.
11. Ken Silverstein, *"Private Warriors,"* New York, Verso, 2000.
12. Michael Isikoff, David Corn, *"Hubris: The Inside Story of Spin, Scandal and the Selling of the Iraq War."* New York: Crown Publishers, 2006.

Government Reports

GAO

GAO–03–695, Military Operations: Contractors Provide Vital Services to Deployed Forces but are not Adequately Addressed in DOD Plans, June 2003
GAO- 04–305R, *"Defense Logistics: Preliminary Observations on the Effectiveness of Logistics Activities during Operation Iraqi Freedom,"* December 18, 2003
GAO–04–854, Military Operations: DOD's Extensive Use of Logistic Support Contracts Requires Strengthened Oversight, July 2004
GAO–05–201, Interagency Contracting: Problems with DOD's and Interior's Orders to Support Military Operations, April 2005
GAO–05–274, Contract Management: Opportunities to Improve Surveillance on Department of Defense Service Contracts, March 2005

GAO–05–275, Defense Logistics: Actions Needed to Improve the Availability of Critical Items During Current and Future Operations, April 2005

GAO– 05–277, DOD Excess Property Management Control Breakdowns Result in Substantial Waste and Inefficiency, May 2005

GAO–05–737, Rebuilding Iraq: Action Needed to Improve Use of Private Security Providers, July 2005

GAO–06–66, Defense Acquisition: DOD Has Paid Billions In Award and Incentive Fees Regardless of Acquisition Outcomes, December 2005

GAO–06–284, Contract Security Guards: Army's Guard Program Requires Greater Oversight and Assessment of Acquisition Approach, April 2006

GAO–06–838R, Contract Management: DOD Vulnerabilities to Contracting Fraud, Waste and Abuse, July 7, 2006

GAO–06–854, Global War on Terror: Observations on Funding Costs and Future Commitments, July 10, 2006

GAO–06–999R, Military Operations: Background Screenings on Contractor Employees Supporting Deployed Forces May Lack Critical Information But U.S. Forces Take Steps to Mitigate the Risk Contractors May Pose, September 22, 2006

GAO–06–1109T, Reserve Fitness: Army National Guard and Army Reserve Readiness for 21-Century Challenges, September 21, 2006

GAO–06–1132, Iraq Contract Costs: DOD Consideration of Defense Contract Audit Agency Findings, September 2006

GAO–07–40, Rebuilding Iraq: Status of Competition for Iraq Reconstruction Contracts, October 2006

GAO–07–235R, Suggested Areas for Oversight for the 110th Congress, November 17, 2006

GAO–07–20, Defense Acquisition: Tailored Approach Needed to Improve Service Acquisition Outcomes, November 2006

GAO–07–145, Military Operations: High-Level DOD Action Needed to Address Long-Standing Problems with Management and Oversight of Contractors Supporting Deployed Forces, December 2006

Military

U.S. Army Pamphlet 710–2–2, Supply Support Activity Supply System: Manual Procedures, September 30, 1998

Cecilia Butler and Sandra Latsko, "Army Total Asset Visibility," U.S.Army Logistics Management College, January-February 1999. Article can be found at WWW.almc.army.mil/alog/issues/Jan-Feb99/ms404.htm

Air War College, Air University, Contractors on the Battlefield: What Have We Signed Up For? Col. Steven J. Zamparelli, USAF, March 1999.

U.S. Army Regulation 715–9, Logistics, Contractors Accompanying the Force, October 29, 1999

U.S. Army, Army Materiel Command, LOGCAP Battlebook, January 31, 2000

USAWC Strategy Research Project, LOGCAP: The Nation's Premier Contingency Contracting Program for Force XXI, Marilyn Harris, Department of the Army, April 14, 2000

U.S. Army Command and General Staff College, Contractors on the Battlefield: Has the Military accepted too much Risk? May 23, 2001

Scott C. Goddard, Major, RA, INF, Australia, The Private Military Company: A Legitimate International Entity within Modern Conflict, U.S. Army Command and General Staff College, June 1, 2001

USAWC Strategy Research Project, Transformation—Revolution in Military Logistics, Aundre F. Piggee, LT. Col. U.S. Army, April 9, 2002

USAWC Strategy Research Project, Civilian Contractors on the Battlefield: A partnership with Commercial Industry or Receipe for Failure? Robert M. Friedman, Department of the Army Civilian, April 9, 2002

U.S. Army Field Manual 3–100.21 (100–21), Contractors on the Battlefield, January 2003

Strategic Studies Institute, U.S. Army War College, *Reconstructing Iraq: Insight, Challenges, and Missions for Military Forces in a Post-Conflict Scenario,* Conrad C. Crane, W. Andrew Terrill, February 2003

U.S. Joint Chiefs of Staff, The National Military Strategy of the United States of America, A Strategy for Today: A Vision for Tomorrow, 2004

U.S. Army Report of Commander's Inquiry of the 724th Transportation Company Hostile Engagement, August 2, 2004. Report can be found at http://www.publicintegrity.org/docs/privatewarriors/PW_Internal_Army_report_KBR.pdf

U.S. Army Command and General Staff College, *Army Battlefield Distribution through the Lens of OIF: Logistics Failures and the way ahead,* Maj. Eric Pl Shirley, January 2, 2005

USAWC Strategy Research Project: *Increasing Combat Service Support Units in the U.S. Military,* Paul M. Burnham, Lt. Col., USAR, March 18, 2005

USAWC Strategy Research Project: *Civilian Contractors on the Battlefield,* Col. Ronda G. Urey, March 18, 2005

Air Command and Staff College, Air University, *Contractors on the Battlefield: Planning Consideration and Requirements,* Major George (Sam) Hamontree III, January 30, 2002

DOD Instruction 3020.41, *Contractor Personnel Authorized to Accompany the U.S. Armed Forces,* October 3, 2005

Department of Defense Inspector General

DOD Inspector General Audit Report No. 91–105, *Civilian Contractor Overseas Support During Hostilities,* June 26, 1991

DOD Inspector General Report No. D–2004–57, Acquisition, *"Contracts Awarded for the Coalition Provisional Authority by the Defense Contracting Command – Washington,* March 18, 2004

Special Inspector General For Iraq Reconstruction

The Office of the Special Inspector General for Iraq Reconstruction Report No. 06–035, *"Interim Audit Report on Inappropriate Use of Proprietary Data Markings by the Logistics Civil Augmentation Program (LOGCAP) Contractor,"* October 26, 2006

Congressional Research Services

CRS Issue Brief for Congress, Defense Acquisition Reform: Status and Current Issues, January 9, 2002

CRS Report for Congress, Order Code RL32370, *The Coalition Provisional Authority (CPA): Origin Characteristics and Institutional Authorities,* April 29, 2004

CRS Report for Congress, The Cost of Iraq, Afghanistan and Enhanced Base Security Since 9/11, Amy Belasco, October 7, 2005

Congressional Budget Office

CBO Study, *Logistics Support for Deployed Military Forces,* October 2005

Defense Contract Audit Agency

DCAA Audit Report, Audit Report of Kellogg, Brown, and Root, Inc., Billing System Internal Controls, May 13, 2004. Audit Report Number NO–3311–202K11010001, May 13, 2004

DCAA Memorandum, Implementation of FAR Clause 52.216–26, Payments of Allowable Costs before Definitization, LOGCAP Contract, DAAA09–02–D–0007, August 17, 2004

ACKNOWLEDGMENTS

Dina Rasor and Robert Bauman would not have been able to write this book without the help of many individuals. Some must or requested to remain anonymous. We wish to give them all a very large thank you for taking risks to talk to us and give us information. We especially want to thank the active duty service men and women who were willing to take bigger risks than civilians to let us know how and why the military system that they love is not working.

We also appreciate the risks that each named source in this book took with their careers. Even though some of them are out of the military or no longer working for a private contractor in Iraq, there may be some type of retaliation on their careers. After spending a lifetime helping people come forward with their stories, we are all too aware of the lengths that bureaucracies and corporations will take to discredit someone trying to tell the truth.

There are also many groups out there who we have relied on for their information and persistent investigations. The Project on Government Oversight (POGO), especially director Danielle Brian, Keith Rutter, Beth Daley and Todd Bowers have been very helpful with information and moral support. The Iraq and Afghanistan Veterans of America (IAVA), run by Executive Director Paul Rieckhoff also have been very important in our research and especially in contacting the troops to tell their stories. Their help in starting Dina Rasor's Follow the Money Project greatly contributed to the writing of this book. Bobby Yen, Ray Kimball, and Perry Jefferies are members of IAVA and their stories were crucial in illustrating problems that troops had in the war.

Alex Knott from the Center for Public Integrity was very helpful in tracking lobbyists involved in the war service industry. John Pike of Global Security gave his sage advice at the beginning of the writing of this book and his very informative website, www.globalsecurity.org was used extensively to look up any type of question on Iraq. Charlie Cray of Halliburtonwatch and the Center for Corporate Policy was generous with his time and his website on Halliburton, www.halliburtonwatch.org also was a great resource of information. Winslow Wheeler of the Center for Defense Information (CDI) has always been willing to give advice and help, especially in untangling the mess of the DOD budget. Pratap Chatterjee met with us several times and his organization, Corpwatch, www.corpwatch.org has been one of the organizations that has done breakthrough investigations on the Iraq war.

We also appreciate the time and help of the majority and minority staff of the House Government Reform Committee. We also would like to thank Neal Higgins of Senator Dorgan's Democratic Policy Committee with his help on investigations and protecting sources.

We appreciate that General Paul Kern and General Wade McManus, Jr. took the time to talk to us and were forthright on the problems that they saw while in the commands.

Our book agent, Laurie Liss of Sterling Lord Literistic, Inc., was very patient with us when we came to her with a very large proposal and big ideas. She helped to focus the book on the important information. We also appreciate the help of her assistant Leah Miller. Our book editor, Airié Stuart of Palgrave Macmillan was encouraging with her advice and blunt when we needed it. She was patient through many rewrites and continually changing information. We also want to thank Chris Chappell, Jodie Hockensmith, Yasmin Matthew, and attorney Mark Fowler, for their great work and patience with our changes and our work with the media.

Dina Rasor has been blessed with many professional and personal friends who have guided her and convinced her to keep going. She especially wants to thank three long term friends, Donna Martin, Danielle Brian and Elizabeth Driver for their support and willingness to listen and give great advice. Dina's long time mentor, Ernest Fitzgerald, taught her most of what she knows about government procurement and whistleblowers (he hates that word and wants to call them truthtellers.) Dina also wants to thank Peter Stockton for his helpful skepticism and great humor in discussing investigations. Dina thanks her church family at the First Congregational Church of Berkeley with ministers Patricia de Jong, Charlotte Russell and Adam Blons. She wants to give special thanks to the church's music director, Larry Marietta and the whole choir who gave her refuge from politics and war at every Thursday night rehearsal making beautiful music. She sends a special thanks to Dr. Jonathan Terdiman of the University of California San Francisco Medical Center for his patient determination to keep her functioning and working.

Dina wants to thank her parents, Ned and Genny Rasor who gave her a great start and has never given up on her for 50 years. She also thanks her two amazing sons, Daniel and Nicholas Lawson for their humor and understanding that dinner wasn't always ready because she was talking to some desperate soldier or madly typing on the computer. They have brought great fun into her life.

Dina has a special thanks to her husband, Thomas Lawson, who has known her since she was sixteen and married her anyway. His complete devotion, love and support have given her the courage to take risks and to keep going despite the odds.

Robert Bauman is thankful for the many professional colleagues and associations who have been helpful in his career as a criminal investigator for the Department of Defense. He gives thanks to the many friends and business associations who have made his post-government career a success. Robert gives special thanks to Danielle Brian and Peter Stockton for their friendship, gracious hospitality, and help during his many trips to Washington D.C. Also, to Donna Martin for her friendship and hospitality. Robert wants to thank his long-time colleague and friend, Bob Kong, for his help as a sounding board, over coffee, on investigations and Defense Procurement issues.

Robert is thankful for all the support his family has given him during the very difficult and time consuming process of research and writing this book. To his wife, Norma, who endured his many absences while traveling the country and spending so much time on the book. She has always been there for him. To his two sons, Blake and Marc, and their wives, Debbie and Debbie, for their wonderful support. And finally, to his lovely grandchildren, Sophia, Luke, and Emily for the pleasures they bring to his life everyday.

INDEX